MAKING WAVES

CLIVE FRESHWATER'S MEMOIRS

1939-2015

Edited by Tom Drysdale

With a Foreword by

Tim Walker, former Principal, Glenmore Lodge

Published by
CAIRNGORM CANOEING AND SAILING SCHOOL LIMITED

Published by
Cairngorm Canoeing and Sailing School Limited
Insh Hall
Kincraig
Inverness-shire
PH21 1NU

First published 2018
© Mrs Sally Freshwater

ISBN 978-1-5272-1517-7

Typeset, printed and bound by
Groverprint & Design, Newtonmore

Typeset in Calibri

Contents

Foreword

I am delighted to contribute this foreword to my old friend Clive Freshwater's memoirs. The title "Making Waves" seems appropriate since Clive was never afraid of engaging in controversy. I wondered if "War and Peace" might have been more appropriate, but that title had already been taken.

Clive was appointed to the instructional staff at Glenmore Lodge in the early 1960s and remained there until 1970. These were pioneering years in the whole field of outdoor education and sport. Scotland was leading the way and it was Speyside in particular where things were really happening - Clive played a major part in making them do so. During this decade the British Association of Professional Ski Instructors (BAPSI, later BASI) was formed; Benmore and Lagganlia local authority education centres were opened; the first mountain leader (summer) course was run; skiing courses for schoolchildren were introduced; the Mountaineering Instructors' Scheme was formed; Ski Party Leader courses were introduced; the first professional ski instructor courses were held; the Mountain Rescue Committee of Scotland was formed; the Cairngorm Mountain Rescue Team was formed; a delegation from the area visited the Avalanche Information Centre in Davos, Switzerland and the first permanent custom-made ski tow was installed on Cairngorm.

The Glenmore Lodge Committee accepted that they might now have to pay instructional staff but it took another fifteen years or so for them to be persuaded that the role of instructor could be carried out by someone who did not live on site at Glenmore Lodge. It was during this time that Clive and his future wife Sally met – Sally was secretary to the then Principal, Eric Langmuir. You may know that the Lodge has been hugely successful as a marriage bureau over its sixty-nine years history.

Towards the end of Clive's time at Glenmore Lodge he and Sally formed the vision for a Cairngorm Canoeing and Sailing School. The purchase of the old Insh Hall and the lease of the old boathouse on the shore of Loch Insh and its surrounding land from the Forestry Commission enabled the vision to become reality. At that time Clive and Sally had very little and the Centre was built up with the help of many friends. Disused telegraph poles, old sheds, cast off furniture and all sorts of materials were pressed into service –

nothing was wasted. As you will read, Clive had a work ethic and a dogged determination which was without equal. During the period of nearly fifty years of its development the Centre has gone from strength to strength and it was fitting that it was Princess Anne, a keen sailor herself and who, I think, has a similar Freshwater work ethic, who would visit Loch Insh and pay tribute to Clive and Sally.

Some say that Loch Insh Watersports replaced National Service. It also became known as the place where you could be fired in the morning and hired again in the afternoon – working there for more than a few weeks was an achievement and a solid endorsement of character. On an inspection by the Adventure Activity Licensing Authority the inspector commented on the maze of corridors and doors within the Boathouse. Clive replied "Yes, that's right; it works well and the staff don't know which door I'm coming through next". Clive was never one to be daunted by authority or bureaucracy and he took on most of the main public agencies in Scotland. They got to know him well and they knew what to expect. His biggest challenge was probably the Spey canoe case, the court action over the right to use the river for navigation, raised against him by the wealthy and powerful salmon fishing interests on the Spey. As it turned out, and as you will read in the pages that follow, those interests took on more than they had bargained for.

During the past forty-seven years, many thousands of people have passed through the doors of the Centre and have come to love the great outdoors. The reputation of Speyside has been enhanced by its existence, local schoolchildren have had access to training there and the use of its facilities and the Freshwater family have played their part in themselves providing an Olympian to join the other sixteen Olympians who were born and brought up in the area.

Although we didn't always agree on everything, it was a privilege for me to be counted amongst Clive's friends. We got to know each other well through BASI, when he was its Chairman and I was a Director. We covered the length and breadth of the country together attending various BASI meetings. Clive proved to be the right man at the right time. He was a strong Chairman and when necessary a formidable one. BASI has been a great success story and Clive rightly deserves his place in their Hall of Fame. Later on we would meet frequently and Clive would give me a weekly phone call, often to discuss his next campaign. These calls always came at irregular times – late at night, early in the morning and often at weekends. My family got into the habit of saying, even without answering the phone, "that will be Clive".

About twenty years ago Clive and Sally came to visit us in Drumullie. Helen and I had just moved into a £200 caravan with our two young daughters whilst we set about renovating an old farm steading. I walked around the steading with Clive as I outlined our plans. Clive noted that the caravan was just about derelict; it leaked; it had condensation running down the inside and Clive noticed that our two daughters were living in a room the size of a cupboard. His departing remarks were "Well done; I like what you're doing; children nowadays have it far too easy. Hardship always does them good."

So here is Clive's story, told in his own words. It all started in a modest cottage in Nottinghamshire in January 1939. Read on…

Tim Walker
Former Principal, Glenmore Lodge
January 2018

Editor's Note

Clive told me late in 2011 of his concern that he had never really told his sons about his family history and his early years and that he had started to compose his recollections. These were partly written down and partly dictated to his long-suffering secretary, Linda Wilkinson. In a rash moment I said I'd be interested to see them. A short time later they started to pop up in my inbox, chapter by chapter. Clive never claimed to be a writing man and often said that English was his weakest subject at school. You wouldn't know that from reading the story that follows. His friend and neighbour Tom Ramage, of the Strathspey & Badenoch Herald's editorial staff, undertook early editing but he has a demanding workload, whereas Clive knew I had retired and assumed I had plenty time on my hands to take over the task. Thanks are due to Tom for setting the pace.

The text which Clive passed to me has been adjusted in only minor respects, other than some infilling in the last two chapters, which were unfinished at the time of his final illness. He wasn't a stickler for spelling (particularly of the names of people and places), punctuation or dates and these have been corrected or adjusted where possible. Any remaining inaccuracies are mine. As many readers know, Clive had an outgoing nature and made friends easily. He was also quick to criticise where he considered that appropriate. Typical targets were often people he saw as bureaucrats, such as planning officers, tax inspectors, some (but by no means all) bank managers and people in local or central government with whom he was involved on official business. I have either excised or watered down some of his comments in that department in the hope of avoiding displeasure or worse.

In a busy life Clive did not have much time for photography. Limited photographic material from his early life is available and some of it is of questionable quality. I am grateful to Peter Wright, the younger brother of one of his boyhood friends, for providing information about some of the photographs of Clive's early years at Mablethorpe and at college. Sadly I have found no photos to illustrate his experiences training the army in Germany and on secondment to the Outward Bound school in the United States, recounted so vividly in Chapter 9. I am grateful to his youngest son, Jonny, for searching through the family records and providing many of the photographs, particularly the more recent ones which reflect so graphically the wonderful environment Clive and Sally created at Loch Insh. I am also grateful to my friend and digital mentor Alastair White, of Gullane, for having edited, sized and laid out all the photographs with such professional skill - for the captions I accept responsibility. Thanks also to Larry Bates for taking time out of a busy life to design the front and back covers of the book. Particular thanks also to Ian Grover of Groverprint for his strong "can-do" attitude throughout the publication process and for going well beyond the call of his original remit in guiding me on so many aspects of the layout and design of the book. I am not aware of any copyright issues relating to the photographs but please let me know if you have any concerns on that score. A few names are lacking from some of the group photograph captions and some of the spellings may be amiss; please let me know if you can fill in any of the blanks or correct any spelling errors.

I am grateful to Archie Rennie for permission to reproduce in Chapter 15 his brilliant verses about Clive's legal triumph in the canoeing case in the House of Lords. Sadly Archie died last November, when the book was still being prepared for publication. You may think that the story of the long drawn out court battle, pursued by the powerful salmon fishing interests on the River Spey, is rather spread out, but that is how it was for Clive and Sally – over some six years they had to endure the daily stress of defending their position against those interests at the same time as developing and running their fledgling business and looking after a growing family. Clive gave his legal team the credit for their success but I think it was in equal measure his tenacity which helped win the day. The story unfolds in Chapters 12, 14 and 15.

Another battle, over the competing developments of Lord Fraser of Allander's Aviemore Centre and the Rank Organisation's Coylumbridge Hotel in the mid 1960s, is recounted graphically in the Ballad of Crampon Creek, recited almost in full in Chapter 17. I regret that I have been unable to trace the copyright holder of this lengthy poem. Sally has told me that Clive did not have a printed version of it but, as with quite a few ballads, he could recite it from memory from start to finish. Read it slowly for best effect, and let me know if you can supply the missing line in verse 20.

Finally, the biggest thank you is reserved for Sally. Her contribution to the development and success of the Loch Insh story is much greater than many people realise. With consummate skill she kept, and still keeps, a firm hand on the tiller of many aspects of the business and she successfully reconciled Clive's often fiery temperament with the creation of a happy and fulfilling home life for the family. I am certain that if Clive had lived to witness the publication of these memoirs he would have dedicated them to her.

Tom Drysdale
tomdrysdale@btinernet.com
January 2018

Introduction

I was born to battle.

All the deprivations, the crippling injury and crushed hopes, the forces of nature and fierce competition, the feudal fishing barons, the rogues and the regulators, the crowds of critics and credit crunchers.

I was always lucky to have an army of faithful friends and family bringing up the rear, but there is a battle I have to fight alone - and after seven decades it's high time I did.

This is my chance, chilling out in the 23 degree heat on a palm-fringed terrace with only spring turtle doves nagging at me. Here, in the heart of the old walled city of Marrakesh, I'm just far enough away to start the long journey to the beginning.

I'm going back for my sons. Like all youngsters, they never have time to ask the important questions until it's too late. Where are you from? What did you do in the war, Daddy? What did you do before *our* warring.....? And until now I haven't had time to tell them. So here are the answers.

Clive and Sally at Loch Insh

Chapter One
The Day War Broke Out

The conflict began in 1939, on a cold January day in Nottinghamshire.

I was a second pincer movement: from very rare conversations I gleaned that my mother had first had a girl, but not for very long. I don't know if the baby was buried – a search through the local graveyard produced no results. I do know that if she had lived I probably would never have been born. The birth had been very traumatic. In those days most babies were delivered at home and, when I look back at the facilities we had, it must have been a very intimidating prospect for my mother in that two-bedroom railway level-crossing gatehouse: a tin roof for a scullery, coal-burning range and boiler for the week's wash and bath. The outside toilet was ten or so yards from the house and seemed much further, as did our water pump. No electricity, just oil lamps and a rechargeable battery to power the wireless set. And yet my birth apparently went without too much trauma, apart from Mum having to be left alone as my father cycled up to the village to fetch Dr Dewar.

World war was soon upon us but I didn't know too much about it. There was a big one-man metal shelter in the signal box which had a wooden floor and the air-raid shelter had no bottom to it, so if it had ever taken a direct hit the whole thing would have gone through to the floor below, where the rechargeable batteries for the Morse kit were kept. There are some incidents I remember clearly, even as a tot of three or four sleeping on the settee (we always slept downstairs it seemed, preparing for the air raids which never came). Probably the earliest memory is that of being woken by a house full of people, mostly in army battledress. A troop train had derailed, its back carriage bogey carving a quarter mile of railway sleepers in half and causing a long delay. It seemed like half the world and his wife were in, getting my water first of all and then getting my mother to boil it while they made the customary cups of tea. I think we finished up better off for tea and sugar than we had been for a long time.

The family history is hazier. I know far too little of my own parents' backgrounds, even though they lived until I was into my late 20s and older. I know my mother was a tailoress in Wakefield and her parents, I believe, had both a farm and a pub, which is probably what attracted my father to her. At that time he was working as a signalman in nearby Ardsley, where the father of little Ernie Wise, Eric Morecambe's "fat-hairy-legged" partner, had once served as a porter. My father had come up from Stamford, where he was one of five brothers and two sisters. I have only met one of the brothers. I know that my mother had at least one sister, whom I visited once when I was five or so, in Wakefield. She was known to me as Auntie Annie and lived in an odd-shaped house – it was pointed to make the Y junction of the road. It had a stone staircase up the outside, with iron railings. We visited there twice by rail, but I never went to my mother's home and I have always wondered if there had been some kind of family bust-up there, when she met up with "Pop" as we fondly called him.

Equally, I don't recall ever going down to Stamford, even though it was barely an hour's train journey from where we were living in Tuxford, better known as the gatehouse at Stone End Lane, where my father was a signalman. They recalled their courting days on Ilkley Moor and at Roundhay Park, a place I would later come to know as a Carnegie College student, training as a physical education teacher. My parents – Ivy Lee and James Freshwater – certainly played golf at that time, because I remember the clubs I was to abuse as a six or seven year old in the fields around Tuxford.

The signal box was across the line, almost opposite the house and higher than us. My father said there was always the danger of enemy aircraft going home and emptying the odd bomb or strafing the line, but again I don't think that ever happened, not on our section anyway. The only thing I do remember clearly is the horrendous noise of the iron ore trains thundering past, which could have had up to 60 wagons, at interminably slow speed. The tin roof of the scullery seemed to bounce with each wagon that passed. There were two sidings on the north side of our gatehouse where Pop used to put the slow-moving goods while the expresses were allowed free run to London and the south. The Silver Link and the Mallard were regular sights, doing the ton within two metres of the house, with something like ten to fifteen coaches: an ear-splitting racket. According to Pop we had a train every three minutes, which is a staggering thought in those black-out wartime days.

Pop worked shifts of eight hours with two other signalmen, who I don't recall ever meeting, and when they had a weekend off they worked twelve hour shifts. I spent quite a lot of time with him in the box, going over each day with his tea in a blue ration bag, mixed with a little sugar, no milk. As the day shift started they would have the kettle on the compulsory fire which every signalman kept, an ample supply of coal dropped off by the goods drivers as they passed the house. A full supply was maintained in the box and the house. Huge lumps of coal would fill a wheelbarrow at one go. We always seemed to have plenty to eat. My mother was a good cook and baker and a highly skilled seamstress. She made most of our clothes. Only when I was approaching my teens did that strike me as an embarrassment, with my friends kitted out in all the latest shop styles. I felt a little let down that she didn't possess a steam iron and couldn't put sharp points on lapels and so on, but she was mustard with a needle! I believe that when she worked in Wakefield she was paid by the suit: she made them for the 50-shilling tailors as they were then, of which she received sixpence (2½p) and an extra shilling (5p) for a waistcoat with sewn buttonholes.

We witnessed some aircraft incidents. I remember seeing a plane going down in flames not more than two miles away, as it attempted landing back at one of the airfields which surrounded us. I remember visiting three or so airfields after 1945 during the victory celebrations, and receiving a huge meteorological balloon from RAF personnel. The thing measured some two feet across and was strongly made, but it only lasted a fortnight or so – it broke my little heart when the thing got caught and burst.

Christmases came and went. One of my early recollections is Pop making toy Spitfires from bits of timber and then painting them in camouflage. I don't think I had any boats, oddly enough, but there were certainly aircraft. When I was five he made a clock with hands that moved. It had a small poem on the back which he painted in white, saying: "Wake up Clive, you are five years old!". It went on to say I should learn to tell the time and that's just what I did, using those moveable hands. It was a pure delight, not least because presents during the war were pretty thin on the ground. Metal ones, of course, were particularly scarce, but I did get a Hornby train set with the very basic circular track, a wind-up green locomotive and two yellow coaches. Probably worth a fortune now, but it did last until our children came on the scene. It was difficult to get track for those models and Pop used to spend his spare time in the signal box fret-sawing, by hand, planks of the orange boxes which anybody from that era will remember. He made remarkable lengths of railway line, their black sleepers pinned down with the cut-off pins Mum used for her dressmaking, and brown painted long strips to make the lines, including curves and points which worked. We could link these together to extend the line hugely – the little clockwork train needed to be wound up more than once to complete the circuit. There were a few other toys, including some lead soldiers which would have been pre-war. They were about one and a half inches high on a lead plate, probably with lead paint and I would probably have put them in my mouth, although I can't say I remember doing so. I also had some small guns which fired matchsticks.

I was playing with the soldiers in the garden one day and firing at one on a fence post when, towering overhead, came an aircraft towing a glider...then another...and another. Soon, as far as the eye could see, there were planes two abreast pulling gliders, each passing directly over the house. Whether they were following the railway line I couldn't say - but it must have been the Arnhem invasion – I really do mean they filled the sky as far my eyes could see, in a clear sky at 2000 feet or lower. As I turned round my toy soldier fell into the long grass, never to rejoin his regiment despite my tireless search for him. Items so difficult to come by were cherished and played with for hours, and any casualties were heartbreaking.

I learned very early that you had to dig for victory. In the garden with Pop, we'd empty the privy into trenches which he had dug, and turn the soil later to plant potatoes. We produced some magnificent specimens. Digging for Britain was the in thing. We had a very fine vegetable garden with a plum tree and an apple tree, and we kept a few hens. Making do was certainly the name of the game. Nobody seemed to complain, everybody doing their bit. We were surrounded by farmland and at the bottom of Stone End Lane the Peel family farmed. They had two sons, Howard, about my age, and a younger lad called David. They were my playmates and we gathered the sheep, roamed the fields, played in the haystacks, worked with the threshing machines at harvest time: we'd gather corn from the stooks and then help (as we saw it) to build the corn stacks. Then the steam engine would trundle away with its flying wheels and belts. We worked around the stack as they stripped it and threw it into the thresher, on hand to whack the rats and mice which came flying out of each layer of corn as the farmers put it into the machine; we'd chase them into the byres and deal with them. There was an old windmill by the railway line, defunct, full of pigeons, which I think may still be there today, probably converted into a private house. I remember on a family shopping trip to Tuxford, on the farm at the bottom of the lane, I saw what I thought was a rabbit (I remember shouting "Wabbit!") and chased the thing until I caught it by its tail. It turned out to be a rat, which spun round and bit me on the wrist. Mum had to abandon the shopping trip and rush me back to the house for Dettol treatment. I was none the worse for it, although it probably gave my parents a heart attack.

The rat took no prisoners but the British did. There was an Italian working on the farm, and when about six or so I used to help him. We'd take the horse and cart carrying turnips and would spread them on the fields for the cows and sheep. I'd be given the privilege of holding the reins while my friend threw the food over the back and sides of the cart. I think the horse knew where to go – I certainly didn't have much influence over it.

When not scattering turnips our only means of transport was Shanks's pony, at least for the quarter-mile stretch down to the A1, where the buses ran between Newark and Retford. We didn't go very often, and when we did it was usually for shopping. Everything was measured and sold in either brown or blue bags and on very few occasions we went to the doctor's house where he distributed bananas to the community. Why they were kept at his house I have no idea – maybe he was seen as less of a spiv, not that I recall any of the neighbours as spivs – but it was his job to give a nice potassium-rich bunch of fives to the locals. My parents seemed to be able to make the things last for ever: we'd have them sliced – always sliced – and hot or cold in custard. I'm pretty sure I was given the lion's share. I can still see the Geest box they came in, and those boxes have only just recently disappeared off the scene. They were recyclable. I don't know what bananas are shipped in now, probably a refrigerated container, but when they get here they don't taste anything like those fresh ones.

Being friendly with the farm also enabled us to go gleaning. Gleaning was a follow-up to the harvesting of the corn and we'd go out with a picnic basket a mile or two away into a field, on a hill looking back to our house, and wander up and down picking up the ears which hadn't been taken away for threshing. This became food for the chickens through the winter. I remember we got a good sackful each time we went, usually on a nice day with a picnic of home-made bread and whatever Mum had managed to save from the week's rations. Certainly nothing was wasted. The bin men never came and if they had they wouldn't have had anything to take away, there just wasn't any wastage.

The fields opposite the line were pasture for the cows and, yes, we had milk from the farm direct. Yes, it was untreated and did me a lot of harm I'm sure...or maybe I'm just lucky. Those same fields had mushrooms, field mushrooms like you've never seen. Pop and I would take our little wheelbarrow over to collect handfuls of them, not to sell but to give to the fireman who came by in the goods train, as payment for his occasional chunk of coal. They were great mushrooms - maggots and all. Once you fried them the maggots soon hopped out and died in the heat – then it was up to you whether you ate the mushrooms or not, but it certainly didn't spoil them.

The fields were ringed with the great hedgerows so tragically missing today. They

Top - Clive - early years

Above – Clive as a growing lad

were so densely populated that Pop enthusiastically taught me some of his bad habits, like bird-nesting and gathering eggs, but always on the basis that you only ever took one so that the bird didn't abandon its nest. I had a considerable collection by the time we moved to Mablethorpe on the Lincolnshire coast - so many that in later years, for fear of prosecution, my father destroyed them all. There were up to 100 of them, including some of the more exotic, such as the Guillemot, which weren't generally found in our area. It was a pastime, it whiled away the hours spent wandering in the fields and a place called Green Lane at the top of the railway, where the family used to go.

Schooling started at Tuxford when I was five or six, but I had no more than a year there. I used to go to the bottom of the road once I'd been taken to school and knew where to go, along the main A1. My parents made arrangements for the family who ran the village shop - I think it was a paper and sweets shop - and for two shillings (10p) a week they gave me a hot lunch, long before school meals existed. It was either that or sandwiches. Amazingly, I had to walk a mile and a half, or I hitched when the massive British Leyland trucks would stop – I'd be about as tall as the wheel arches and would haul myself into the deafening cab for the trip up to Tuxford. Looking back, it was simply never seen as a high-risk situation, roads and rogues not a consideration then. Even into my teens the question of any molestation never occurred to me. I have to say that the old brigade put a lot of the molestation mania of today down to the media. The drivers in those days were very helpful and used to drop me off at the school gate, one or two of them picking me up on a regular basis – they giving *me* the thumb-up and not the other way around. Just as well, because there was no school bus. There may have been a bus, but it was never at the right time - some things don't change.

I didn't get on too well at that school. I felt intimidated. I wasn't very academic and perhaps that was the problem. I could read a little, but not as much as some. There weren't any sports so I didn't get my chance to shine. I did that outside school – I can recall one snowy winter playing at the Hollyhocks, an undulating area of grassland, when a few of us forgot about time: when we finally returned to school an hour late we got a bit of a roasting. I haven't forgotten many names, but the name of the people who fed me has gone. Maybe it'll come back to me as I ramble on. The food was good, I remember that. Their daughter was an attractive 20-year-old and I suppose even at seven I had a bit of a crush on her. We were well looked after at the shop, dried if we got wet and sent on our way home or back to school. I don't remember travelling to or from school in the dark at any time, nor do I recall being off school for very long.

Some early adventures have stuck in my mind. Pop, being on the railways, got free privilege passes (a third of the fare - they'd come in useful for me at a later date). I know we had been to Blackpool and not liked it, especially my father after I'd grabbed his hat and thrown it out of the window, the way little lads do. Nothing else remains of the place in my memory, but I do remember an expedition to Newquay, after changing at mighty London. My parents seemed to know the Underground as if they'd been brought up on it but then Pop was not frightened by time-tables and knew exactly how to work any rail system to his advantage. I remember being woken up as we trundled along near Penzance, where the railway runs close to the sea. It was dark but moonlit and Mum woke me and put me to the window to point it out. It was the first time I'd ever seen the sea, but I was soon back to sleep in that cosy carriage amid the sunny posters of shiny resorts the railway would take you to (oh, for some copies now – at today's prices they'd fetch me a new car).

As we pulled into Newquay Station (unchanged to this day) my father picked up our tin trunk (it still sits in our workshop at Loch Insh) containing all we needed: food rations, primus stove, bottled fuel, tent, all packed into a piece of metal three feet long and 15 inches square. How we got it from the station to Trennance Gardens I don't know. There were few taxis about. We struck camp in a field on what is now a mobile home stance, at an angle of at least thirty degrees. The farmer gave us a bale of hay I recall, and the tent was very small and white, with a two-stick support, no fly-sheet, no groundsheet and just a rug to cover the hay. And I slept like a log. Every morning I was given three thruppeny bits (amounting to a total of about 4p in today's money) to go down the boating lake (still there) to get myself an hour on the paddle boats, which were utterly fantastic. What Mum and Pop got up to in that time I have no idea – they didn't say and I didn't ask. I remember, too, the bowl of Jersey milk, cream nearly half an inch thick on it. I wasn't too keen on the cream but my parents made good use of it on the scones. They would come down to the lake eventually and we'd go off to various places. There were no fewer than seven beaches and we'd take in a different one each day. The house on the island was there; the mainland bridge was there. We surfed – you could get a little surfboard or inflatable which, in shallow surf, was great fun bearing in mind that I couldn't have been any more than seven at the time.

We enjoyed it so much that we went twice to Newquay, before deciding to try Mablethorpe, nestling between Skegness and Cleethorpes. It was closer to home, only 70 or 80 miles and virtually a direct line took us to Thirsby, where we'd change for the Skegness/Mablethorpe branch line long before that war of Beeching's broke out. It was a wonderful introduction to a totally different coastline over on the east of England. The water was muddier but it was a great place to explore. I would go down with Mum in the school holidays and camp in that tent, which we pitched between all the grander ones and the caravans – we weren't jealous. We made do. I do remember we were pitched on a caravan site at the north end of Mablethorpe and a gale hit the whole site one year. The neighbours rallied round my Mum, with Pop still working back home. They found every brick they could and built a wall, which not only shielded us from the wind but also held down the edge of the tent to stop it blowing away. It worked brilliantly. Mum probably had some sleepless nights on those summer trips, but I was always straight out the moment my head hit the pillow.

What we couldn't explore on those lazy, hazy days of summer were the sand dunes. They were sealed off for minefields, in preparation for any invasion: those majestic sweeping sands would have made ideal landing grounds, with warm shallow waters trickling over that concrete-hard base and only a few pill-boxes to worry about. As it turned out, the Germans never did invade Mablethorpe – instead, we did. After our two summer holidays, my father heard there was a signalman's job going there and landed it. The Freshwaters were coming.

Chapter Two
A Salt-Water Home

The Freshwaters were no strangers to conflict. My grandfather, whom I never met, had been a regular soldier, fighting in various campaigns of the 1800s, including Afghanistan (remember the days when the British were fighting there...?). Pop told me he used to talk of his time in the Middle East. I have vague memories of visiting the family home in Stamford but none of meeting any of his family. Of his brothers, the one closest to Pop was, I think, the youngest. Horace spent his whole life in India with the Army and had ended up as a major. After serving he saw out his life in Northamptonshire. There was Bill, a railway driver out of Peterborough. He was the only member of Pop's family that I did ever meet. It happened when I was playing professional football in Grimsby. He came to the ground, took me home with him and I stayed the night, but I never saw him again and we didn't keep in touch.

The oddest, saddest thing about my side of the family is that none of them kept in touch, neither my mother with her side nor my father with his. We had one or two cousins who visited after we had moved to Mablethorpe, but they never seemed very friendly affairs – it was as though there had been some bust-up which had sent them all on their separate ways. It was never spoken about. We just got on with our lives.

Tuxford had lots of high points for me, especially the lifts I would hitch, both on the footplates with my father and in the wooden guard's vans which used to bring up the rear on the goods trains. They always had a fire and rattled along – bone-shaking at its best. It was always much more fun than walking between home and the station. The last time I was there, with my wife, Sally, and at least two of our boys, we arrived at my old home only to find it had been completely flattened: the place had been reduced to nothing more than a pile of red clay bricks, since they were planning to straighten the line for speeding up the 125s. While we were there one came through, announced only by an ominous rumbling on the rails from something like a mile away. It then rocketed through at more than a hundred miles an hour. Suddenly, my childhood proximity to the line struck me as having been shockingly close. I don't know how I survived, walking along that track unaccompanied as a very young boy, and blithely hopping across time after time to see Pop in the signal box. Of course, the track is now automatically operated with just a flashing light and a barrier.

There was an incline, I remember, on the crossing and in that record-breaking winter of 1947 we were still there, because I recall sledging in the snow for weeks. There were not too many motorists in those days, but all of them seemed to have got stranded at one point. We didn't have a car then and didn't get one until I was well into my 20s. My parents didn't drive. There would be the occasional lift on the road but we travelled essentially by rail – it was easy and, with Pop's connections, very affordable.

Wintry pasts remind me of Christmas presents. There would usually be one, maybe two, with the obligatory large stocking hung at the end of the bed. My first Meccano set, probably the Mark I or II, gave me endless pleasure, just as Lego has done for youngsters over the last couple of decades. Meccano was a treasured possession in those days and later sets were to constitute some pretty advanced engineering projects, complete with electric motors. A little railway set, coupled with Meccano and Pop's wooden tracks from those orange boxes, ensured that I had a very good early supply of play equipment – even if there was a shortage of playmates. But we were to move into a far more populous area before much longer. Mablethorpe, the seaside home of our happy holidays, became home itself – after spending just the occasional holiday weekend with us, Pop accepted the post and we moved to the coast for good. Professionally speaking, it was actually a downgrade, his salary actually dropping in 1947 to something like £6 a week, or at the very most £7, but the accommodation was upgraded: until then we'd stayed at a caravan site but now, at the south end, nearer to Sutton on Sea, we took a room – literally a room – with the owner of the site, who shared his kitchen and dining area with us. But there was still no electricity, the trusty old Tilley lamps still working away for us. Before long we moved nearer to the centre of town, on Wellington Road, but still sharing with an old guy in our "digs" near the primary school, where I was to study for the next four or five years.

The one incident I remember in the new accommodation involved not so much eaves-dropping as an overheard conversation between my parents, another man and the owner of the house as they sifted through a handful of black and white photographs. The old man, possibly Polish but certainly foreign, was showing them snaps of the graves at Belsen, or some similar hell-hole. Once they realised I was in the room I was quickly dispatched, but not before catching sight of the horrendous piles of naked bodies. That was probably my first exposure to death and the war, although nothing was ever said to me about the pictures and I certainly didn't ask questions. It was only later that I put two and two together and realised what it was all about. My only earlier experience of death came at Tuxford, one Christmas, when my father came in, closed the kitchen door and exhibited two of my chicken friends hanging feet uppermost, ready for plucking. The image remains with me to this day, but it's never put me off eating chicken.

The school at Mablethorpe was pretty spread out, 1930s style, with a veranda hall linking all the classrooms to the headmaster's office. Mr Wilson was his name and he had written a very graphic account of the floods on the east coast way back in the 13th century, well before those of 1953. I never saw the account myself, which he'd printed off in the school print shop, but it explained how half the town, including the church, had been lost under the sea. I did see some of the stumps from the forest which had been swallowed up, but I never heard the church bell tolling, which locals said I might hear one day on a very low tide.

Primary school rang the changes. I found I had a lot more friends and had a lot of fun exploring, although the regime was quite strict. The deputy head, Stivvy Stevens we called him, was a stern disciplinarian, with one hand on his cane and the other tugging your ear should you ever step out of line. His able assistant, Mrs Mason, would walk round the rows of boys in assembly during singing, sorting out the droners. "You're a droner!" she would proclaim victoriously, before leading you out of the hall. The better singers were led in the other direction, hand-picked for special – and always remarkable – annual performances of Gilbert & Sullivan operas. It was quite an undertaking, but in those days everyone who went to school had singing lessons as well as the normal academic studies. The primary was attached to a secondary school, so it was able to offer all those subjects so sadly missing today from school life: gardening, home economics (baking for the girls) and crafts like metal and woodwork. Not the academic type myself, I was easily distracted by the other pursuits which included fishing, football and helping an old boy on the beach – he had a 30ft double-ender and used to take visitors on boat trips in the summer.

Mick Slater taught us as best he could, with Nelly Mason shrieking over her own class in the next room - the school was prefabricated and in no way soundproofed. Mick was an ex-RAF pilot who'd done a one-year teacher training course after the war. He too was a disciplinarian and Freshwater's backside often saw the underside of his slipper, not for any wrongdoing but always for wrong spelling. Spelling still beats me. Fortunately I now have secretaries to make life (and sitting down) easier, and they have Dictaphones to spare them from my spelling. Despite the footwear, Mick was a good teacher, especially games – in those days primary teachers held their own games sessions, of which we got two a week. As boys (I can't remember there being girls although I'm sure it must have been a mixed class) we could play soccer and cricket and do some running. Oddly enough, I invariably got headaches when running, so I was put in goal. It was either that or leaving the pitch, besides I was big built and well suited to the position.

I definitely inherited my sporting interest from Pop, but he told me of one position he hoped I'd never get myself into. It was while we were visiting his old stamping ground in Stamford, at his house on the edge of Burghley Park, that he recalled one game that was very nearly his last. He'd been playing with his brothers and they had him up on a stool near the park gates, with a rope round his neck. They kicked the stool away and only rescued him in the nick of time. Just through the gate was the entrance to the cricket ground at Burghley House and he'd go to the pavilion when the gentlemen were at play against the Burghley Park families or invited guests. He had no fears approaching anyone and before long he was whitening boots and pads (for a small consideration) and even bowling in the nets for their batting practice before each game. He also told stories of half-crowns (12½p) being put on the middle stump, which he'd be given whenever he bowled successfully at it. It wasn't unusual for him to earn up to five bob (25p) a time. This was an age when halfpennies and farthings were worth something to young lads – tanners (5p) and five bobs were a lot of money and, with his skills, Pop never went short.

One of his brothers worked in the local brewery, another as a funeral director's assistant. Bill was on the railway, Horace in the Army, and the fifth brother fell into a vat at the brewery and was asphyxiated. A tough business then and, for some, it still is today. As for their two sisters, I think I may have met one but I have no idea what happened to them, sadly. Apart from a cousin in Newark-on-Trent who died in the late 1990s, I have had no recent contact with any family members beyond those already mentioned.

Pop's exploits and his outgoing manner made him a very good mixer and he'd get on in all levels of society. I know he was good at games and had a good eye for the ball, although I never did actually see him play. He and Mum always encouraged me to go the way I wanted and there was never any pressure regarding academic exams. They worked hard to provide for me and, out of respect for them as much as anything, I tried to provide for myself.

By the time we got to Mablethorpe Mum had put on a fair bit of weight. I think I first noticed it just before we left Tuxford. Having seen their wedding photographs (which sadly disappeared somewhere between our seaside home and Pop's later move to

Scotland) I know they were extremely slim in their young days. There are still pictures of them in each other's clothes standing by a tandem. Using each other's things could sometimes be very practical indeed: as a young girl Mum had been kicked by a horse and it had left an ulcerated wound which proved horribly painful for her, but which magically healed when, having used up all her ointments, she resorted to using Pop's hair cream. Whatever was in the stuff, it took the pain away and the wound healed up. She never had a problem with it again, apart from the scar it left on her skin.

How Mick Slater's slipper never left a scar on my bum I'll never know. Having been taught a modicum of psychology at college later, I look back on his methods and can't help thinking of Pavlov's dogs, who had obviously decided amongst each other: "Hey, if we get this right we can programme this guy to bring us some food by ringing his door-bell!". What Mick taught me – at least, what his slipper taught me – was to avoid writing down words I knew I couldn't spell and just to write the ones which I could spell. That left me with a pretty limited vocabulary and that perhaps explains the lack of a permanent imprint of a slipper on my bottom. Nevertheless I have to confess that later at college I earned only an E minus for English Literature. My consolation is that I once watched a TV programme featuring the education of Jack Charlton, Greg Dyke and some other celeb. Dyke admitted to being in a class of 35 and ending up 35th in most of the exams. I wasn't quite that bad, but as far as English was concerned I wonder if I might have been dyslexic all my life. Our eldest, Duncan, was identified as being severely dyslexic when he finished up at Aberdeen University. The slipper, for all the occasional discomfort, didn't hold me back though, and I've yet to meet anyone claiming that corporal punishment at school psychologically harmed them, through either the stick or Scotland's favoured tawse. So long as it was deserved, it was seen as fair retribution. For Britain's sake I hope it all goes full circle eventually, because the system we have at the moment certainly isn't working (but that's enough politics).

To help pay my way through school my mother got a very modestly paid job at the railway station looking after the ladies' waiting rooms. I don't know why, but my father never wanted her to develop her sewing skills commercially. We could have had quite a cottage industry in our industrious cottage, the place usually looking like a tailor's workshop, with part-rolls of material all around it. And cobbler's, too: Pop had his own last and knew exactly what to do with strips of leather, soling and heeling like a real professional – and God help me if I ever damaged my home-made shoes playing football.

By the time we got to Mablethorpe things were a little easier, but Mum could have made a really good living as a tailoress. People used to bring her their clothing, trousers and jackets, for altering. She was so quick, her fingers so nimble - and heaven help you if you ever went too close to the Singer, her sacred treadle sewing machine. She could also run up a coat for herself in next to no time, as she did the night before the Coronation in 1953. It was full length and pretty heavy for her solo trip down to The Mall, where she stood to watch the procession. I had it a little easier, watching my first television in my neighbour's house, next door to what had become our third home in the town. We had moved from Wellington Road into our own accommodation, which was good but also very cold, one of six properties built out of sheet asbestos about a foot off the ground and like a fridge in the winter. I don't remember any fire. There was one bedroom, a small kitchen and a parlour. Mr Page, next door, was a bit better off than us and had very kindly invited me in to watch the big event, which in the end occupied some thirteen hours of TV viewing. It was a very small black and white screen with an awful lot of speckled interference, but you could see what was going on and I found it very interesting.

We had good friends around us. Jack Durrance, Les Hastle and another family, all pulling together through those hard times. We survived there for a couple of years before moving out to a pre-fab, one of a batch of twenty built at the north end of Mablethorpe. It meant we were back to walking nearly two miles to school, but it never seemed to matter if you set off at the right time. In the winter there was a stream, or a "cut" as we called them in Lincolnshire, which froze over and we could slide our way to school (didn't have skates then). It was all great fun getting there. That cut has been filled in now and replaced by an underground drain which serves the marshland into the sea. The great thing about the new pre-fab was that it had electricity. Oh, the thrill of running to that switch on the wall. By now I must have been ten years old and life was becoming a little easier: no more paraffin lamps, cleaning lenses and protecting mantles, and an open fire which gave you hot water while it heated the bedroom. In the bathroom, no more tin baths. The kitchen had an electric cooker and a washing machine, a fantastic improvement on what many people had put up with immediately after the war.

Scoffed at today, ridiculed even at times, the pre-fabs were loved by those lucky enough to have them as their first homes. For starters, they weren't crammed in against each other; they had an ample garden with a front lawn, drainage and water supplies, all of them comfortably detached, with no bother from their neighbours. My parents stayed on in theirs and, even after Mum died, Pop kept it on until he finally came to stay in Scotland.

We were all coming through testing times. Even young Freshwater.

I enjoyed school immensely, with little pressure from my parents or the other pupils, although there was quite a push to get everybody through the all-important final primary test, the legendary 11-Plus. I wasn't expected to pass, but my recollection of the exam was that we had a few "dummy runs" and a lot of it was not so much writing as working out formulas, both mathematical and verbal. When the results were given to my parents it was more a case of nonplussed than 11-Plus - their surprise bordered on amazement that one Clive Freshwater had passed and won a much-coveted place at Alford Grammar School. Not that *they* coveted it much – I think they'd have been just as happy to see me attend the local county secondary. But Alford, some eight miles inland from Mablethorpe, taking in the best brains from the Spilsby, Skegness and Longcastle catchment area, had quite a reputation, its regime reputedly the making of pretty well every pupil who went there.

And now it was my turn to put that reputation to the test.

Chapter Three
Life's A Beach And Then You Dyer

It was good, having three educations. School was enjoyable during the week, then I would be back beside the seaside with my other teachers, developing the other skills which I would come to rely on. One such teacher was Eric Tustin who put me through the mincer in the butcher's shop. After two years he gave the joint the chop, opting for fish and chips instead. I went with him as an errand boy, delivering wet fish and being his general dogsbody in what was one of fourteen such shops around the town: the summer influx of 80,000-odd working-class families called for lots of fish and chips with their beer. As I have told many of those toiling away at food preparation today, it wasn't unusual for us to provide a ton of potatoes a day, most of which I had to rumble and chip. I also had to collect a four-wheeled trolley from the railway station once a day in the high summer, with as many as fifteen to twenty seven-stone boxes of wet fish in all forms. We had the largest wet fish bale in town, landing me the task of not just preparing the wet fish and chips but of delivering wet fish every day to some twenty guesthouses for their middle class customers. And then there was my other classroom, the one which was to complete my education and set my true course in life: the beach.

For all the study and the work, we found plenty of time for sport at the weekends. Football was for Saturday, but the rest of the time was devoted to another abiding passion: canoe-building. My canoeing exploits started with an old fuel tank which came off a Meteor aircraft belonging to Max Appleby. I cut it in half, but it was too unstable and before long I was determined to make my own craft. I have often related how, having designed my first canoe at school in art lessons, I brought the thing to life in the Mablethorpe village scout hut, where the father of one of my pals, Willie Hewson, was the scout master. At the tender age of 14 we acquired a couple of long planks of wood from a builder, an old floorboard from a house, which he kindly cut up into stringers, and other pieces which we used to make a hexagonal frame for the shape of the canoe. There was no plywood for us in those days and even if we had got hold of any, we had no fret-saw to cut it. We could only work in the evening, when we got the key to the hut, and the only glue we had was the stuff used on furniture (it was made from animal hooves, melted down in a double pot over a gas ring). I remember it took as much in thruppenny bits for the gas as it did for the rest of the material – 10/6d for the gas and just ten bob for the materials).

The frame made, we had to skin it and Willie's father contributed a fly-sheet of an old tent for the deck. Another friend, who I'd worked with at the butcher's and now had his own shop as a pork butcher, provided us with the old blind from the front of his premises. It was quite heavy and certainly heavier than the fly-sheet, so this formed the hull. Having tacked it all together we then knew we had to paint it with something waterproof. We had some black pitch which did the job and Willie and I were now the proud owners of what was initially a one-man canoe. It was pretty square or diamond shaped because we didn't believe we could bend the timber around the frames to make it more aesthetically pleasing. But our maiden craft lasted us several years and a modification to the cockpit enabled both of us to travel together. Willie was smaller than me and sat up front, initially for canal trips in Mablethorpe and ultimately out to sea. It wasn't long before we were taking our big leap into the great unknown, with a camping trip up the coast, my parents following on foot to see we didn't get into difficulties. Our only difficulty was getting well and truly rooked: we camped in the churchyard at Theddlethorpe, under the trees, and there must have been a thousand of the birds in them. What a sleepless night. But we had negotiated our first big expedition successfully and there were to be many, many more – the big adventure was under way, the canoe and I destined to be lifelong friends.

The next craft came from Willie's sister's boyfriend, Jim Foster. Jim had been three years ahead of me at Alford and I think had just taken up his first position as a PE teacher. He was another keen sportsman, a very able athlete and footballer. Jim produced the £14 for a PBK17 Percy Blandford kayak, which came in kit form with all its timbers and frames cut from plywood. We assembled it in Willie's home, between the front door and the back door. The frame must have lain there for two weeks, but his parents were very accommodating - each time they went into their home they had to dodge a 17-ft canoe frame. But eventually it was finished, with fine lines and proper green waterproof canvas for deck and hull. It was a three-seater and, as we showed the folks, the time had certainly not been wasted and the disruption had been well worthwhile as we were to use that canoe extensively over the next three or four years, sometimes on excursions of seven miles or so along the coast, past the bombing ranges at Theddlethorpe and Saltfleetby.

We would often spend the day in a run-off from the Fenlands. At low tide in those

Top left - Clive and his "Pop" with his first canoe, built by
Clive and his friend Willie Hewson

Top right - Clive at sea in the first canoe

Above – The first canoe and its owners

days the cut, which was anything from two feet to chest deep, would be full of sheltering flounders and we made ourselves strongads – spears with many forks like an inverted rake, but with the points going downwards with barbs filed into them. So, as you walked up the run of the stream, jamming away with your strongad, you'd eventually go through the fish and pull it up before placing it in your canoe or bag. Some days we'd catch 20 or 30 fish. They were good eating, usually a pretty substantial catch at up to two pounds in weight. Occasionally, instead of going up by sea, we'd go further up the Avon, transporting over the pumping station dam and paddling back along the cut, some five miles back to Mablethorpe. It was a good day out to say the least: the best part of 10 or 12 miles would have been paddled, with up to a couple of hours spent fishing.

The beach at Mablethorpe had been my favourite haunt since the age of eight or nine. There were double-ended boats available for hire so, at the time I wasn't at the fish shop, I'd have been down there, initially with my parents and latterly with my friends. Mother would come down with cold salad in jam jars, with fresh potatoes, peas and whatever meat was going. I was always fascinated by the boats and became friendly with Harold Teanby, one of the boatmen. He had quite a few boats under wraps and piles of driftwood in his yard. A friendly old boy, he endeared himself to my parents with his kindnesses to me. As I got older he invited me to join him on the boat and by the time I was 15, in my canoeing days, I was helping him with his 30 foot three-ton double-ender. It was kept on a pair of lorry wheels with a railway sleeper between the axles and we'd launch it by running it off the concrete ramp down to the water's edge and charging in. We used a rising tide and as it came into the promenade it filled a concrete spillway half-way down the beach, which took the water from the Fens. We found harbour alongside and attracted the public via metal-wheeled gangplanks - not so much a trip round the bay, more a trip towards Spurn Head and the top end of Mablethorpe, usually a half-hour journey.

Harold's boat had a little seven-horse Austin, non-marinated, in-board motor, which started with the cranking of the engine and off we went. He charged two bob (10p) per head and carried up to a dozen trippers. Then, at the end of the day when they'd gone for their tea, we'd run the boat onto the beach and sit with it while it dried out. As the tide fell back the sand became concrete hard, then it was a matter of digging under the prow, jacking it up with a large block of timber which had to be carried down from the prom, along with the chocks and blocks which went with it, to rig it high enough for the axle to be inserted underneath. Then we'd pull it up to the back of the boat, put the rope on and accost fifteen or twenty people to help us haul it back up to the promenade. It was never very difficult; there were plenty of volunteers, mostly miners, strong fit men who'd do the pulling, and within ten minutes we'd be back at the resting place, above high tide and set for the next trip. If the weather was good we'd go out every day.

I remember our best day. We finished up and Harold was always very fair, very generous in my estimation: there was a third of the take for the boat, a third for the owner and a third for the mate. On this day we took about £35 and I got £12. I went home with a handful of money, to the astonishment of my folks, since Pop was only on a tenner a week by then. I was encouraged to stick it in the bank, which I duly did. In addition, as I mention later, I had income from the station luggage runs and that supplemented any spending. Being the seaside, there were of course the dreaded slot machines and being youngsters we knew just which ones to play, which ones paid out, and if we didn't make a lot of money we certainly didn't lose much either. The operators were never too keen to see us because they knew we'd be winning, which was not their idea at all. The pinball machines were also susceptible to celluloid film as much as pennies and that wasn't entirely encouraged by the operators either. I used to deliver fish to one of the owners and behind his fenced house I would pass these dustbins full of pennies, halfpennies and thruppenny bits. The story goes that they were delivered to the bank in the bins - buckets of money, in gambling.

Life on the beach was buckets of fun, a heady mix of leisurely, lazy days, adventurous sporting ones and hard-working ones which did me absolutely no harm at all. After a day at the fish shop we'd go out on the town, round the amusement arcades and helping our friends who had the odd stall here and there, gathering the crowds to encourage them to put their hands in their pockets and try their skill with darts, airguns or whatever. One of our members, Jack Durhams, had a whelk stall, at least his parents did. Jack seemed to spend a lot of time working there until the late hours, 11 o'clock not unreasonable. He was a bright lad, did very well at school and became a teacher. Many of the Alford boys became teachers and it was essentially through the good offices of the headmaster, H J H Dyer, or HJH for short. One thing is for sure, I can't remember any boys who came out of that school without a job, since Dyer seemed to have his finger in so many pies. He could speak on behalf of his pupils so enthusiastically and convincingly that no employer would turn them down.

So it was with us athletes. As I went through the school I became the games player, the captain of hockey, soccer, athletics. We all had the uniform with colours that you wore on your cap as it was a very traditional education in those days, inherited from the university graduates whom most of the teachers had taught at Alford. As I got into the sixth, Dyer and his wife Edna were the main teachers of history and religious education. During my time at Mablethorpe my parents had been regular church-goers and I had been a three-times-a-day attender: morning service, Sunday school and evening service. I finished as the head choirboy, lighting and snuffing out the candles. I was also the bell-ringer: we had a peel of eight in Mablethorpe Church. Dyer guided us through the Bible with his many quips, knowing the New Testament backwards the way he did. In many ways he had the school sewn up, but considering his time there it was hardly surprising. Not only did his wife teach part-time, his sister was the secretary. Occasionally she would come into class and speak quietly to him, which resulted in the instruction: "Right gentlemen, carry on reading pages (x) to (y). I will be back in half an hour. I'm just off to remand a fellow...".

He was the local JP and would get up on his "sit up and beg" bicycle and trundle off to Alford Town Police Station to put someone behind bars for a short period, eventually returning at the end of the lesson. We'd then put our books away and await the next member of staff. I gather the boss also used to sit on the bench at Lincoln Assizes, which were held quarterly, and he'd be off in his little grey Austin. He never had driving lessons, so the car would go out of the yard containing kangaroo petrol, lurching forward until it got running properly. I don't think he understood what a clutch was. Anyway, he would drive to Lincoln for a couple of days and sometimes on his return he would tell us of the "blackguards", as he called the prisoners he had dealt with. One amusing incident involved a neighbour in Mablethorpe who owned donkeys – Donkey George, we called him. I had worked for him briefly as a herdsman, as he owned twenty or so of them and they'd had to be rounded up from the field, taken to the beach and brought back at the end of the day. I lost interest in the job, or at least my backside did, since we had to ride bare-back on the tarmac and it was a very unsettling experience which put me off riding, probably for life. But George clearly profited from it. Too much, it appeared: he had not been paying his national insurance stamp so was brought up before HJH Dyer JP. In his defence George explained that he had understood the contributions to be "voluntary". Back then the weekly wage ranged from £12 to £15, so he was duly fined £200. When asked if he wanted time to pay he assured the court "No, that's all right" and from his inside pocket produced a wad of notes. The boss found it all quite amusing and it became a regular story among our friends and neighbours.

Top – school sports day cup winners, Clive on right

Above – Mablethorpe football team with Cup -   Goalkeeper Clive, back row centre

Money flooded in from Sheffield Grammar School, too. After the storm of 1953 they sent a donation to Alford, to be divided among those who had lost possessions. The gesture prompted a new inter-school friendly between ourselves (250 pupils) and Sheffield (600-1000). We always gave them a good game but I don't think we ever won. It was all good education and by the time I was fifteen I was playing in the first team as a goalkeeper as well as 'keeping for the local Mablethorpe side. Through this I attracted the interest of Skegness Town and then, at the age of 16, that of Scunthorpe. The trial I had with them didn't amount to anything, but while I was at Skegness we played Grimsby Town "A" team; they had a good strong side and inspired me to play well enough to save a penalty.

Shortly after the match the club contacted me through my parents, asking if they could come and see me. At the time Skegness were being managed by George Raynor, among his stars the coloured comic Charlie Williams, who had been centre-half for Doncaster Rovers (and who was to go on to TV fame in "The Comedians" and "The Golden Shot") and another Doncastrian, Alec Jeffrey, who had been an international prodigy until breaking his leg. For some inexplicable reason it had failed to heal and he had settled for the insurance money, thereby ruling himself out of any more league football. Thus his appearance for Skegness, where he was an outstanding passer and shooter of the ball - way above the standard Lincolnshire and the Midland league played at. It was all terribly sad, but while he was there, in one of the evening training sessions there was a young Hungarian refugee from the uprising of 1956, looking to join Skegness as a goalkeeper. He played in a kick-about and, diving at the feet of Alec Jeffrey, broke Alec's other leg. Amazingly, Alec came back from that and played several more seasons. Indeed, after I left Skegness, Charlie Williams, ever the funny man, would join him on stage at the Derby Miners Welfare Home in Skegness to entertain holidayers from Rotherham, Nottingham and Doncaster. Despite being in their mid-thirties they both went back and signed for Doncaster, playing a few more years before Charlie retired. I heard recently that Alec had died of Alzheimer's disease, but would long be remembered in other people's memories. The obituary referred to his confession that he'd never get a job down the pit because the foreman would never have been able to find him in the dark. Sadly, innocent jokes like that would now be dismissed as "racist" and be frowned upon by today's modern, unhappy audiences.

Anyway, I too became a happy Skegness player, thanks to George Raynor, which made me pretty special, since he was: in those days it was invariably the board of directors who chose the teams, but George was the first manager to insist on picking his men. As a result he would never manage a league team, even though he was brilliant enough to get Sweden to the World Cup final in 1958. I once went to his home (probably had a few hours to kill before training) which was nothing pretentious, but I met his wife in the sitting room where pride of place was taken by a large, solid silver football for his success in the competition. It bore the signatures of the whole team, who were only bested by the legendary Brazil. He had certainly been a great catch for Skegness and they prospered under him until Sweden grabbed him back for another spell, which peaked with a 2-0 thrashing of England at Wembley, their first defeat to a European team there for years.

All the same, my stay with him was all too brief because I was approached by Grimsby's manager, Alan Chiltern, the former Manchester United centre-half. He came to our little pre-fab – I say little since he must have been at least 6ft 3in tall and virtually had to crouch to avoid damaging the ceiling. We discussed the move with my parents and his secretary noted everybody's approval. I had to sign professional forms but, of course, was still involved with Alford Grammar and the move needed HJH's approval. That was very enthusiastically given, since the selection of one of his boys for Grimsby was a great accolade for him and the school. More significantly, the boss knew only too well how helpful the move would prove for my family - better than most, he knew the sacrifices working class families made to give their children a decent education.

Thanks to football I promptly became one of the best-dressed fifth-formers at Alford. Brian Locking, the centre-half at Skegness, was transferred with me to Grimsby for the princely joint sum of £500. I got a signing-on fee of £30 and £3 a game, plus another £3 if we won. At that time you could buy a pair of shoes at Saxone for £5, a good jacket or blazer for between £5 and £7. My first seven appearances were for the reserves. Grimsby were a second division club in those days, when there were only four divisions in the English league. The reserves played in the Midland league, where most of the pro teams from the east side of the country had their reserve teams. We won our first ten games, the first defeat coming, I think, at Peterborough. I remember playing Boston, who needed just one more goal for the 100 that season, and putting in the performance of my life to keep my sheet clean. We won the game 1-0. I reckon if they'd played all night they would never have got past me. Nobody was beating Freshwater that day.

Not long after I joined Grimsby the senior keeper, Harry Williams, was injured. So was the second team's goalie. Grimsby were playing Leicester City – who were pretty high in the second division at the time - and someone sent me a copy of the city's evening paper headlining that "Schoolboy of 16 is Grimsby's only fit goalkeeper". I had only been with the club a fortnight and came pretty close, but in the end Harry played – with a broken finger, I later found out. We lost, I think, as we would have done even if the great Freshwater had played. Leicester had an infamous centre-forward in Jack Froggart, who was renowned for his hustling and bustling of goalies. While I was tall and reasonably weighted, I was still fresh and fragile compared with those big burly forwards of the 1950s and all keepers were fair game for them. Nevertheless, for two years I enjoyed my time "standing between the sticks" as the boss put it, both for Grimsby reserves on Saturdays and the school mid-week. Alford had built a seriously strong team by then, which swept all before it in inter-school contests.

Dyer talked a robust game too, and had twice stood for parliament. He hadn't succeeded in politics but had won his battle against smoking – much to our amusement he would proudly announce that he'd given it up when he was twelve. His delight in the political cut-and-thrust was all too clear when the monthly debate got under way: the main hall was transformed into a parliamentary chamber, with healthy verbal war declared after one of the masters had chosen the topic. Three or four students would be asked to propose and defend a motion, while a Speaker would endeavour to keep order. After an hour we'd all be asked to file out and register our vote. Long before televised sessions from the House of Commons, it was all very interesting stuff, where the intellectuals would cut their teeth on their journeys to university and law school and even, ultimately, parliament itself.

There were school trips. I went to Dublin, 40 or 50 of us spending a week or so at St Stephen's Green. I particularly remember a boat trip from Bray around Ireland's Eye. Having worked on the little double-ended craft at Mablethorpe, I was impressed by the skill of the boatmen amid some daunting waves on the cross passage. The boat rolled dramatically and at times seemed likely to capsize with its fifteen passengers, but we made it safely there and back. Another day we visited Phoenix Park Zoo, at that time one of the country's largest open zoos – or "safari parks" as we call them today. In the Fifties the animals seemed very exotic. We climbed Mount Sugarloaf, a neighbouring hill in the Mountains of Mourne, and even in those days the path was severely eroded and quite steep in places. It's probably been concreted over by now...or it's been lost completely.

The boss came with us to see an Australian test match at Trent Bridge in Nottingham. Although I loved playing cricket, a whole day sat watching it was certainly a test. And in those days you were allowed only to clap, there was no chanting or shouting – even talking in the crowd was frowned upon. I was to return to Nottingham later, somewhere in my career between professional footballer and teacher, to live in digs along the Fox Road, which gave its name to an end of the famous ground. I could see why: the three-storey house looked nicely along the pitch and we could watch for free from the bedrooms on the top floor, making as much noise as we liked.

When the end of my school career was nearing, the boss again wondered how I would end up and suggested that, with national service due to end in a year's time, the best thing for me was probably a job as an uncertified teacher, back at my old primary school in Mablethorpe. He felt my exploits at school and an outward-bound centre had been sufficient grounding. Two years' conscription, either in the RAF or the Army, while educational and interesting, would perhaps not be as valuable as teaching. It's hard to believe that headmasters could have that kind of influence in those days, but the boss certainly possessed it. I was now established in Grimsby's reserve team, now playing second division football, so being based at Mablethorpe would facilitate both the sport and the teaching. Having had an interview with Saltley College and been accepted, a year's teaching for me would be of benefit. It certainly did benefit me, but whether it benefited my charges I'm not sure. In those days there was a streaming system, even in primary school: if children were not best suited academically, they were selected out to classes known as ESNs or (look away now, all you politically-correct modernists) "educationally sub-normals".

I had a dozen of these children, a nice small class which I ran at one end of the assembly/lunch hall. To say my lessons were challenging and disruptive would be an understatement, because at the other end of the room there were another thirty five, in the grip of a "Miss" whose voice could break glass at fifty paces. It simply wasn't possible to talk to my charges when she was screeching, and of course at the end of the morning session and the start of the afternoon one I would have to set up my tables and chairs before even trying. I followed the set curriculum and was expected to encourage them in all subjects including English, maths, some geography, history, art and PE. Because of my involvement with Grimsby I think many of the teachers – while shocked at my return to their school, knowing I hadn't been the most able of their own pupils – were nonetheless pleased to have my services as a physical education teacher. So I taught most of the PE for the senior boys and girls jointly, all the lessons taken outdoors with no indoor facilities available in those days. Everybody got at least one session of games each week, which suited me. I enjoyed that year. I'll have made a few mistakes I'm sure, but the children and their parents remained good friends after I left and I suppose that's the best compliment I can give myself. Many of them went into jobs around the town and for many years I'd see them on my frequent visits to my folks.

Soccer continued. I would hitch the 30 miles to Grimsby on Tuesday and Thursday nights, getting home on the last train at 10.30pm – and, having been teaching at school from 9.00 am, that made a pretty full day. One particular training session, I remember, was tragically delayed: in February 1958 we were warming up when the manager called his babes together to announce the Munich air disaster, which had wiped out Matt Busby's team. So many wonderful young Manchester United players, primed to claim England's first European Cup, had perished on the city's blizzard-blitzed runway. The grim announcement cast a shadow over that training session and blighted British football for years. Busby first had to rebuild himself and then set about restoring England's European ambitions. It was to take the great man ten more years to claim the cup for England – but not Britain, Scotland's Glasgow Celtic having claimed that honour just one year earlier. It was all an eye-opener for me. In those days, long before saturation TV football, I had been wrapped up in my own little world, until that horrific night.

As far as Grimsby were concerned though, it still was a small world. When I told them I was moving on in September, to a college which would only allow me to play for them, the club didn't want to let me go. Grimsby suggested I quit the educational trail and join the RAF, where they could "arrange" it that I stayed at a bombing range just outside the city, nicely available for the Saturday fixtures. But I had made up my mind. I was very grateful to the club for what they'd done for me – and wanted to do for me – but my parents had done far more to get me this far and I wasn't going to let them down. Much to my surprise, eight weeks after I had departed I received a card asking me to call at the ground. Even though I hadn't been picked for all that time they insisted on paying me. It was a very generous gesture and a real golden handshake. It almost gave me second thoughts, since in those days the maximum wage was £47, when people like my father were pulling just seven.

But the Freshwater course was set. I was bound for Brum.

Chapter Four
The Dyer Is Cast

Yes, bound for Brum, but first a few more recollections of Mablethorpe.

It might almost have been HRH Dyer - that's certainly how he ruled his school – but in fact his initials were HJH. I don't know what they stood for but I do know what *he* stood for: in his forty two year reign as headmaster of that proud 400-year-old institution he stood for no nonsense whatsoever. He was the boss and every boy knew it. His management style made an indelible impression upon me. Behind my back some call me "The Bear", but he was dubbed "Chis" and, again, I've no idea why. It was just the word which went up if he was ever about to descend on you from a great depth: yes - his office was at the bottom of the staircase of the three storey yellow-brick Elizabethan building which had been inspired, I understand, by Lord Cecil. Our house names were Cecil, Travers and Spanning. I was in Travers, along with those whose forebears had been there, as was the rule: had any more Freshwaters gone to Alford they too would have been in Travers. Your house name became the focal point for in-school competitions, especially sporting ones. Dyer's influence on me wasn't just managerial, it was just as much recreational, since he was of Oxbridge descent and had won a half-blue at cricket. He enjoyed watching sport and perhaps the fondest memory I have of him is his conviction that taking part in sport was every bit as important as achieving academic success.

At Assembly every morning a hymn was sung, with Mr Dyer a lay preacher along with two of his teaching staff, an English master Ken Lewis (a very amiable chap) and Mr Bourne our geography teacher, who wore a dog collar and insisted on some rather antiquated and hilarious pronunciations - I'll never forget his version of Massachusetts. I suppose it's remarkable that some fifty years on the names of my teachers readily come to mind, for no other reason than that they were outstanding characters, as much as outstanding teachers. There was a strong tradition of versatility in the staff, no more than fourteen teachers but all seemingly expert in several subjects. Tommy Williams taught French, German and Latin. Mr Milner taught maths and art. I was always top of his class, with 10 out of 10 each week – and yet I remember copying a picture of an eagle in flight

HJH Dyer, Clive's charismatic headmaster at Alford Grammar School, who had a major influence on his choice of career

Henry James Herbert Dyer was born in Leamington Spa in 1902. He attended Leamington College and Keble College Oxford, where he was awarded an MA degree. He studied law at Lincoln's Inn and was called to the Bar in 1931. He taught briefly in Huntingdon, Coventry and Bradford before being appointed Headmaster at Alford Grammar School in 1935, a post he held for 32 years. He was appointed a JP in 1944 and two years later he became Chairman of Alford Urban District Council. He was appointed President of the Incorporated Association of Headmasters in 1958. In the early 1950s he stood unsuccessfully as Liberal Parliamentary candidate for Louth. In the next election he stood equally unsuccessfully as a Labour candidate. He was eventually elected to Lincolnshire County Council as a Conservative and to East Lindsey District Council representing the Mablethorpe Ward. He became Chairman of East Lindsey District Council and remained a councillor until 1984. He died at Alford in 1995. See Lincolnshire Life magazine, January 2016.

from a Scottish advert showing purple hills. I had never been to Scotland and sadly neither had he, because I was ridiculed for their colour. It was only in later years when I moved to the Highlands that I realised just how unfair the criticism had been. All the masters with the exception of dear old Milner were strict disciplinarians, wore the gown and used the stick.

While I was there we got our first full-time PE teacher, who also taught geography and played county cricket for Lancashire. He was a fine coach and between him and HJH they ran some pretty energetic sports sessions. In my early days at the school we had no showers or changing rooms, but woe-betide you if you came without your kit. One poor lad from Mablethorpe, the son of the local chemist, Bunjey Knowles, was rather over-protected by his parents. His mother was restricted to a wheelchair and it was perhaps understandable that they didn't want their boy coming to any harm. On rainy days in his first summer he turned up without any kit and the boss, when he found out, wrote him a letter warning that if it ever happened again he would be "sent down". Knowles was blissfully ignorant of the term and duly turned up again kitless – and was promptly expelled for two weeks. Nobody got out of physical education.

In the bad season, when the football pitches were cut up, cross-country running was the order of the day: seven miles up Allsby Cross and back. I can't say I was a great runner, but if I came in the first 15 out of 60 I was doing well. I was simply not designed as a greyhound, yet I did enjoy it and it got the circulation going. Previous problems I used to have with headaches seemed to have passed, but by then I was well and truly shackled with my goalkeeping reputation. So it was that one cold October day after the school holidays I was selected for an inter-school match with Louth Grammar. The boss came into the classroom and announced that he wanted Freshwater and Noel Barker, another hefty, tall lad, whose parents ran a bus company in Mablethorpe – and still do - Noel now the remaining son who manages the business. There was to be a trial for the 'keeper in the under-14 fixture. I remember it was drizzly wet, the pitch soaked and the boss in his gown while we turned out in shorts and blazers. We were taken by the captain, Charlie Beech, one at a time. Charlie clattered the ball at us, not exactly from the penalty spot but just to see how we handled the ball. Eventually the boss and his captain decided that Freshwater was the one and he personally took me aside to demonstrate how I should handle the responsibility too: he expected me to pick the ball up with my feet together when bending or kneeling down and never, ever with my feet apart. That, I suppose, was my first lesson in goalkeeping.

We played Louth two days later on the Wednesday afternoon. Being the under-14s we played on the poorest of the pitches, the first team on the best of course, the reserves on the second best. Our pitch sloped at about 20-degrees, with the mud in the goalmouth just over my boots. Despite the conditions, we won 14-1 to complete a great day for Alford. The next morning at Assembly HJH announced, in his rather high pitched voice after the hymns and prayers and academic notices, that "We had a good day at Louth". And yet he finished his declaration with an ominous demand that Freshwater was to report to the headmaster's study immediately after Assembly.

We are talking about a man who had been at the school for twenty five years and ruled it with a rod of bamboo, a man who some ten years before had caned one boy so effectively that his reputation had allowed him to lay the cane down altogether for the next decade. Tremulously, I approached his dungeon, tapped on the door and waited to be ordered in. He was sat at his desk, which was set at an angle across one corner, and he eyed me sternly. When he rose he stood six feet tall with one of the straightest backs I've ever seen – I wasn't to know then that the posture was fixed by a plaster-cast jacket from hip to chest after a bad fall (although I was fated to share the experience a few years later).

"Well Freshwater..." he grumbled. "Why the one?"

As it turned out, he had simply wanted to have a friendly chat and, as ever, sport seemed the perfect opener. He wanted to know just how I was getting on in the school, how my parents were and generally to put me at my ease. As I have reflected over the years, I think he realised our financial situation and wanted to bring me into the body of the kirk. He certainly became a very good, fatherly friend, for all my dismal showing in the academic fields. It's the old story: very good at art, woodwork and metalwork, average at a lot of other things and very poor at others which just didn't draw that vital spark of interest, except perhaps science. I was very keen on science.

Back at Mablethorpe "sport" gave way to recreation, once the homework was out of the way. Obviously we got plenty homework but it was usually rushed, or simply copied, often just hurriedly done on the bus. Most of us got jobs. Many of my friends worked as bus conductors in the summer holidays, because they could all write standing up on a moving vehicle, which in those days the clippies had to do, filling in their time sheets. I earned pennies, sometimes more, at the weekend. In the summer trippers came to the town, a popular resort for all the working class families from Nottingham, Sheffield, Doncaster, Rotherham, Lincoln and Barnsley. They came by train and a gang of twenty of us would wait with our four-wheeled trolleys (pram wheels, a bit of wood and a rope).

Top - Sports day at Alford Grammar

Below – Summertime at Mablethorpe

There were only two taxis that I remember, so with 500 people coming in on a train there were a lot of suitcases needing to be carried. From the age of twelve until about fifteen I'd stand on a Saturday morning saying "Luggage on the barrow, sir?" and all of us would get at least one lift. We would then walk them to wherever they were staying – sometimes right to the opposite end of town – for a few bob. Four shillings (20p) maybe. On a very good day five. With Pop still on £7.50 a week and Mum on two shillings an hour it was very good pocket money for me.

I later discovered my true entrepreneurial spirit when I found an old three-wheeler delivery bike at the back of a restaurant, bought it for ten shillings, put a new inner tube in the back tyre, converted it to a flat trolley and took it to the station, where I waited for luggage to come in. I found I could do two trips, since I could get back quicker before the tail-enders had left the station. So, from earning some £1.50 a day I was moving up to £3 or so. The tricycle served as a good explorer during the week. And for off-duty we had a hut which went onto the platform, enabling us to go off exploring or fishing, with a dynamo providing lights both on the road and inside the "building". It was hard work pushing the thing, but always worth it!

I was thirteen or fourteen when I got offered some work as a butcher's boy, running errands and helping out in the shop, cleaning bones, making sausages, generally dogs-bodying in the back, and going out on the rounds to guesthouses, delivering their orders on my bike by using its front carrier. It was my Saturday morning job courtesy of the London Meat Company. I remember an inspection of the shop ended in the sacking of the manager: they'd discovered some bones filleted out of the pork and lamb had too much meat on them, which Freshwater was scraping off and putting into the sausages. The poor chap was dead meat and in came Eric Tustin in his place. He was a big man, 6ft 1in, 18 stone, a jovial chain-smoker who, like all jovial chain-smokers, didn't stop coughing until eleven o'clock. In his bantering way he would discipline me and kick me from one end of the room to the other, getting me started if I were ever in after 7 am. I then did the rounds with him and enjoyed it immensely. But I remember only too clearly one very hairy moment: it was 31st January, the day of the great floods in 1953. There had been an international football match at Lincoln, an under-21 game between England and France I think. I went to watch with a bus party, having finished my round. On my return home I was met by a deeply concerned Pop and Eric – they wanted to know if I had the money from the rounds as I hadn't cashed up. Sure enough, I still had it in my pocket, a little matter of £35 or so which I had completely forgotten about. My luck had certainly been in,

Top – Mablethorpe station in the old days. Clive worked there
as a self-employed Saturday porter in his early teens

Above – Clive as a teenager in Mablethorpe

with no pick-pockets operating at the ground - at least, not near me.

But there was an ill wind that day, for all that. It had been a bitterly cold blast since the morning, but little known to me it was whipping up a big storm out at sea. By the evening the waters had risen catastrophically all along the coast. By 7 pm the temperatures had plummeted and the waters were smashing the concrete defences as if they were made of nothing more than plaster of Paris. Nobody was ready for it, since there had been no warning of any kind. As my friends and I struggled up the street against the winds we noticed that water was flowing into the main street. Would you believe it, the local cinema was showing "Hurricane Island" as we braced ourselves to watch the tide rushing into the town? We were soon hurrying to a friend's place, where his folks ran a fish shop. It all ended up with Freshwater being trapped in there for hours by sea water, as it rose some eight feet, cutting off the electricity as it came, the water pressure building up so much that manhole covers were simply blown out of their housings.

It was a horrendous night for Mablethorpe and Sutton on Sea, with no part of the region keeping its feet dry - the inundation carried on two miles inland as the military arrived to help the locals battle with the elements. The next day, amidst all the terrible disruption and destruction, we were horrified to learn that some locals had not survived and that 200,000 acres of farmland had been devastated, with hundreds of animals lost. I know now about the true scale of the horror. At fourteen my world was very small and it was a long time before I realised that we had received only one blade of the double-edged storm: the high tide and severe European winds had caused a storm tide in the North Sea, with the water level exceeding 5.6 metres above sea level. In all, 1,835 people died in the Netherlands and 307 over on our side in Lincolnshire, Norfolk, Suffolk and Essex. Another 28 died in Belgium. And many more died at sea.

Fortunately for me, life continued as normal at Alford. I sat various "O" levels, English, maths, geography, history and religious education, and passed all of them but English, which was always my problem. The boss had taken me into his study and asked what I intended to do with my life. I didn't have much of an answer and I don't think many of us did, probably don't today at that age either. I remember him saying "Well Freshwater, I think it would be best for you to be a physical education teacher". He had clearly given the matter some serious thought, having already sent me on a course to Aberdovey Outward Bound School a year early, as a mere fifteen year old. I had survived an expedition over Cader Idris in North Wales, which had earned me a good report. I had enjoyed it, although it had been a very challenging ordeal and just my trusty old fishing jacket (which I have only recently discarded) saved me from hypothermia. Swimming in the Dovey in winter was a very sharp start to the day, but that was exactly what Outward Bound meant. The course had exploited the great outdoors precisely as Kurt Haan had intended – a rigorous month of hardship, which did none of us any harm. Satisfied with my good report, Dyer had ideas for me to go on to college and, like Jim Foster, Ron Atkinson and Malcolm and Jeff Hill before me, I was encouraged to look to the future as a PE instructor.

But there was a problem. You needed to have English, so the boss sent me for another test at Skegness Grammar, which was run by a different board of examiners, and there I managed to scrape through. A bit like John Major really, having six "O" levels and never going on to any higher qualifications. Here the true word spoken in jest involved Tommy Williams, the French and English teacher, who didn't think there was much point in my doing French as I was so bad at English, and that's what I tell my friends now - I am very good at opening doors and shutting windows in French, but that's about it. Nevertheless, physical education was to be my vocation and I remember going for an interview at a Church of England College – Saltley – in Birmingham. This was HJH's choice and I didn't realise what the connection was until later. There had been a very substantial redbrick house built in Wellington Road and I used to deliver fish there in the summer for Canon Platton, but didn't meet him or his family until I got to Birmingham. There wasn't an interview as such - I was simply taken for tea to the principal's residence at the college. We discussed this and that but I don't remember any of the details, just taking the train home and hearing a few days later that I had been accepted. The connection, it turned out, was that HJH was a lay preacher and when Canon Platton came to stay for his summer holidays he took on some of the boss's work around the diocese, presumably to give him a bit of a break.

It was through the church at Mablethorpe, Mr Dyer and my parents that I joined the choir, eventually becoming head choirboy. I remember a very nervous introduction to a solo rendition of *Ave Maria* before a full house, but I think that was the only time I ever had to go it alone. There was another friend of the boss, Jack Parkinson, the vicar at Trusthorpe and a tremendous character. I think he was a councillor, and he ran a great youth club two miles from home, with a five-night programme which I contributed to a few times. I seem to remember being a robber in *Babes in the Wood*. My friends today consider me a bit of a heathen, but I really did have quite an ecclesiastical background and was ultimately confirmed by the Bishop of Lincoln. Rather touchingly many years later, after moving to Scotland, my parents received a photograph the boss must have found, of yours truly with the bishop in Lincoln Cathedral just after the confirmation. Before the college interview Mr Dyer had decided to keep me on for a year as a groundsman: "You can do religious education and history, with English as a back-up". I suppose that had been to justify my staying on. It was very important to him, retaining the boy who captained his treasured teams. Oh, how he wanted to carry on beating Skegness and Louth, Spilsby and Horncastle.

Winning was everything. You only had to look at the cricket pitch: school pitches simply didn't produce bowlers' footprints up to the crease, but Alford's did. We had a great seamer in Bill Yates, who was encouraged to play like a true pro from the start. He would measure his run-up, had his peg down and bowled full-pelt to whoever had the misfortune to be batting. We had another lad, Howard Crowe, who was a good friend and an even better spinner, so the boss had us watering the wicket at the uphill end so that it would take spin. As the pitch dried out it became lethal. The boss would turn up with another staff in whites – everyone always wore whites, right down to the boots – complete with six stones each for keeping count of the overs, and there was a scorer, someone injured or not good enough to make the team. If Yates was bowling he was ordered to "bowl at the legs" and if he hit them within half an inch of the wicket the appeal would go up and so would his finger. On the other hand, when we were batting, on the walk in the boss would say "Pad up, pad up!" and even if the opposing side just about took your leg off, when their appeal came the boss would simply be looking the other way - such bias! In cricket, timing is everything and the boss knew exactly when to call it: on one occasion we were being beaten at Horncastle, which was a good thirty -mile trip courtesy of Hunt's Buses. They had declared for 160 and at tea we were 100 behind with seven wickets down. Right after tea another one went down and the boss stepped forward to remove the bails and end the match a couple of hours early. "My boys have a long way to go to get home" he explained. At the following morning's assembly, our competitive headmaster included in his announcements that the cricket team had played a successful match against Horncastle, securing a "moral victory". That's how he was and all the other schools knew him for a bit of a rogue. Similarly, I gather that when he was sitting at Lincoln Assizes he would go into the education offices to get his requisitions and breeze around the various departments telling them exactly what he wanted for his school. He was 110% for Alford and its boys and would proudly issue me with each season's hard-won new football, cricket bat and ball with the instruction that I was to go out there and win.

Alford one and one for Alford!

Chapter Five
Freshwater Tastes Saltley

I went to Saltley to drink deep from the spring of knowledge, but that wasn't quite how the principal saw it. When I chose physical education, technical drawing and craft as my main subjects, he declared: "It seems some gentlemen hope to go through college without reading a book".

There was an element of truth in that, since I had never been the academic type, but I was only too well aware that there was plenty of hard study ahead of me, since my course included the dreaded English along with religious education and basic science. Besides, if you were doing it right, PE contained plenty of physiology and psychology even then. It was a pretty arduous in-depth course and I was more than ready for my two years at the college. It was located near the Alum Rock area of Birmingham and was something of a rock itself, a three-storey chunk of granite which had stood for 100 years, proving itself an ideal teacher training outpost. Of the 400 students, though, only five of us had not done national service – the vast majority of them had seen the world, so I was only too grateful I'd at least had some Outward Bound experience, if only for that month. What also made things easier for me was that, unlike those worldly ex-servicemen, I had at least had some teaching experience: standing before a class and speaking was not difficult for me, while the old soldiers of Saltley were complete greenhorns. So things actually evened out pretty well.

I made plenty of friends. One of them played centre-half for Coventry, and there were two other pro footballers as well, which broke the ice. We had a pretty good team for our Wednesday sport sessions. We'd play Birmingham City "A" (the thirds), Aston Villa, West Brom and Wolves in the college league. There were several other colleges we'd mix with for dancing, especially Anstey all-girls, the sister college to Saltley. In years to come many of them would stay at Glenmore Lodge during my time there, all of them escorted by Barbara Rylands, one of the head lecturers and captain of the England ladies' hockey team. We'd go to their dances and they'd come to ours, always heavily chaperoned of course in those discreet days. Girls were not allowed in rooms except at Shenstone – but all the mattresses would have to be left outside in the corridor and everyone had to be out by 10 pm.

Coventry Tile Hill was a mixed college and newer than ours. We'd go there for inter-college swimming matches, which were quite popular. Dave Bowker was our star, the British breaststroke champion. He made a phenomenal sight doing dolphin kick under the water, dominating the gala. These were all great events for us, as were the other inter-college competitions involving soccer, hockey and athletics. They were also contested at a very high standard. There was a lad called Roberts who was a member of an acrobatic team. He was no more than 5ft 3in tall and I recall our first encounter: we were practicing in one of the gyms and I heard this strange thumping sound, only to look up and see him bounding across the floor on one hand. And he could carry me (two stone heavier) while he did it. He was also a tremendous juggler and could catch a football on his forehead, roll it onto his neck and do anything Beckham can today. He wasn't a brilliant tactical player, though, and didn't make it to the football team (and with only one hand free wouldn't have been half the keeper I was). All the same, he'd be there at the games and would play with the ball outside the changing rooms, much to everyone's amusement. The visiting team would take note of his skills and we'd say: "Yes, he's quite good but not good enough for the team", which always put them nicely on their guard. As I said, there was a lot of psychology in my course.

We staged marvellous smoking concerts amid the cherry blossomed boughs at the end of the summer term, with various girlfriends invited. Young Roberts would do his music hall act, including brick-carrying and hoop-spinning on his legs, feet and arms. He really was a superb juggler, but what became of him as a teacher I have no idea. I do know that he could always come up with something to hold his students' attention.

Another young man whose skill (if not his name) sticks in my memory would recite wonderful monologues and they gave me a real taste for the things, although it was only when I came to Scotland that I first discovered the king of them all, Marriot Edgar, whose works were made immortal by Stanley Holloway. *The Battle of Hastings*, *The Magna Carta* and so many others go down very well and I can still remember the words after all these years:-

> *The reign of King William the Second*
> *Was a bit of an uninteresting affair*
> *There's only two things that's remembered of 'im,*
> *That's 'is sudden death and 'is red 'air.*
> *He got 'is red 'air from 'is mother,*

The crown what he wore were 'is dad's
And the arrow that came at the end of the reign
Were a well-deserved gift from the lads.

All very droll and, with the right audience, a lengthy haul through all thirty-odd verses. It was a passion which was to serve me well, especially in Scotland when I became involved with the folk club at Carrbridge, where I learned to play the guitar too. My experience in the choir was to prove useful, since although there were lots of guitar players, not so many played and sang at the same time. The monologues were always popular and one I picked up, on the development of Aviemore, I have added later in these memoirs for posterity's sake[1]. It was written by two members of the Scottish Sports Council for a Christmas concert, with apologies to Robert Service's *Shooting of Dan McGrew* and *High North Trail*.

Living on the West Midlands trail was an education in itself. Birmingham was a frantic, filthy place: in my bedroom, on the window sill, I had some big plates (I still have them) and without a word of a lie, if the window was open on one of the smoggy nights we would hear pieces of soot dropping onto them. You couldn't see from one end of the corridor to the other with the lights on, nor your hand in front of your face. It was just as well we moved about a bit for teaching practice. The list of schools we visited was very wide-ranging, from very good to pretty awful, your stay generally one or two weeks until, for your final practice, you'd spent a whole month there. The last school I taught at had just moved into the comprehensive system and, because I was the largest of the four students, the deputy head chose me to substitute for him. There were four streams of the twelve year-olds, i.e. four classes of about thirty five pupils, streamed on behaviour and not academic ability, so he had all the hooligans, as I saw them. On the first day, while he was teaching, they were playing darts, dominoes, cards and the like and I found it all quite astonishing, though I said nothing. It turned out that leaving them to fiddle around with their games was the only way he could get them to concentrate on anything, but I found the whole thing a nightmare from start to finish. I had a month of prepared lessons which I never taught, since I had always been told never to teach unless you had your class's reasonably undivided attention.

It was all pretty unsettling and after a couple of weeks I was quite disturbed at my inability to teach anything. There would regularly be three boys outside the door, one along to the headmaster's office for disciplining. Two boys disappeared once and I asked the others what the problem was, only to be told: "Oh, they're bookies' runners, Sir.

---

[1]See Chapter 17.

They've gone round the council estate to pick up the bets, but they'll be back this afternoon". It was with real trepidation that I came to prepare my geography lesson for the senior education lecturer's assessment. I first had to prepare the class, pleading with them to bear with me since I had a very important man coming. "Oh yes Sir, we know. He'll be coming to see if you are a good teacher. Well, we won't let you down, Sir. We won't let you down". But I wondered about that, having seen only too graphically how wrong things could go.

Came the day, came Mr Callbeck, the man who passed or failed the student teachers, and with him was Noddy Turner, who had a terrible affliction: the nickname said it all, as his head bobbed up and down in silent and uncontrollable acceptance that while he was something of a playwright, he was nothing as a teacher. The lesson began...and there wasn't a sound from my charges...only polite, urgently silent hands, which shot up in rapid succession, young shoots of earnest enquiry bursting forth, thirsting for information from the learned teacher. I was staggered, but managed to carry it off. At one point Noddy got carried away too, nodding off on a set of cupboards at the back of the room, head still for once on his hand, his elbow resting on the cupboard. "Make yourself at home, Sir! Make yourself at home...!" laughed the kids, at which he jumped to his feet and stood straight against the wall where he should have been. But Freshwater, I'm glad to say, got the nod from Mr Callbeck and the memory of that primary class has stayed with me to this day.

As I said, my two subjects over and above PE were technical drawing and craft. We had a very good TD teacher and a celebrated master of pottery and metalwork (I only did the pottery). One of my friends, Jerry Pettigrew, had worked for Jackson Boilers in Leeds, who produced the big stainless steel vending machines used in most 1950s cafes. He was a draughtsman and so having him as a buddy was a tremendous advantage: his skill and speed were pure quality. He passed with distinction and took me with him. Jerry was keen on football and would pump me about John Charles, the centre-forward for Leeds and Wales, since he idolised the Leeds team. Jerry played in the college team but wasn't the most fluent of footballers, only just holding his place for the two years he was there. I gather he later became a prison officer, his father having been a police inspector. Talking of prisons, one of our lecturers had been a POW in Colditz, where to amuse himself he had fashioned an 18-inch long xylophone, which he had somehow managed to smuggle out with him. Music was all the rage with us at college and the jazz band was in great demand at our functions, such as those smoking concerts. They had a very busy itinerary at the

Top – Swimming team at St Peter's College, Saltley. Clive third left, back row

Above left – Clive with a canoe frame at St Peters College

Above right - Clive's contract with Leeds United, as reserve goalkeeper, aged just 22

weekends, going to the Lord Mayor's banquets, for example, with a five-piece line-up to entertain and earn some vital student money.

The college was heavily church-orientated. Where it wasn't cornered by the main line to London or the Morris Cowley metalwork and paint-spraying factory it was hemmed in by the Catholic church with its full set of chiming bells, operated electronically on a keyboard. They would ring for both services and lessons, particularly early morning communion, where you were all expected to turn out at least once a month. I don't think I managed to do that even in those days, and would regularly get a little note from the Principal to remind me of such. The chapel, which housed 400 students, was an awesome place when it was full at the end of term, for the carol service and other commemorative events. The college was originally built in virtually a circle and there were attractive features like the quadrangle of grass which you always had to walk around and never across. You'd be in serious trouble if you didn't keep off that grass – perhaps even getting sent down for a fortnight just to cool your heels. We had another quaint tradition: once a year we gathered at one end of the college corridors in pitch darkness, hands on each others' shoulders and, without speaking a word, would march around all the corridors to a finish in the quadrangle for hymn singing. They were fine old traditions which have, perhaps like the building itself, been blown away nowadays.

I enjoyed my time at Saltley, but on my first holiday home I realised I was free to return to Skegness for football if and when needed. I began training with them again in the run-up to the season, getting myself properly fit. By the time I returned to college I was quite a substantial 400 metre runner, much to the amazement of many who had fancied their own chances at that distance. I wouldn't say I was the best, but I could always finish in the first four. I was fit enough for Skegness too and they played me a number of times. George Raynor was still in charge and gave me plenty of opportunities. Of course Skegness had other attractions: from the age of fifteen a few of us would get on our bikes in Mabelthorpe and cycle the fourteen miles to the metropolis for its Winter Garden dances overlooking the Lido and its magnificent swimming pool. We'd carry our suits and dancing pumps in our saddlebags and change in one of the many alcoves around the boating pond before dancing beyond the midnight hour. If we didn't attract any female company we'd change clothes again later, get back on our bikes and rattle home by the light of our battery headlamps.

Eventually a great friend from the fish shop, Ron Silcock, who'd taught me to drive in the fish van along disused roads, had a bit of luck. He came across an old but immaculate Rolls Royce in the garage of one of the people he delivered to, and successfully offered £100 for it. He was a ladies' man if ever there was one (certainly more than me) and proudly showed off his dead-cert machine: it had a vertical windscreen with a central wiper at the top and an engine you could fry eggs on, it was so clean - and of course it proved a lot more successful in attracting female interest than a couple of old bikes with battery-powered headlamps. We young folks certainly put on the style, but at ten miles to the gallon (when it was 2/6d a throw, and rationed) we couldn't put on too much of it, despite what Lonnie Donegan said. You had to be very careful with the coupons. Ron was to end up with his own butcher's shop, opposite the old fish shop where we'd met (in fact, it was that very shop where we got the blind which went into making our first canoe).

Back at Saltley, we had a lecturer who'd been to "Carnegie", a college in Leeds that I hadn't heard of, but one which was to become highly significant to me. His name was Black Jack, after his fine dark hair (which ironically had all but gone by the time I met him). He had a polished face, I remember, and a dry humour which matched it: when one of his students fell from on high off the wall bars, smashing his own face into the floor, Black Jack was unimpressed. Asked by the unfortunate, much-bloodied boy if he thought the casualty's nose was broken he sighed: "I don't know, Mr Horridge. Go and see Matron". Then he carried on with the lesson, as if nothing had happened. The show must go on, that apparently was the Carnegie creed. When another lad fainted in a lecture on a particularly warm day and clattered onto the floor we were told: "Leave him where he is. Loosen his tie. He'll be all right." And Black Jack simply carried on again. The youngster did rally, eventually, and only then was he helped out of the room by two of the students. The Carnegie creed intrigued me.

At that time a third-year course was being designed for teaching and particularly for physical education. Loughborough College, York College and Cheltenham were the main athletic centres but to get into Carnegie you had not only to finish your course, you had to go for an interview, which was 90% physical examination: if you couldn't produce head springs, hand springs and cartwheels to a sufficiently high standard you didn't get in, not even if you had a sporting background. Loughborough tended to take sporty people and was easier to get into, since it would always benefit from the kudos earned by its students' international successes. Carnegie's education was the more traditional and disciplinarian: I learned that missing a lecture more than once would land you in serious trouble, and there were lots of them. They started at nine in the morning, with two before lunch, two after lunch and one in the evening, all of them 90 minutes at least and very intensive stuff. I remember the immense relief after my interview, and the intense pride on finally hearing I had been chosen as one of the successful 120 new entrants. My friend Jerry from Leeds, though, did not make it. Despite being a super-fit athlete he just wasn't well co-ordinated. But I was a very happy lad, for all that. Freshwater had shown he was worth his Saltley. He'd made it. He was bound for Leeds.

Chapter Six
Following Leeds To Nowhere

The city which promised so much was fated to break my heart and nearly my back, but there was no hint of that on my arrival, with its soft landing among those gentle Leafs.

Mrs Leaf was a real life-saver. Carnegie College's draconian code was all-encompassing and we were supposed to dress smartly as well as behave it – a real challenge when proving your sporting prowess in all weathers - but my landlady was up to the task. Not wanting to live in at the college, I had chosen digs at Headingley. Mrs L had been a tailoress in her time, just like my real Mum, and her husband Jim had been a tailor's cutter. Two other students shared the digs with me and the Leafs made a wonderful job of sheltering all three of us. For a small consideration Mrs L would launder our muddy, sweaty clothes, a huge help considering the exacting dress code at Carnegie: grey flannels, navy blue blazer (single breasted, no vent) and black polished shoes. You could go for lunch in your track suit, but you had to have your blazer on in college for dinner. And the track suits, which had to be cleaned at half and full term since they were regarded as formal dress, were cream, of all things, and had to be treated with the utmost respect. In fact, I still have mine, complete with its rolled silver badge, the "Welsh athlete, Dai Scobolos" as we jokingly called Discobolus, the discus thrower of Greek legend - the Other Place (Loughborough) had "the ice cream man" bearing the Olympic torch. There was intense rivalry in those days, because we were the special ones. Today that's all been watered down, with the multiplicity of colleges. Carnegie was so special that it only had about twenty staff, with Boufler as Principal. The Vice-Principal was Johnny Dodds, a very effective hit-man handling any breach of the college's multifarious conditions.

The yearly photograph, I remember, was taken outside the front of the building, which was one of fourteen red brick blocks initially built as a hospital. Each had a different name, ours being Carnegie Hall. The others were used by Leeds Training College and much more ramshackle affairs. Our Principal had us all lined up for the photo but before the shutter could open there was much to be sorted out: throat zips had to be precisely half-way drawn and then a boy was sent up to the bedrooms to pull the drapes half-closed.

That was the sort of regimentation which applied in the great and good college.

The only freedom came when we attended the city hospital for our anatomy and physiology, which was just the same as the first year course for medical students. It involved being lectured for two and a half hours by a brilliant surgeon in his white coat and starched collar. There were three green roller blackboards, no notes, and by the end of it all the boards would be crammed full: remarkable drawings of joints, the respiratory system and the nervous system would complement detailed notes in an amazing jigsaw of knowledge. It was almost impossible to keep up as the information flowed, especially with the distraction of the adjoining mortuary: we could see the bodies on the slabs through there, where the dissecting was done. When he needed to illustrate a particular fact about a particular joint, the surgeon would simply go and fetch one to show us. What turned stomachs wasn't so much the sight of a dead, detached limb in his hand so much as the stink of the formaldehyde preserving it, although I wasn't as susceptible as the others, having spent four years as a butcher's boy, When the surgeon fetched in a head, clutching it in two halves, I was not among the students who went running from the room. He did it for effect: a certain graveyard humour of course, but also to ensure that nobody forgot their trip to Leeds Infirmary. Whether that kind of thing still goes on I wouldn't know, but I certainly found it an unforgettable introduction to the human body. And there was more: I remember even more clearly how some of us slipped away for a bit of surface anatomy. We were free enough to escape into Leeds for some extra mural studies at the City Varieties of "Good Old Days" fame. What a good old days it was, observing some very beautiful living bodies. Of course, in those prim days of the 1950s the nudes weren't allowed to move, so we had some highly animated comedians between the static displays, but it was all very educational for us lads.

Having settled in at Carnegie, I was warned by the old stagers always to leave my Saturdays free. Putting your name down for anything would commit you to that particular college club and there was only one club I was interested in. I took a day out to visit Elland Road, home of Leeds United F.C., where the new manager – one Don Revie – was just settling in too. He wasn't there when I called, but I introduced myself to the man I understood to be the chairman, a Mr Wilkinson, and told him I'd heard the club were looking for a new goalkeeper. It paid off: after confirming that I was no longer tied to Grimsby and had been given a free transfer, I was signed as a Leeds keeper at a fee of a fiver a game, with a £3 bonus for a win, which seemed fair enough to me, considering it had been two years since I'd been at Grimsby. At that time Leeds were in the second division, but Jack Charlton and Revie had bigger ideas. I think I only met the Don once as I wasn't in the first team, merely "on the books" as a regular A team player. I played a couple of games, hoping to make the first team. It was a world away from Grimsby: much higher standard, totally different pace. One of the A team made it into England's 1956 World Cup team. But the real golden boys of Billy Bremner and his like were yet to come. The keeper was having a miserable time of it then, having lost his confidence, and I played through that season, mainly in the A team but sometimes with the reserves. I remember playing against Sheffield United reserves and telling myself I could live with the pace. Ignorance is indeed bliss.

While with the club, I'd go down in the evenings to train under the stand, outside on the cinders with a couple of coconut mats down, catching fast low balls alongside another young groundstaff member, one Gary Sprake. A pleasant, quiet lad some two years younger than me, he'd just come to Elland Road and was acclimatising like me. Gary was destined to make the grade: he ended up as one of The Blessed United, winning all those major titles and progressing to international level as the Welsh number 1. I shared his ambition. I dreamed of becoming a full-time footballer too and playing all the way through to retirement, but first there was the matter of that teaching certificate to address.

The problem was, Carnegie was more rugby-minded, with a number of top-of-the-range players including Chalky White and Bernard Braintree (who played for Headingly) and a lecturer called Jack Malpass who was a bit of a comedian (and I don't mean funny ha-ha). While all the children at Birmingham had been divided by behaviour, at Carnegie the students were divided by size, so most of my section were at least 5ft 10in, but Jack Malpass was oblivious to the fact, and was determined to see us all as delicate dancers. He was to lead me a merry dance, all right: the dance of death for my football career.

He had been brought into the college on a trendy bandwagon of "movement and dance", and was nothing less than a missionary of gentility and grace in a jungle of gorillas. It was summer, I recall, and we were all to pretend to be monkeys, jumping up and down the wall bars. Carnegie's gymnasiums were very high affairs and there were plenty of them. I was coming down on one occasion and missed my grip, landing flat on my back from a great height. After forcing the air back into my lungs and finally lifting myself off the floor I checked for injuries and seemed to have escaped anything serious. I carried on with the lesson, but not long afterwards I got a groin strain, which kept me from playing football for a while. When I did get a game again I was soon doubled up in pain and had to leave the field. For six weeks I shunned all serious sporting activity. On my return to Leeds, against Hull, I could hardly kick the ball by half-time, although the pain had by then shifted to the back of my pelvis. I ended up at the Radcliffe with Pennybacker, the world's leading neurologist, who was so thorough he probably even x-rayed my x-rays, but the injury never really righted itself. Looking back now, I think the fall had damaged tissue in my joints, which had created lesions. What I can tell you is that the first fifteen years are the worst, but by then you have learned to adjust, to go with the weather, as it were, and the weather certainly has a say.

It was a crushing blow, giving up football when I had been so close to arriving at the top level. I still wonder how my life might have gone if I had been there with Revie, as he'd taken the club on that roller-coaster ride to the pinnacle of English soccer. The consolation for me was that I passed out from Carnegie A1, even with my statuesque 16st 3lb, a statue for six months, courtesy of a plaster jacket from neck to groin. That was an experience worth a book in itself: standing there starkers, suspended by my chin in the plaster room at Leeds Infirmary, with an audience of at least four nurses while someone slapped plaster around me. It proved utterly useless and was incredibly itchy. I was to get the thing removed at Grimsby Hospital on going home but for six months I at least made a good dartboard for my friends - down at the New Inn for a half-pint, they would occasionally lob darts at my back, or even my chest.

I made some really good pals at the college, one of them for life: Bill McGuiness was a breath of fresh air with his infectious, all-consuming enthusiasm for life. It would probably be more accurate to say that he and I forged our close friendship outside college more than in it. We met in the great outdoors at the start of term, since the college had been overbooked and the first two weeks constituted a standing camp: there was a large marquee alongside two smaller tents and an open fire on the Harewood estate near Gassington. It was a terrific introduction for me, with my background of outdoor activities, and I had found it all pretty easy while everyone else struggled initially, lighting fires and cooking over them. At the end of the year there was lightweight camping but, because of my back, Bill took me to the checkpoints (I think there were three) and he was impressed at my ability with a primus stove, cooking a three-course meal in a set of dixies after catching some trout on my fishing line.

Back home and plastered no more, I took a summer job as a swimming instructor and lifeguard at a swimming pool in Mablethorpe. It had been built by the millionaire behind The Golden Sands holiday park (there's one in every self-respecting seaside resort,

I expect). He was an interesting character, living at the "posh" end of Sutton on Sea, and had flown in the original air races to South Africa and back. He had a couple of planes which he flew around the area. I got pretty high too, thanks to the codeine I pumped into myself in fours to help me cope with the constant pain in my back. I walked with a terrible limp around the pool and can't have instilled much confidence in my charges, although things were always a little easier for me in the water. As I said, I went to see Pennybacker, the neurologist, but he gave me little hope, other than to say that I would learn to live with it all. He was right, but it certainly didn't go down too well at the time and I was left to ponder just what kind of future lay in store for me. I came across one possibility, leafing through The Times Educational Supplement in the autumn: there was a job for a hill-walking instructor at Glenmore Lodge, an adventure centre up in the Scottish Highlands. The combination of Outward Bound with map-reading, hill-walking, camping and canoeing seriously appealed to me, and I didn't want to think about the pain it would probably bring me. I applied. When I got the job, I still didn't want to think about how painful it might be: I simply wondered what to pack.

It wasn't to be my first time in Scotland. There had been that bitter sweet introduction to Badenoch and Strathspey in the spring.

As part of my teaching practice with Carnegie I had been at Wakefield Grammar School for Boys for a week and the secondary modern at Pudsey (where star England paceman Freddie Truman had gone). There was a PE teacher called Jim Starkey, who led brief expeditions north of the border for small groups of boys, and he had invited me to join them on one trip. Remarkable as it seems now, we journeyed all the way to the Highlands in a Leyland minibus, camping on the way up at Shap, arriving at Kingussie on the day the shinty team were playing Oban Celtic at Fort William in the cup final. We camped at Miss Gair's farm, by Tromie Bridge, and Jim had made arrangements to collect food from various suppliers, after which we walked back into the deserted town, where the solitary firemaster, somewhat the worse for drink, was attempting to hang some bunting in time for the victors' return. We took in a film at the Victoria Hall. I can't remember what it was, but I remember the squeaking of the spools on the projector. We came out by ten o'clock and the town was really stirring again. Going into Volante's for something to eat we heard that Kingussie had won the Camanachd Cup for the first time in sixty years. I still have the happy event recorded in my trusty old log book. And then the team arrived home, still in their strips, having called at every hostelry on the road back from the Fort. The captain, still in his boots, studs and all, held the cup aloft as he tried to pass me in the doorway and as I grabbed it he tipped it and soaked me in whisky. That was my first encounter with the water of life – until then the only drink that had passed my shoulders was half pints of lager. Some 40 years later I was chatting to local shepherd Donny Ross at Leault and related the story to him. "Do you know who it was, that did that to you?" he asked. "No", I admitted, "I never found out." And he laughed: "That was me!"

I had been properly baptised by Kingussie on my first visit, anyway. And what a night it had turned out to be, with the A9 closed at the Duke of Gordon, all traffic respectfully diverted down Spey Street all the way to Duke Street, to allow the pipe band and the eightsome reels right of way through the town, cheered all the way by a thousand delirious fans. It was a magical atmosphere and made a huge impression on us Sassenachs. Little did I know then that I was destined to meet a lot of those faces again over the years. The following day we rested at our tents and on the Monday we packed our kit and set off for an expedition, stopping off at the Clarkes' farm at Achlean and leaving our valuables with them, which Jim often did on his trips. Then it was the footpath up to the lochan at the top.

By now I knew my back injury was going to be painful, especially on the downhill trek, and even with the codeine it didn't ease. I survived though and we got down into the Lairig the next morning, up the other side, over the Fiddler's Burn and down to the Shelter Stone. It was a pretty momentous day for me. The next morning was a bit of a shock, though. Freshwater in lederhosen and shirt, with no trousers in his pack, discovering four inches of fresh snow. We had to pack up our tents – Blacks' "Good Companions" with A-poles, cook breakfast and then get up over the top and back down to the pass. We had no ropes, no ice-axes, and it was terrifying. All the joy and merriment of our introduction to the Scottish Highlands was forgotten as we shivered in tearful fear at the danger we had put ourselves in. One boy slipped and fell some hundred yards, fortunately his fall finally broken by a boulder. It was the closest I have ever come to a serious incident in the hills and showed me only too graphically how disasters can happen to complete newcomers in the Highlands. We did get back down safe and sound, but I was severely shaken and the memory has stayed with me and protected me from complacency for all these years. I'm not sure how affected our leader had been, with his army and marine background, but the boys were all very traumatised by their experience. The Highlands had a savage beauty, all right – and if you wanted to know what that really meant, you simply took them on in your lederhosen. Anyway, we marched out by Strath Nethy and came to the Bynack stables, a haven after the night's traumas, to celebrate with a right good sing-song. After sleeping like babies we walked the next morning to Feshie Bridge. Jim went to fetch the bus and I carried on with the boys to Glen Tromie, passing this little tin building with green doors and wondering what it was doing there, on its own in the middle of nowhere. Later I found out it was called Insh Hall.

Back in Kingussie, I ate the blackest, toughest steak I'd ever seen at the Char Hotel...Star, sorry, but since I'd been on iron rations for four days it went down fine, with a pint. We met up with some of the locals again, the joiner Donnie McDonald inviting us to join him and his brothers at a dance at Aviemore. I was only wearing moccasins, Millets trousers with brass buttons and a black polo-neck sweater which a girlfriend had knitted for me in my goalkeeping days, so I felt very self-conscious, but he said I'd be fine and I'm glad to say he was right: I turned out to be the best-dressed man there, apart from the paratrooper in his red beret, gaiters and boots. The dancing was sweet and simple too: a quickstep the length of the dance floor, about turn, straight back up the other end. I had a great night. The following morning we struck camp and headed for Oban, which was not without its surprises: within half a minute of pitching our tents one of them had gone up in flames. There had been two boys in it, but they had dived into their sleeping-bags as their cover simply drifted with the wind and went up in smoke. It was a lesson for us all. Only after that final drama did we at last enjoy an uneventful journey home to Leeds and Pudsey.

I had enjoyed my taste of Scotland and was ready for that autumn advert when Glenmore Lodge needed a walking instructor. I applied immediately and was invited to work with them for two months, no interview necessary - in the pioneering days at the end of the '50s the outdoor adventure world was very short of instructors. The omens were good, as illustrated by my demonstration: during an open day at Carnegie I had to pitch a tent for a special guest in the gymnasium, using drawing pins, and fry him some pancakes on a primus. The VIP was a red-haired gentleman called Dr Stuart MacIntosh, from Glasgow – the man who, with May Brown, chairperson of the Scottish Council for Physical Education, had established Glenmore Lodge.

MacIntosh, through his directorship of the education authority, had put up a fair chunk of money to provide courses at the Cairngorm Hotel in Aviemore for young and old from Glasgow. They had moved swiftly into Glenmore, to what is now the youth hostel. There are photographs there now of those early days, with the long shorts and the camping, skiing and climbing. They were the formative years of the present Lodge, which went up in 1958/9, a brand new, purpose-built timber-clad centre on the Colt House system, using natural materials and designed by architect Jim Scott, who became another very good friend. He was one of a few members of the Scottish Sports Council's committee who used to come and stay with us at the Lodge, to learn how the place ran and get to know the staff. The only criticism of the place I heard was that the sound-proofing wasn't too hot.

The new Glenmore Lodge was aimed essentially at school parties. From October to December there was a month of boys and then a month of girls from Glasgow, all aged about 15. Instructors were assigned two children from each school. Of the first group I was destined to meet, thirty two out of the sixty four would have police records. It was going to prove very educational.

Chapter Seven
No More Mr Nice Guy

I arrived nicely at Aviemore station and was met by a volunteer, who drove me away from civilisation: up a hill road which, although metalled, was narrow and twisting, as if feeling its way round a crystal loch iced by snow-topped hills swathed in soaring Scots pines, where the world smelled a whole lot fresher than Birmingham or Leeds. The Glenmore Lodge cook, Mary Brown, fed me and asked if I was going into Grantown with the rest of the staff during their change-over period and, rather than be left there in the middle of nowhere on my own, I piled into one of the two Land Rovers. The locals called it "Planet Lodge" and leaving it unattended wasn't going to be the end of the world: the staff were mostly volunteers, a motley crew of enthusiasts who were either on the committee or just up for a short spell.

In town we headed straight for the Palace Hotel and ordered a round of drinks. "Eight whiskies and what will you have, Clive...?" I asked for my usual half a lager, and when the second round was brought in I again declined their offer of the local poison - Glen Grant, in those days. Two bottles of the stuff were collected for the journey home, which we took via the local cinema (the YMCA hall). Then I was offered another choice: I could go back in the Land Rover taking the road, or take in the sights in the other car over one of the rough hill tracks, which I declined – I wouldn't even enjoy it today, but with the state of my back then it was out of the question. Back at the Lodge everybody piled into my room for a housewarming party, keeping me out of my bed until two in the morning - and until two bottles of Glen Grant had been all but drained (not with my help, although I suspected it wouldn't be long before my self-discipline gave out enough to taste of the craitur).

The Principal at Glenmore was Geoff David. Although a retired naval officer, he was not strong on discipline, having lived a world apart from his charges. The one with the worldly wisdom was Aviemore family man Jack Thomson, a Glaswegian himself, ex-tank regiment and ex-Duke Street Primary (the one next door to Duke Street Jail). It was Jack who educated me in the Glasgow vernacular, without which I would have been completely

in the dark in dealing with my new street-wise charges. The trick with those kids, I quickly
learned, was that in the first week you didn't smile - by the third you had them eating out
of your hand and at the end they were in tears at having to say goodbye. Like them, at
Glenmore I learned one of the most important lessons of my life: playing Mr Nice Guy
simply doesn't work.

The schools all came by train. The pupils paid £1.50 for the full week's course, the
rest subsidised by Glasgow (Dr MacIntosh's team). They were met at the station and
escorted by instructors who had been sent to the city to collect them, a task I was to share
at a later date. We had a four-ton truck with canvas sides and central seating, and driving
it was an education in itself, with its crash gates for gears and double de-clutching. There
must also have been a bus for the children – all 64 of them – although the thing doesn't
spring to mind. What an experience it must have been for those children, meeting up with
each other for the first time on the train, probably on their first ever trip outside the city.
They were put into patrols, billeted four to a room and one to a bed, which was an even
stranger experience for most of them – both the boys and the girls, although never there
at the same time, wanted to share beds, since that was all they'd ever been used to in
their tenement homes. At the Lodge they tasted a certain luxury, since it was a very
modern, comfortable place, with under-floor heating and purpose-built for them. But the
place was baptised in ice: those first winters really tested it to the limit, with their fierce
winds and plummeting temperatures - there were even times later on when we had to
turn off the heating to cut costs. Other than that it was perfectly adequate, with its drying
room, ski and climbing room, lecture room, lounge and dining room.

Breakfast was a revelation. I remember watching one lad with his kipper, doing
what came naturally: cutting it into four pieces and scoffing the lot, head, tail and all. It
was quite an eye-opener, watching a smoked herring skeleton disappear down a
Glasgwegian throat. I'm not saying they all ate like that, but nobody else seemed fazed by
it. They were a wild bunch to begin with and it was always a problem getting them to bed.
Lights out was at ten o'clock and there was no TV in those days. The idea was to have
them running from the moment they got out of bed until they got back into it, and they
only had half an hour at the shop to buy sweets. The middle section of the building was
used as the last resort for the pupils who wouldn't quieten down: the trick was to isolate
the trouble-maker and have him sleep on an unheated, stone-slab floor. It did the trick,
although today you'd probably end up in the European Court of Human Rights. As far as
we were concerned, the trouble-maker was the one infringing people's human rights and

he was the one who had to end up in the dock.

All the pupils were offered an extensive programme: lots of walking and at least three camping expeditions culminating in a two-night overnight. The climbing was low-level but there was no canoeing at that time of year. Plane table surveying was a relief exercise so they didn't have to walk another ten miles. Most of the expeditions, though, were pretty expansive and, with no transport laid on, every part of the activities was walked. A day round the corries was a day walking from the Lodge, round the northern ones, down Lurcher's Burn and back, although that trek would come towards the end of their stay. They were all issued with boots and clothing of much poorer quality than today's, but it did the job. There were always incidents of course, but every time they seemed to involve the trouble-makers. I think the girls must have come in October and the boys in November, since there was snow on the ground and the river was iced up.

Jack was out with them one day doing geology, pointing out to them the stratification of the bank where a swirl had undermined it, creating a big pool some six feet deep. I was in "Ben the Hoose" and it was just getting dark when this body appeared in the doorway, shaking with cold and soaking wet. Cosby, his name was. You always remember the ones who were a problem. "Good heavens Cosby, what's happened?" I asked. The stuttering reply came: "M...Mr Thomson th...threw me in the r...river, Sir!" I gave it a second's neutral unbiased consideration and totally agreed with Jack. The boy had obviously deserved it and I ordered him to go and get dried in the drying room, which he duly did. Later that evening, in the staff room, I asked Jack what had happened. He explained: "The boy'd been throwin' stanes in the river aw' day and splashin' everybody. I telt him tae stop it and come ower tae me, but he jist ran aff. So I got efter 'im, and made a splash mysel'...".

They were a strange and wilful lot. On one of my trips with them to Bynack Stable they enthused about the place, but only because it would be "a great place to do a job, Sir!" Explaining just what kind of job, they boasted about stealing from Woolworths ("Woolies"). They had songs about stealing from Woolies, Glasgow street songs celebrating their own particular culture. So it was a rather foolish Principal who allowed his unprincipled charges to go down to Sandy's shop at the campsite, some half a mile from the Lodge, *en masse*. I had been into Inverness in the Land Rover. I was conscious of a police car behind and I suspected they were following me. But it turned out that sixty of the boys had been allowed to go to Sandy's store and hadn't just nicked a bag of sweets, or a box of sweets even, they had virtually stripped the place bare. You hardly ever saw a police car up the glen, but that fateful day an officer just happened to be visiting the Lodge, so was right on hand to round them all up on the road after Sandy's call. On seeing the car, the boys scattered in all directions, dropping and dumping their stash as they went. By the time I got back there were two police cars at the Lodge and our evening programme was being revised.

Having led us all a merry dance in the afternoon, the boys' evening country dance was off. Jack and I had put in a lot of time with them, teaching them the steps – even persuading alternate boys to play out the ladies' parts – but we had to take steps to recover all the loot and that was to take until one in the morning. They had hidden the stuff in the most obscure places, but we recovered about 90% of it all. Our friend Cosby was one of the ring-leaders and I noticed, years later, how he'd been "mentioned in dispatches" for serious assault in Glasgow. For all that, most of our charges returned to their gang-riddled city knowing that there was a much better way to live. Out of the first group of girls who came to the Lodge, two returned to work there for some ten to fifteen years and one of them now lives in Aviemore, happily married with a family. The other one I lost track of after she finally emigrated.

After those first two pre-Christmas courses, I applied for a job in Nottingham, as did another Carnegie man - he ended up at the grammar school and I landed the secondary modern post. I managed to find digs nearby, which served me a cooked meal each night. I wasn't into getting a flat for the duration and probably couldn't have afforded it anyway. Teaching didn't pay much and Glenmore paid half of that, although they were generous enough since they relied so heavily on volunteer staff.

I started teaching at Gedling Secondary, where a Mr Pursclough was headmaster. The deputy head would stand at the door as the children filed in and grill any pupil who had turned up out of uniform, which I thought was a good start. The first assembly in the autumn term saw the head address the whole school of up to 500 pupils and explain to those who had failed the 11-Plus that their selection for the school suited their abilities. It was a pleasure to work there because the discipline was good. The children were encouraged to engage in practical skills which suited their capabilities and it was reasonably academic too. We had several pupils who transferred to the grammar school and a number who took 0 Levels at the end of the year. Gedling was one of the better examples of a comprehensive education after my earlier experiences in those larger schools (especially Birmingham) and what I was to see in later years. But it's not my job to change the world, thank the Lord. I have always felt that everything which gets bigger just gets tougher to manage and has nothing like the quality of a smaller more focused unit.

I spent eighteen months at Gedling, where I was in charge of physical education. It was a demanding job and I had a part-time assistant initially and eventually a full-timer. Cherie Simpson was a bright spark, married to an electrician, and we were a good team, with a good sports programme and the support of many other teachers who'd come along to help out when we needed them, especially on games days. We also had a janitor who played professionally with Nottingham Forest and he'd help coach some of the boys. In those days a janitor who taught was frowned upon by the authorities, but I managed to persuade the Head to turn a blind eye to it, since it eased the load and was certainly an advantage to the youngsters.

In time I had the resources to take a wee flat in town, overlooking the legendary Trent Bridge cricket ground. There were quite a few of the single Notts Forest players in the same block and, since I'd remained in touch with Leeds United, they arranged for me to have some physiotherapy with them at their own ground. My back wasn't healing, but then I wasn't really giving it the chance: I was just too enthusiastic about playing, which always aggravated the injury; the pain was always there but I was young and in teaching, and both the work and the play mattered more to me. Sometimes far too much: I managed to break both my arms in one week, teaching western rolls on coconut matting in the gym.

There were more pleasant breaks. At Easter I was straight back up to Glenmore, for long lovely walks in the spring snows on expeditions with adult groups. I could only spare two weeks, but they were blessed with wall-to-wall sunshine and I was never out of my shorts. There was a new Principal, a PE teacher from Galsby called Alec Dalrymple. He was a very different kettle of sharks when it came to discipline and seemed to like my attitude, which was to prove very advantageous for me. Anyway, after that glorious fortnight I returned to Nottingham, blissfully burnt to a cinder. Back at school everyone wanted to know where I had been for my holiday, having wasted their time going abroad to stay the same colour as before. They didn't believe me when I told them.

Before long I heard of the new vacancy at Glenmore. Alec wanted me to go for an interview and I jumped at it. Afterwards he admitted that the interview had not seemed to go too well, but he'd told the panel that I was definitely the one he wanted. So after eighteen months' teaching in Nottingham, I was finally back at Glenmore Lodge as a full-time instructor – and student. Climbing, for example, was something I had never seriously experienced, so the mountaineering adventures were new territory and over the next six or seven years I was dragged up many steep rock faces by the experts like Hamish MacInnes and his wife and Molly Porter, John Cunningham and Fred Harper.

The small amount of training we did have was usually little more than an attempt to frighten the life out of the newcomer. One memorable incident I remember was with John on the Polldubh Slabs over in the Nevis range, where he had separated us all into groups up above the Lochaber mountain rescue team. I was aware of them watching my feeble efforts to climb the first pitch, getting the shakes and asking John to get himself above me, sensing I had little more than a couple of minutes before "peeling off". He quickly circumnavigated the route to the top, with the rope attached to me, then threw down a loop allowing me to clip into a karabiner and get some support. He then did the next pitch solo for me, putting in runners, and I duly followed. At the next pitch, the final crux to the top, he had mentioned there was a jug at the top to pull myself up, but by this time I'd become aware of the 500 foot drop (having started on a sloping grassy embankment). Somehow reaching the top and putting my hand over, searching for the jug, I found a hole that I could just get my forefinger into. "That's it!" he said, again having to come to my aid, helping me to scramble for dear life over the top edge. I was now aware that the rescue team had stopped practicing their stretcher lowering and were standing waiting for the accident to happen. We never did meet up with them, but I can imagine what they'd had been saying.

I was to get my own back on the Cunningham boy, when his turn came to flail around, in a canoe. Some time afterwards it was decided that we'd go to Knockando on the Spey, launching at Ballindalloch and paddling the three or four miles down-river. I recall Jack Thomson falling in and swimming most of the length of the last rapid. We had been practising cutting in and out of the eddies beside the rapids, and having demonstrated a clear cut-in, I encouraged the rest to follow me. Cunningham came, and keeping his canoe perfectly flat, swung into the eddy, with the natural result that gravity promptly flipped him over, after the build-up of water on his after-deck. He came up spluttering and cursing since, although a regular mountain goat up on the heights, he was no swimmer down below. We dragged him out and he continued on the trip with a glower at me. In the end though, we had a good laugh about both situations. The poor old lad had badly bruised legs from rumbling down the 100-yard rapids, but he survived his ordeal as unscathed as I had survived mine. We were both learning the ropes, in our different ways.

There were so many incidents with different people, stories exchanged back at the

Lodge which would, in fact, fill many books in capturing the incredible diversity of the characters and the challenges they faced. At first the Lodge had primarily served school parties from Glasgow and the inner city areas, but it gradually developed to cater for a huge range of people, including physical education students from Dunfermline College in Edinburgh, Anstey College in Birmingham (the sister college to Saltley, where I had been trained as a teacher) and the Irene Marsh College in Liverpool, which happened to be run by the sister of May Brown, one of the founder members of the Lodge in the old youth hostel (it was only natural that this should have inspired her to bring her girls to Glenmore). They were very enjoyable weeks with those 20-year-old PE students on their fortnightly stays, and in the summertime we probably had 12 weeks of such courses, where lots of liaisons were forged with the instructors, including yours truly. Some lasted longer than others. We were always invited to the May Ball at Anstey, and on one occasion we drove down in John McPherson's car (he was at that time courting a young lady in Birmingham) with a group of instructors who had worked on the course including myself, Cunningham and Dougal Haston. We met up with Dougal in Edinburgh late at night, with nowhere to stay – but Dougal had the key to the Scottish Mountaineering Club's library, which was a hallowed place and not to be abused. Nevertheless, needs must when Dougal drives and we slept on the floor, escaping unseen in the early hours. Few believe this actually happened, but it's quite true and that's where we spent the night.

Dougal Haston was one of the top climbers of his day, having climbed the North Face of the Eiger. Others we were to rub shoulders with included Tom Patey, the first up many Alpine ranges, who was a doctor from Ullapool and a real Jekyll and Hyde character, always appearing in his climbing kit on Speyside but only in his pin-stripe suit back at Loch Broom. The climbing of the Old Man of Hoy (a TV first ascent in July 1967) was a Patey and Haston production along with another old friend I will talk more of later, one Eric Beard, with whom I formed the Wild Rover Folk Club at the Carrbridge Hotel in the mid-sixties. Beardy was a fell runner but served as anchor man at the top of the Old Man with a 1,000 foot rope should things have gone wrong. He spent the best part of four days encamped on the top, probably singing some of his folk songs, having been dropped there by helicopter, while the rest of the climbers went back to the bottom and prusiked up the next morning. (Dr Prusik was an Austrian climber who designed a special sliding knot which locks under pressure and can be used to form a loop).

But canoeing was my forte at the Lodge and I was put in charge of kayaking. We had six NCK racing kayaks (made from plywood and extremely unstable) and four double kayaks, which were folding boats made by Tyne, known as Tyne doubles. Both were fairly unsuitable for teaching, as the NCKs had to have long, tubular airbags alongside to stop them capsizing as soon as the students sat in them. However, the pictures are in the Lodge today so that's how canoeing started there. Shortly after I arrived, fibreglass came on the market and I was encouraged to go down to Scott Bader, the resin manufacturers in Northamptonshire. I spent a day there with the lab technicians in their smart white coats and they taught me all about fibreglass, resins, fixing agents and gel coats. We made a small moulding which represented the nose of a canoe and it was used for many years as a demonstration model for teaching. Shortly after that I went on another trip, to Whitehall Outdoor Centre, where Eric Langmuir had been Principal before coming to Glenmore. I then met up with a young instructor by the name of Brian Hall, who had acquired a copy of the Hunter Supreme, one of the first fibreglass kayaks to be made in Britain – by, I believe, the same person (Keith White) who became known to canoeists as KW and his craft were KWs, versions 1, 3 and 7. Many of them were copied and modified and we used a fleet of these at the Lodge for many years. The first Hunter Supreme was made under Brian's direction at the Outdoor Centre. I brought it back with me on my car and proceeded to make another mould. We made three or so of them, but at the same time the best kayak was the Klepper T67, a folding canvas canoe, and having made canvas canoes as a young boy I decided to take drawings off the frames and make a rigid version of the T67. About the same time we had two Hunter Supreme fibreglass boats and those T67 rigids.

George McLeod, an instructor at Glenmore when I first went there, had been the handyman and had just departed for his second tour of Antarctica, working for the Falkland Islands Dependency Survey. He was a dog team handler and a surveyor and would go on two-man expeditions for fourteen days in the frozen wastes, doing what surveyors do, in some of the most appalling weather conditions. He had a tremendous photo collection and a great gift for presenting them. George had known the old canoes and so when he returned in 1962 we decided that on his day off we'd go canoeing with Duncan Ross, who wasn't a great canoeist but had more experience in the doubles. As all instructors do, we had breakfast and studied the map. We then decided on the Findhorn. An Ordnance Survey map doesn't actually tell you a great deal, so we loaded a trailer (a big heavy iron machine with Land Rover wheels) and took our boats down to a point on the river by the Nairn road bridge. By the time we had organised ourselves, and with no spare food or hard hats, no map and compass, no torch, we arrived at the back of

Top—Ray Pettit, Division 1 slalom canoeist, in full flight on the Findhorn

Above—Glenmore Lodge – as it looked during Clive's years there

lunchtime and set off.

I think George had fallen in three times before we got round the first bend. He wasn't pleased about this and couldn't understand how anybody steered a fibreglass canoe. The expletives continued until eventually he began to get the hang of things. The Findhorn is not exactly the easiest river in which to learn your first slalom techniques, and it was an overcast day and, as I said, we weren't best prepared. We wore gym shoes with holes at the ends for drainage and sported flimsy little inflatable life-jackets with nothing on our heads. But we coped with most of the rapids and did portage round Randolph's Leap at Logie, since the water was so low - in those canoes it just didn't seem possible to get through, and it certainly looked very dangerous. The point was proved down by Logie House, where we lost a paddle. We were at least prepared for that, with a spare one handy, and we carried on through one rapid after another until it grew dark. When we couldn't see, but only hear, a thunderous rapid waiting for us round the next bend we called it a day. There happened to be a sandy beach right there complete with, astonishingly, an access ladder some 30ft high, made from two pine trees stitched together with planks of wood, possibly there for pretty hardy fishermen, but we tied our three kayaks to it and climbed out. With no compass for guidance we made a stab for the Grantown-Nairn road through the forest and set off to walk to where we had left the trailer, thinking we would make it as far as the mouth of the river. We then tried to hitch a lift but, as you can imagine, there were few people on the road at that time of night and those who were almost went off the road trying to avoid us. We walked some three miles to our car and arrived back at the Lodge at four in the morning, hungry, not especially cold but very tired. Next day was also a day off, two together being very rare, and we went back to finish the trip, but this time with hard hats and a lot more respect for the environment.

There were many other canoeing exploits, often with students. A great friend was to come on the scene later in the '60s: Ray Pettit was a division one slalom paddler of no mean ability and a brilliant teacher. His forte was one-handed rolling and we'd go to various venues to demonstrate this skill, which was something of a novelty then. The Inverness swimming pool was a popular venue, as was Loch Imrich near Newtonmore, which was so green that when you capsized you disappeared. Ray had terrible sinuses for weeks after demonstrating at this pond.

We had so many superb trips. Senior boys and girls would be with us for a fortnight, the first week for training up and the second for expeditions. We canoed the west coast and into Loch Maree, where we fished in the evenings and sneaked off to the

Loch Maree Hotel for a beer. I remember putting the boys in their tents and seeing to their food before crossing the loch, first setting our secret lines, not realising that in those days the loch was a seriously prestigious fishing run, with up to six boats and ghillies. It was a damp day and we were pretty wet, but a guest directed us into the residents' lounge, where we were promptly ushered to the public bar, a room the size of a bungalow bedroom with bench seating around it and a portcullis type window. I ordered four pints of lager, to be asked who the "second two" were for. "Once you've poured them they'll be for us", I explained. The first one didn't touch the sides, with closing time then just 9.30 pm. All the time the ghillies were eyeing us suspiciously, and although they saw us the next day when they were out fishing, they didn't see Liam Carver relieving us of our overnight catch in exchange for fresh supplies and provisions.

The journey home was epic. Having studied the tides, we reckoned it would be high water and that there'd be no rapids under the bridge but we couldn't have been more wrong, and by the time we got there we were committed. Most of the boys capsized, although the double canoe survived - with the hole at the bottom full of red "man o' war" jellyfish. Nobody was seriously hurt, but we were metaphorically all at sea exiting that loch - with two days of the *literal* thing to come!

After prodding our way through the rapids we finally made clear water, and the journey home was all "pain sailing" - that's not a misprint, the experience hurt and I never forgot it. That's the thing about being a teacher: you're always learning.

Chapter Eight
Punting, Shooting And Fishing

One of the many terrific characters I met in the early days was Duncan Ross, who had also learned his lesson on the Findorn, as narrated in the last chapter. The son of the head forester at the Glen Tanner Estate on Deeside, Duncan was a real dead-eye Dick. Three times Scottish small-bore rifle champion he could handle a shotgun too and had been selected for the Rome Olympics. But he hadn't gone, his Olympic dream shot to pieces by this unsporting life: during a shoot-out at Bisley, some champion shit (that's not a misprint either) had stolen his personalised scope, and with it his faith in the great Olympic ideal. But Rome's loss was our gain.

An RAF pilot after the war, Duncan had landed at Glenmore and he became the most solid of friends. We enjoyed a drink together and he taught me the basic skills of poaching, fishing, fly fishing and shooting. Glen Tanner at that time had nine gamekeepers and after the hunting, shooting and fishing brigade had been up for the "season" in August he would phone his father and we'd be lined up with a private keeper to take us "walking up" for grouse, accompanied by his father and the dog. There was also duck-shooting in the evenings, which proved great sport, and fishing at Loch Morlich – fly fishing in the old Norfolk and Clyde rowing boats which we now have at Loch Insh for fishing. These were two clinker-built boats which we knew were the original sailing craft from Glenmore Lodge, with gaff rigs, built around 1947 when the first lodge got started. Duncan and I would finish a day's instruction on the loch (he was more of a sailor than a canoeist) and would take the Clyde – a fine drifting boat – and row to the top of the loch some three or four times until we felt we had enough for supper. We'd take the fish to our rooms and cook them in a frying pan on the primus, much to the housekeeper's annoyance. They were great suppers, the fish all a pound-plus and we'd maybe have four of them. They were delicious, with the lovely pink flesh of the brownie and really acceptable after a hard day's rowing in those stiff breezes.

It was summertime and the fishing was easy. Nowadays it's tailed off, but in those halcyon times the odd salmon was even caught off the beach at Loch Morlich by spinning –

not caught by us, I should point out, but by the handyman at the Lodge, who was a keen angler. I think he caught at least two, on a quill, which is not the heaviest of lures to launch into the water. Of course there were plenty of expeditions. In 1964 I went over the pond to the American Outward Bound school in Minnesota[2] and brought back a little folding rod, perhaps a foot long when collapsed, with a good reel, so on virtually every canoe trip down the river it went with me. We were able to cast here and there, and with nobody around in the evenings I probably fished half the pools on the Spey (a point which didn't come out in our court case in the 1970s, mentioned in later chapters). Invariably I'd pick up at least one fish, of about 10-12lbs. The handyman, Jim Bedford, who preceded the salmon-catcher I just mentioned, was an avid fisherman who dreamed of catching a salmon but, sadly, never managed it. He'd collect us at Aberlour and after a successful trip I'd make sure he didn't turn my canoe over but place it on the rack the way it was - all the others would be emptied and turned upside-down. Then I'd store the fish in the fridge until we had a weekend free of school parties: they supplemented the centre's somewhat monotonous diet - a five-day programme with a five-day menu.

The group outings from the Lodge had their uses, though. Springtime walking in Glen Feshie could be very productive. I remember we'd have groups of girls from George Watson's Ladies' College in Edinburgh (14-15-year-olds) and would camp at the Ruigh Aiteachain bothy. Expeditions further upstream would lead to a little fishing in some of the more distant pools and, since the girls were only interested in sunbathing, we'd make the most of it, since young girls stripping off acted as the perfect decoys when the gamekeepers were around. We'd sometimes pick up two or three fish, not that we ever told the girls. We'd hide our catch in a mossy stream overnight and collect them quietly the next day. "Mr Ross and Mr Freshwater went fishing but they didn't catch anything" the girls' log books would record, in all apparent honesty. Three fish of a decent size, in a rucksack already weighing upwards of 40lbs, were always good to off-load in the vehicle before heading home.

Older girls made even better decoys. On a more private expedition we took along my girlfriend, Lolli Sergo - she'd come over to Boat of Garten as a ski instructor for Badenoch Ski School, working for the Swede Toby Leising, and now lives in the United States. Duncan and I had made an early start and left Lolli to break camp as we headed off a mile upstream to fish. We hadn't caught anything when she arrived and, as she came down the bank, she slipped on wet rocks, putting her hand out to break her fall and breaking her wrist instead. It was a clean break and fortunately we had a first aid kit, so

---

[2]See Chapter 9, below   68

we strapped her up and asked her to sit and rest while we caught a couple of fish. On the way home we stopped at the little bridge by the gamekeeper's house for a rest and a drink. He had obviously gone to look for us and had doubled back. As he came over the bridge he saw Lolli with her arm in a sling and was neatly distracted, accepting our explanation that we had had to leave early because she had broken her wrist. Poor Lolli went off to hospital and came home with her arm in plaster – but with the free hand she gamely cooked our salmon.

Who needed television in those action-packed days? On another occasion, in the same area, walking out successfully with a tasty fish in our bag, we were offered a lift in a Rolls Royce which was making its way from the "big hoose". The toff was off for some fishing himself but we declined the kind offer, lest the smell alerted him that we'd beaten him to it. Once again we avoided detection and walked off nonchalantly - all part of the game in poaching for the pot, as opposed to the nasty commercial version. Most of the streams and rivers around Glenmore took their fair share of trout and salmon at the back end of the year, when they swim up to spawn, and we had plenty of expeditions in the autumn, teaching girls from Glasgow. I remember taking the girls downstream below Ryvoan bothy, where we used to watch sea trout from banks which were extremely under-cut. We'd lie down and put our arms under the bank, which went back for a metre or more. The fish were like torpedoes, leaving a wake on the surface as they shot under. The trick then was to demonstrate how to put your hand in, pull the tail of the fish out gently, grab hold and throw it up onto the bank. Many say it just can't be done, tickling trout, but it's perfectly practicable, providing you have the nerve to hang onto the fish when it kicks for freedom - of course the girls just squealed as soon as it took off and they usually dropped it. Still, we usually got one or two and would cook them on the bothy fire. This would always go down in the log books. Most of the other instructors were taught how to guddle trout by Duncan, some even to guddle bigger fish such as salmon if they could ever be found in the rocky streams.

Our fishing stories are so many; sadly with declining stocks they probably now outnumber the fish using the Spey. There would be a story to tell virtually everywhere we canoed, but our shooting trips were no less fertile. I remember one occasion, when shooting duck for the pot, that *we* were the ones who ended up getting well and truly stuffed.

One of our favourite watering holes was at Jimmy Ross's bar, the Rowanlea in Carrbridge, a late-night spot if you were counted among his "guests". We met Jimmy

Murray there, who in partnership with his brother had a farm down by the River Dulnain. The night we met him, we came across a four-wheel-drive tractor parked tight up against the front doors of the hotel. Inside, we heard that Jimmy had been banned from driving a car on the road. Later that night I ran him home in style, courtesy of our host's car, leaving the tractor safely at the hotel and forging a life-long friendship thanks to the Lodge's favourite watering-hole (our second choice being the Struan House Hotel, also in Carrbridge and run by Karl Fuchs and his wife Eileen). Before long Duncan and I were shooting on the Murrays' farms, which straddled the Dulnain, and on one particular evening, in October I recall, we arrived to find Jimmy's wife had some seriously tasty venison cooking on the Aga. The boys had caught a roe deer in a snare on a fence – not an unusual practice in those days when the farmers were hard-up, and a neat way too of picking up the odd pheasant.

Duncan and I had gone downstream and bagged a couple of mallard, but were instructed to sit right down and help deal with the venison. Only when we got back to the Lodge did we remember we'd asked Elsie, the cook, to prepare a couple of duck for us when we got back. She had made a magnificent job of it, complete with silver salvers: the cruet was out, and there to go with a whole duck each was a pile of bread and all the vegetables under the sun. We felt obliged to eat every scrap. The next day I heard that duck-filled Duncan was at the quack's. Dr MacDonald duly confirmed that his problem was definitely over-eating and the cure was to lay off food for two days until his stomach had digested its contents. Naturally there wasn't the slightest sympathy for the patient back at the Lodge, just three-course hilarity. Jimmy Murray, as I said, became a stalwart friend and considered Duncan and me as his sitting tenants, even though it was technically quite illegal. Fortunately, his real tenants at Seafield Estate, a syndicate of eight guns, very seldom appeared and certainly never in the evening for duck. And, after all, we weren't interested in anything else.

One of the other "blackguards", as my old headmaster would have described him, was George Waddle. He was the son of a very well-to-do farmer, who had land across from Jimmy's. He was a rather spoilt gentleman who didn't have to work, but he was great company and was one of the witnesses in the court case which we shall come to later. His father had a Rolls Royce and they used to take the fishing at Knockando, some of the finest the Spey had to offer. In the 1930s, when just a boy before the war, George had witnessed a double canoe coming down the rapids and capsizing, losing pretty well everything. Some time later a wallet was found which belonged to the canoeist, complete with name and valuables inside it. This was returned to the rightful owner and the reason George was taken as a witness was that he was one of the first people to see a canoeist on the Spey – a very handy man to have on our side in the action which was ultimately raised against us. He was a likeable character with a strong family, a niece, Christine Stoddart, who became a ski instructor, and a cousin who runs a coffee shop in Aviemore. All in all, they were a fine close family and I was asked to attend his funeral, since there were going to be so few there who knew him. I was very touched that Christine contacted me from Australia to see if I would go up to Inverness for the service. It was the least I could do. He was a wonderful character.

I like wonderful characters, such as those I met at Jimmy Ross's bar in the Rowanlea. Jimmy had been a member of the Scottish Badminton Team along with Alistair McIntyre, the owner of the Carrbridge Hotel. Jimmy had a favourite trick: in the bar there was quite a high pelmet round the door, some seven feet off the ground, but he could stand in front of it and high-kick his toe to the top quite effortlessly. Of course, the exercise only started once people had had half a dozen whiskies and were beginning to feel they were Athlete of the Year. I watched many people catapult themselves to disaster in vain efforts to match Jimmy. Stories abound of the nights spent there, with music into the wee hours. Once the real locals had been turned out of the bar, the visiting guests from far and wide, Glenmore Lodge included, would be allowed to stay, especially if they had a musical background. I wasn't especially able, but I did play the guitar in those days, a bit of a three-chord wonder, and Jimmy's was the first bar that I ever played in "publicly". Duncan, equally, tinkled away on the guitar as did George McLeod, but there were others of far greater ability. Andy Muir, a jobbing builder from Boat of Garten, was a jazz pianist and there was an upright in Jimmy's bar.

Another of the celebrants I've already mentioned. Tom Patey, an upright and well-respected GP in Ullapool, would travel down in his pin-stripes and then, after that long and winding road, would take very little time to unwind and change into the multi-coloured climbing sweater which featured in several of his instructional films. He had climbed with the best in his day, experts such as Joe Brown, Hamish MacInnes and Dougal Haston. Haston, as I've already said, was a person we rubbed shoulders with at the Lodge and whose company we enjoyed immensely. Like many climbers he was actually a bit of a loner, but a brilliant rock climber and snow-and-ice climber, having made several attempts at the North Face of the Eiger. On one attempt his partner fell and broke his leg and Haston abseiled off the mountain carrying him on his back. Some will remember his epic climb of the Eiger direct with John Harland, the American ace, where it almost became a race between the American team and the German one. The conditions were appalling and, I'm sure, absolutely terrifying. Nearing the summit, Harland fell to his death and Haston and the rest of the team continued to climb, both teams as I recall opening up a new route, marking the time when climbing techniques and hardware were rapidly changing. Tom Patey, on the other hand, was of the old school, scaling the heights virtually in hobnail boots. He had climbed many first ascents in the Alps and had written his own book, almost finished it, when he himself was killed abseiling from The Maiden, a sea stack off Whiten Head on the Sutherland coast. His karabiner had not been correctly closed and he fell to the rocks below. On his travels around Europe he always had his trusty accordion with him and he was, without a doubt, one of the finest bar musicians that I have ever heard. He was a very good composer of satirical songs, many listed in books, such as *Onward Christian Bonnington* to the tune of *Onward Christian Soldiers*, and others which in their day were brilliantly cutting and humorous. When he appeared in Carrbridge it was always with a bottle of whisky to hand. He chain-smoked, as most doctors did in those days, and with a fag in the corner of his mouth and smoke stinging his eyes, he played every sort of melody from Austrian drinking songs to Scottish ballads, to the delighted accompaniment of the bar-room choir.

Jimmy's bar only held about twenty people, or thirty standing. On one occasion Tom presented a young American lady and asked if I thought Jimmy would lend her his fiddle – he was a gifted fiddler and a huge fan of jazz ace Stephane Grappelli – but Tom knew that while guitarists didn't usually mind lending their instruments, fiddlers could be a very different matter. But Jimmy handed his over when I asked, and the bar was treated to an astonishing burst of virtuosity. When the young lady, known as Mary Ann, had finished, the applause nearly took the roof off the place, after which she confessed to me that she had played with the Philadelphia Symphony Orchestra. She became a very close friend of Tom and appeared with him at many venues, finishing up at Kinloch Rannoch school as a music teacher – within two years her class were gold medalists at the Mod.

I lost touch with that Mary Ann, but there was another one. The second Mary Ann became a girlfriend of mine when I found that she, too, was a musician and enjoyed the Carrbridge folk nights. She was in air traffic control at Lossiemouth and it was her job, on night shifts, to watch for and intercept the Russian Bear bombers as they broke into British air space to test our defences. She had signed the Official Secrets Act and would say nothing about her work, but she sang like a canary. We used to go on pretty lengthy pub

crawls, following the musical spots, and I developed quite a repertoire of monologues –
some two or three hours' worth – which, delivered Stanley Holloway style in my
Yorkshire/Nottinghamshire, accent went down very well, even among the Scots (providing
I spoke very slowwwwly). The pieces were quite a hit at Jimmy's and Karl Fuchs's bars. Karl
was often seen on advertisements for McEwan's beer and with some justification: after a
day's skiing on the hill he could be found, still with his top-of-the-range ski boots on, in his
bar with a crate of beer by his side, drinking with his friends. "McEwans is the best buy, the
best buy in beer!" was the caption, and it was Karl who was pictured, skiing down
Cairngorm, a fine figure of a beer drinker. He had been a class B racer in the Austrian ski
team and was a beautiful, hugely competent skier. His wife Eileen, a true Oxbridge
academic who had graduated in history from Newnham College, Cambridge just before the
War, ran the hotel and he was one of the finest hosts in the Strath. Karl was one of my
skiing tutors – he'd take ski instructors and give them an hour or so of advanced
instruction - after the official lessons had finished. In those days there was great
competition, with ten ski schools on the go on Cairngorm. Ten good skiers coming down in
line, one behind the other, was an impressive sight, an alpine tradition, imported from
Austria and Switzerland.

Frith Finlayson was another instructor, and there was quite a bit of aggravation, a
real competitive spirit between them all, but I tagged along and picked up all the advice I
needed. They were all good friends of mine. The joke was that Eileen (who must have
seen me skiing) said to my wife Sally: "You know, I'm surprised Clive is such a good skier for
a big man". All I can say is that if I'm big now, Karl was my equal - and more - with that beer
barrel apparently sewn into his sweater. All the same, I should point out that on run after
run down the White Lady I never once saw him stumble or fall, and his favourite tutorial
saying was "Let your ski stick touch the snow, 'twas like an electric shock." He was
wonderfully artistic in his execution of the most beautiful turn, the classic "stem
Christiania" or stem christy.

Most of the Lodge staff enjoyed a night out in Carrbridge's two watering holes.
The village was the hub of the Scottish skiing universe then and Aviemore Mountain Resort
was not even a twinkle in the snow. The Coylumbridge hotel hadn't been built; in fact
people had only just stopped walking up from Glenmore to Cairngorm, thanks to the
installation of that long and winding road. Mind you, the A9 could be pretty long and
winding too after a heavy night. Epics at Jimmy Ross's place included one I sadly missed,
when he challenged the whole bar to a 100-metre "handicap" (a race with bets taken). For

Top – Ski instructors 1986. L to R - Dave Jacobs, John Gibbons, M.A Harper, Clive

Above – Ski instructors 1987. L to R - Tony Burley, Mark Bishop, Caroline Sterritt,
Duncan Freshwater, Bronwyn Crymble, Clive, Alan Bell

the start, somewhere between one and two in the morning, he was given a ten metre advantage – which put him roughly outside Carrbridge police station, which I understand was not manned at that moment. He was good for a "place", finishing in the top three.

The next evening I was there, sitting in the corner, when two policemen entered. Jimmy stood with his arm across the bar door speaking to them, with his back to the people in the bar. The policemen were pointing towards me and a few others who, not being residents, under the law as it was in those days shouldn't have been in there, but they eventually went away. Mine host fetched a couple of doubles from the optics and joined the throng again, explaining that the officers of the law had been concerned about the noise the night before, and wondering about the presence of Freshwater and Carver after hours. But he had reminded them that, any time a mountain rescue was called for, it was the Lodge staff who were always first on the scene to help.

Another fond memory I have of Jimmy's is the night Winnie Ewing dropped in. She was a young prospective MP for the burgeoning SNP. Like so many politicians she could talk for Britain - well, Scotland in her case, obviously. After saying her piece she was informed that it was gone ten and time for the music to strike up and for others to pipe down. So, naturally, she kept on talking – and was promptly thrown out. Jimmy escorted her, and whoever she'd been button-holing, through to the front bar, which was unheated and rather lonely, a place reserved for special occasions and this was most certainly one of those. I reminded her about it some 40 years later at a funeral in Inverness, but strangely she didn't seem to remember it herself.

The Carrbridge Hotel was a much bigger establishment and around 1962/3 Beardy and I decided we'd start up a folk club. It was to prove a great success and provided years of wonderful music and camaraderie. There was him and me, Willie and Lorna McKenna and, later on, Donny and Arthur who were to blossom as The Trampies. And there was banjo player Sandy Moir. The group played good music and songs which kept things loose and light in the days when you could do that – long before the music had to become sober and meaningful and ethnic and tragic. We were dealing with holiday-makers in the main, and they wanted to sing along most of the time, while always happy to sit back and listen to a special presentation as long as the piece wasn't too long. So every Tuesday and Thursday throughout the winter season Carrbridge was THE place to be. The hotel held dances and if you didn't have your ticket by 4.30 in the afternoon you were unlikely to get in, as the place only held 250. They'd come down off the hill and head straight for the village to grab theirs. There was always a good quality ballroom dance band and a jazz

Top – Carrbridge Folk Club, 1960s and 70s, L to R , Neil Hall, Arthur Maclean, Clive, Lorna McKenna, Mugsy Morgan

Above – Clive, playing the Gibson guitar which he bought in Duluth, Minnesota when on secondment to the Voyageur Outward Bound school

band and they were tremendous nights, if a lot of hard work for us: Willie, the boys and I should have got into the Guinness Book of Records for the miles we covered over those years, hauling 100 chairs a time to and from the dining room for our modest three-shilling (15p) fee. It was well worth it, though, and I don't recall any unpleasantness at the club, no interruptions or disruptions other than the one guy: he came straight off the rigs with a bank-roll and a bottle of champagne, a pain who wouldn't put a cork in it; so we ended up calling the boys in blue; they sent along a 6ft 5in local bobby who peered down at the 5ft 8in rigger before picking him up by the lapels and pinning him to the wall. "My father's the Chief Constable..." warned the lad who'd put the pain in champagne. "Oh really?" came the reply. "I've been wanting to meet you for some time!" And he rammed him against the wall even harder. The "chief's son" was marched away to the cells on the Thursday and didn't reappear until Monday morning, having been treated to his "father's" hospitality for disorderly conduct and given a two-year ban from the hotel. Such was the quality of policing then. It's not at all bad now but the politics, of course, are more correct these days and keeping order can be a lot more fiddly.

Talking of fiddles, I must mention Neil Hall, the tourist officer in Aviemore. He was a fine musician, another member of the team. He's there with us in a Boathouse photo on one very successful New Year's Eve, when the McIntyres who ran the Carrbridge hotel would confess they'd get an even better trade on folk nights than they did at the Hogmanay dances. Alistair McIntyre had been a Scottish internationalist at badminton, which was a very useful sport to have before skiing had taken over in the Highland winters. Sadly, he'd had an accident with a friend who had a new Jaguar. They'd gone for a drive and crashed, leaving Alistair a paraplegic. His lounge and bedroom were directly above the ballroom and over the years he must have learned every song we played, whether he liked them or not.

During my time at Glenmore Lodge many musicians passed through the doors. Len Partridge was one of the finest guitar players whose company I have had the pleasure to share. He reputedly taught Bert Jansch to play (remember Pentangle?) and was a close friend of the Corries. His infectious style had most of the staff at the Lodge learning to play the guitar. He started when the Edinburgh fringe began, but never agreed with charging people to listen to music, so he never pursued a commercial line, even though he would have been in great demand. Len was unusual in those days, in that he had a pony tail tied with a black ribbon and people would very quickly stop talking when he started playing. He was a great friend and sadly the last time I saw him he had last a lot of weight, had arthritic hands and was no longer able to play.

Another musician to come to the Lodge was John Pettit, a captain in the Gurkhas. In the sixties he used to come and camp and ski at Glenmore. He was a seasoned soldier, having served with his regiment in Borneo for most of his career. I think he was an Oxford graduate and had been the forerunner of satire in the London clubs, before That Was The Week That Was. He wrote lyrics and executed them very professionally. His guitar playing was more in the classical style. He had spent a lot of time writing songs which were pertinent to his surroundings, so when staying in a tent in Borneo he wrote *Chocolate Box Girl*, which was about a girl on the cover of the box he had with him. He also had his skiing song:

> *We all joined the party to learn how to ski*
> *We set off for Europe all ski clothes and glee*
> *But it soon was quite clear I had not been much good*
> *In trying to steer those damn long lumps of wood*
> *The girls in the party would all laugh at me*
> *And bat their young eyelids at those who could ski*
> *Especially the skilehrer, a handsome bronze shark*
> *Who instructed them daily and into the dark.*

So it went on, but it involved considerable professional yodeling, which I was never capable of.

Back to Jimmy Ross: he was seldom away from his bar but one day we encouraged him to visit Glenmore and indulge in some canoeing and sailing. On that bright sunny day when he came to Loch Morlich there was a slight breeze and I took him and his crate of beer canoeing first. The old boathouse, with its tin roof and wooden floor, was our hospitality tent and the hospitality duly flowed. Afterwards we went across to the Alt Mhor, the river running into the loch at the far end of the beach, which has a large shallow bend as it enters the loch, and of course Jimmy fell in. There was a great commotion. He grabbed at the middle of the boat as you do when you've never canoed. As it rolled over, Jimmy's feet rose into the air and, thinking he was about to go under, he started shouting and swearing for dear life. I slowly paddled across and suggested he stood up, which he promptly did, with the water coming all the way up to his knees. Much laughter. In the afternoon he went sailing with Duncan. We had four Wayfarers at the Lodge and they were always sailed at the end of the day in a small triangular race around the loch. It's a difficult loch in the wind, its light air swirling in totally unpredictable directions, and very few people could beat Jack Thomson who, like George McLeod, had been there since 1947 after leaving the army. Jack was a very good sailor and teacher and extremely proud of his fleet. You were encouraged not to take a boat out unless you were pretty good yourself. So the race was on and, in the final run to the line in front of the boathouse, Duncan and Jimmy were lying about four lengths behind Jack when their boat caught a strong puff of wind, which lifted them past Jack right on the line. I can say there was no favouritism: it was just a genuine, fluky result. Jimmy never forgot it and that evening, back at his hotel for what I well recall was an exceptional night, he celebrated by playing his fiddle specially, resplendent in his Bermuda shorts and Trilby hat, and recounting the story several times over. Jimmy was the only man I knew who drank Canadian rye whiskey and Coke, and I clearly remember him finishing his last tune while leaning against the wall and slithering to the floor, still playing his fiddle. In the morning he was found alongside eleven empty bottles of cola and two of whiskey. Astonishingly, we were found on parade at the Lodge as usual for a full breakfast, ready to carry out our daily duties. We were young and fit then, in our twenties and ready for anything.

Chapter Nine
Fresh Fields For Freshwater
AMERICA

Around 1963 I met up with Tom Price, who was the acting principal warden at Ullswater Outward Bound. He took an interest in my canoeing activities and suggested that I would be a welcome addition to the newly developing Outward Bound movement in America, in particular in Minnesota and up into Canada, where the whole emphasis was on Canadian canoeing. There were three Outward Bound schools in America at that time, in Maine, Minnesota and Colorado. The latter was mostly mountaineering and winter climbing. It was staffed by my great friend George McLeod, an ex-Glenmore Lodge instructor and member of the epic Findhorn first descent crew with Duncan Ross and Rusty Bailey, former Benmore and Glenmore Lodge[3].

Once officialdom had been cleared in 1964 I was able to go to Minnesota, where I received my work permit and contract from the outdoor centre there. The principal at that time was Bob Pye. He was very friendly and a dedicated youth worker who had been at Minnesota Outward Bound since its beginning. His son and daughter-in-law also worked alongside him, with several other British instructors supplementing the American ones, who were all 1000 Lakes men and women.

The journey out was interesting in itself. At New York there was a bus strike, so getting into the city from Kennedy Airport could only be done by cab. Fortunately I got a Scottish cabbie, who took me to the head of the New York subway, where he refused to charge me, insisting that it had been nice speaking to a Scotsman.

I stayed two days in New York with a gentleman I had never met before but who happened to be the boyfriend of a folksinger I had met in Carrbridge. He was an artist and after I had helped him carry 8' by 4' paintings to an art gallery he offered to take me on a tour of the Big Apple. First stop was the bank for some cash. After crossing the road on a red light we were met on the other side by a large New York cop, who took out his notepad to charge us with jaywalking. I was dressed only in shorts and a shirt, with no passport for identification, but as soon as I spoke he asked where I came from. When I said ~Scotland" he said "OK, on you go". Later we went on to do the tourist spots, taking the Staten Island

---

[3]See Chapter 7, above

Ferry to the Statue of Liberty and climbing to the top. We then scaled the Empire State Building – by elevator. At that time it was the tallest building in the city.

It was a great city but I needed to travel to the west and after picking up my rucksack and guitar I flew to Boston, where I caught a Greyhound bus. The very last section of my big trip, I decided, would be a hitch-hike. I was picked up by a Minnesota miner and taken to his home for lunch. I remember his three attractive daughters and his wife saying a prayer before we ate. She said to me "So you're from Scotland. You speak very good English!". Ah, the delightful parochialism of the Mid West. I really had fallen on my feet, since the lady of the house was due to drive into Ely that afternoon and kindly offered me a lift to my final destination.

Ely was noted for canoeing and fishing. I was met by a vehicle from the Outward Bound school and was driven the twenty or so miles up dirt track roads into the centre of the forest. The area was very remote and we did not see any other human beings for a month, although we often saw moose crossing the road and the occasional brown bear.

The courses lasted a month. We had a shake down for staff in the first week and "drown-proofing" was an essential part of the course for both staff and students. This meant swimming the length of the lake for about a mile fully clothed including boots, undressing in the water into swimming costumes and then swimming back to the pontoons, where you completed an hour's drown-proofing. This was hanging like a cocoon in the water and just coming up for air on a regular basis. If you could do this you didn't have to wear a life jacket. You carried one but didn't have to wear it on the trips, except when you were negotiating the rapids. Drown-proofing was done in pairs, one swimming and one paddling the canoe to supervise his buddy.

Every morning we had a short run. This was at the time I had just completed my BASI grade 1 ski instructor qualification and had a severe shoulder injury, together with my existing back problem, so I was excused the mile run, choosing to swim instead. There were some great characters among the local instructors, who were known as "the 1000 Lakes personnel" since they had canoed over a thousand lakes. Minnesota number plates are marked as "10,000 Lakes" with the number underneath.

We had several short overnight trips, just to get used to the travel conditions for later in the course. The only canoes we had were 18 foot Grumans, which carried three people and Duluth packs (named after the port city of that name on the shore of Lake Superior) – box shaped packs which when full of food and equipment could weigh up to 100 pounds. It was an extremely physical experience, as was the ropes course which instructors and youngsters had to get used to, youngsters being aged 16 to 24. Their background could be anything from borstal to public school and, on occasions, one or two just released from prison. They all mixed in well. There were three to a canoe and two instructors to a group of twelve. One of the boys in my second trip had previously completed the cross-Canada race.

A typical expedition would involve over 400 miles of paddling and portaging. This was all pre-planned with the boys, in between teaching camp craft, first aid and canoeing. Camp craft was primarily with single centre pole tents and square pyramid rig. Cooking was done on an open fire which was surprising, being in a forest area which had a huge fire risk. The pot packs were carried by one of the boys which was no mean feat, with each pot large enough to cook for fourteen people.

I remember the first excursion. We had driven to the starting point, around 30 miles away from the school. For the first three days the temperature was 103 degrees in the shade (about 40 degrees centigrade) and while sweltering in that aluminium canoe you noticeably lost weight. We ate a very healthy diet, with one portion of flapjack with peanut butter or jam for lunch and one square of chocolate. Drinks were from the lake, sometimes with lemonade crystals to enhance the flavour. Breakfast was dried foods (egg and bacon) with a porridge mix. Out of the ten days, four were devoted to fishing. It wasn't too difficult, with the lakes full of pike and a very edible beast called walleye, which is a large version of perch with very sweet meat, rather like plaice.

Portages varied in length from 100 yards to four miles. The itinerary always had to include certain disciplines, such as an overnight paddle, so you chose long lakes, where you could just paddle without having to portage. From memory Lake La Croix (the crooked lake) was one that we took on. On one evening, a beautiful moonlit night, we witnessed the most spectacular Northern Lights that I have ever seen. Four mile portages were another challenge and, in the tradition of the outdoor school, once started you didn't stop. It was a fairly broad footpath but carrying the canoe for that length of time was an experience you didn't forget, especially with black fly and mosquitoes as company under the canvas. We carried chemicals with us which were very effective. Although they stung your sweat pores, at least they kept the mosquitoes off. Out there in the big country everything that flew stung you; mosquitoes, birch fly (black fly) by the thousand, deer fly and horse fly. The deer fly always bit you on the top of your head if they could get at it, so hats were essential. Some of my students couldn't put a penny coin on any part of their body without covering a bite. Other hazards of the swampier parts of the portage were the leeches, so the first thing you had to do when you got up was to brush the things off. One portage in particular was a nightmare, where at times we were waist deep in sludge too thick to paddle through and we had no option but to negotiate it by simply walking through it.

Half way round our 400 mile adventure we had to identify a place where we would do a three night solo. This meant that we would put the boys out at strategic places around the lake where we could see each one, but where they could not see or contact each other. Trying to move through the forest, where we had practiced map and compass, was horrendously time consuming and tortuous. The forest was very dense and in the run up to the training of the second group we lost two of the lads. It took us two days to find them and we had to bring in aircraft to see if they had lit a fire to show smoke above the trees.

Progress could be as slow as half a mile an hour due to the density of the forest. We chose Montgomery Lake for the solo, a high point for us with an electric storm brewing from the west. After duly putting the boys out we returned to our position on the hilltop and within half an hour the electric storm was upon us. There was a great black cloud as far as the eye could see, blocking out the horizon. We had watched this all day from our position. For twenty four hours it rained with lightning like I had never seen before, to such an extent that we dared not stay in the tent with the aluminium pole – instead we went down and stood in the hollow all night with our poncho rainwear, squatting amongst the trees. Our tent didn't get struck; we could have stayed there but we were exposed on the highest point on the island.

On the solo the boys were each issued with a small tin foil dish with which they could cook. They were each allotted five matches in a waterproof container and a very short length of fishing line with two hooks but no food – it was up to them to catch their own. One of the easiest to land was the crayfish. These tasty fellows resembled large shrimps and were delicious but fiercely fast – and when we went to catch them they would leap backwards with a flick of their tails. The easiest way to catch them was to ring bark a birch tree, taking off a tube of bark and putting it over the crayfish, then placing your hand inside to catch it. One boy caught a rabbit and brought it back to camp as he had used all his matches. The only protection from the elements was a 6' by 3' groundsheet, which was part of the pack. You can imagine what it was like, with the birch fly, black fly and no-see 'ems, which are smaller than midges and could penetrate through the midge barriers on the tents. The American tents had smaller mesh than I was used to, so that once you were in the tent and you had used up the "black flag" spray (which could virtually kill a deer) it certainly cleared the tent out. It was more comfortably habitable but I shudder to think what the "black flag" did to our nervous systems.

You had to put the kettle pack in a very precarious position close to the tent, so that if brown bears came round looking for food (never keep food in your tent) they would go to the kettle pack in the food store and hopefully knock over the pan with the cutlery in it, making a loud noise and waking everyone in time to frighten them off. We never actually had to deal with that but I was later reminded of the potential danger with the accident involving a polar bear in Svalbard, off northern Norway, in 2011. In May and June, before the berries are out, the brown bears are certainly looking for food.

So we progressed. Lake after lake, portage after portage. A lasting memory – sad in some ways – is the comparative tedium of the scenery. Minnesota is so flat and on Lake Montgomery we had a high point of 50 feet. The rest of the time you are on lakes within a ring of trees and with no hills. We used to watch the deer swimming across the lakes on the marshes. Some of the boys we were with used to swim alongside a moose, then jump on its back for a ride – making sure they disembarked before its feet touched the ground.

Canadian canoeing wasn't done on windy days, so it was quite calm when we were paddling although we did put up a little canvas to try and get some wind. It isn't all lakes: there are rivers and some of them are massive after the winter snow and frosts. Sudden thaws can create potentially dangerous conditions on rapids which you would normally portage round. On one occasion we rescued a group of Indian paddlers who had come from a reservation. They had been shopping and two of their canoes had capsized but we managed to help them recover their goods.

The whole area was famed for well known trappers of old, known as the Voyageurs. The groups in the Outward Bound school were named after some of them: I think ours was Henry, a famous trapper. Their canoes were 20 man craft, carrying 2 to 3 tons for bringing back skins from Canada. They were huge canoes, which also capsized, and to this day there are diving interests at the bottom of these rivers searching for their valuable cargoes of axe heads and European metal tools.

All groups were scheduled to return home on the same day, to a great homecoming and a positive banquet. The school had a wonderful cook, a woman with fourteen children. All food we had in camp was home baked and there was as much as you could eat.

My accompanying instructor was Chuck Kurkowski, a 1000 Lakes man. We never used the map on our 400 mile journey, although we did have it with us. As soon as we hit the lake from the portage, Chuck would say "Portage over there" and we'd head down and across the lake to a blaze on a tree, nothing more, no great pontoon, just a tree with an axe mark. Some years later Chuck came to work at Loch Insh. He was great company.

Another young man who was a botanist shared our bunkhouse accommodation. He would go off into the night with his lamp and map to trap moths and butterflies. He had a wonderful collection of these exotic creatures – exotic to me anyway – which were actually commonplace around the site. I recall one evening being rather alarmed at what sounded like a brown bear trying to open the metal grills on the windows. I then realised it was a mouse that had got inside a metal waste bucket in the bedroom. Panic over: your mind plays strange tricks in the dark.

After two weeks the girls came into camp. Their time at the camp never crossed with the boys', which was perhaps a good thing. The girls were aged 16 to 25 and would be on shake-down for the two weeks we were away. There were some amusing pictures of the girls trying to lift the canoes, which weighed around 60 pounds. Some of the girls had slipped and the canoes had landed on top of them, legs sticking out either side of the boats. The girls would cover less distance than the boys, cooking by fire and having no food drops. They left as we arrived.

For safety some of the experienced staff stayed in camp in case of emergency. I recall them paddling on one occasion to evacuate a person who had split their leg with an axe and the speed at which they covered fifty miles was quite remarkable. Float planes also provided a safety service in the case of fires. Float planes were quite popular in that area and you would occasionally see them overhead. To summon assistance you would light a fire in an open space to raise smoke, but that wouldn't necessarily bring anyone down to help you. There were no mobile phones and no radios and you were on your own for ten days.

After two days off we had a trip into town for a beer. You could only buy the stuff if you were over 21, a law strictly enforced, so the instructors had a night of living the high life. Next day it was back to work, a new group starting again with a shake down, map and compass, axe use, etc.

Sadly I had to come home early, as the Lodge wouldn't allow me to stay the two months. It was in the middle of the second trip, having crossed the border between the United States and Canada (as you could then and probably still can) without any checks: you just paddled across through the lakes. We had a paper pass from the school as authority to be in Canada. However, coming back I was to change places with a guy who took over my paddling and I took his large Cadillac. Having taken my personal belongings from the rucksack I set off for the school. This meant very quickly learning how to drive on the right hand side of the road. And what a culture shock it was – the Cadillac an enormous beast compared with my Morris Traveller.

During the trip I had the radio on, naturally. It was a beautiful day and I heard that I was in the area of "Scotland", with Loch Ness, Fort William and Fort Augustus, etc. There were so many Scottish names (McKenzie, McDonald and so on) on the post boxes as I drove past. These must originally have been families cleared from the Scottish Highlands. On the radio they announced that "In Fort William there has been a baby snatched from a pram outside a supermarket...". I didn't think much about it but there was a great deal of fuss on the radio. I drove through the Canadian passport control and after half a mile I reached the gates of the American frontier. I had no passport and as I walked into the control point I realised that I didn't know the car registration number. The next hour was spent talking my way in while the guards were on the phone asking for a clear description. I was one of the few who managed to get into America with no passport and no visa, just a piece of paper that allowed me to canoe in the Minnesota lakes. The Principal of the Outward Bound school must have given me a good reference.

And so to the final journey home, on a flight from Duluth to Boston, then to the UK via New York. While in Duluth I had my flamenco guitar to hand as I was now doing a lot more folk singing, but that instrument, with its nylon strings, was never very good for folk singing, with or without a microphone. Having walked the streets of Duluth I came across a music shop and ventured in, to find a Gibson, for which I exchanged my guitar and gave them £40 as well. The Gibson has stayed with me ever since. Sadly I don't play it now but it must be worth at least £1000 today. It has always been the *crème de la crème* of guitars. I became quite attached to it as it helped me to get started at Loch Insh, with the folk singing at Carrbridge and the Aviemore Centre.

At Boston the plane broke down and had to have an engine replaced but we stayed on board. Having brought the precious Gibson along with me in nothing more than a cardboard box I was asked by the hostess to entertain the rest of the passengers and so I did, with the best Scottish nationalist, anti royalist songs that I could muster, much to their amusement. I gave them all the songs that were popular in the sixties plus the Glasgow street songs I had learned from the schoolboys and girls who came to Glenmore Lodge.

And so a great educational chapter ended for me. Before I left I was asked if I would like to go back and be a roving ambassador in the Outward Bound movement in America. They had so many contacts and business people supporting the movement and, having completed the course, I was considered a good candidate for the cause. Looking back now, I have to concede it would have been a wonderful opportunity for me, and all of it paid for. What might have been is still what might have been, but one thing is for certain: I wouldn't be here at Loch Insh if I had taken up their offer.

EUROPE

One offer I did take up was the military's. Not canoes this time, but skis. I had a fine time working for the Green Jackets in Germany.

There were three occasions where BASI were asked to provide trainers for a course to create instructors for the British Army. There were several centres for this in Bavaria, including one in Sonthofen, one of Germany's southernmost towns, and I had an unforgettable fortnight at the Vedack hut, half way up the mountain; a hostel style Tyrolean building at the top of something like the White Lady ski run, but with no facilities whatsoever and only one access by T bar. This hut was used by hikers in the summer and hired by the army in the winter as a sleeping base at the centre of the ski run.

My introduction, with Doug Godlington, came in running what was known as a ski party leader course. The army provided their best 'squaddie' skiers along with a corporal and captain to keep them in order. I think we had twenty four in total (twelve in a class). This particular regiment was based in Berlin at the time of the Berlin Wall, where they had one or two notorious prisoners to look after, notably Rudolf Hess, Hitler's one-time deputy, who was held there for many years. The American and British armies took it in turns to cover the guard duty, including some of the potential ski instructors on our course.

I had to get myself by train to Munich, disembarking at Ulm and then taking a branch line to Sonthofen. On arriving there I had to get my skis on, rucksack in hand, and ride the T bar approximately 1000 metres to the hut. I didn't have any difficulty with this, but gathered from speaking with Doug that on the day before there had been a hilarious introduction to the T bar for the squaddies. In typical military fashion they had arrived in a four-ton truck; on disembarking they were issued with skis and boots and told to march round the car park until they got the feel of the skis; after about half an hour they were reintroduced to their suitcases and told to pick them up, catch onto a T bar and head up to the hut.

Those of you who are skiers will realise this is no mean feat if you have only worn the skis for half an hour. The better ones set off first, got fifty yards up the hill and fell off, letting go of their suitcases, which promptly became lethal weapons, hurtling down the track and knocking the other students down like skittles. The suitcases ended up at the bottom, having all blown open, exposing the contents to the elements. A dozen so-called potential ski instructors were left to walk down the slope with their skis to sort everything out. Doug related this story many times and it was evidently a sight for sore eyes. Eventually they all walked up with their suitcases and skis.

The hut was quite different from most places one might sleep in. For starters it had no heating. It had a lino floor, which was about an inch deep in icy water. We had good quality sleeping bags and the army boys had the usual army issue. There was an oil-fired stove at the end of the room, but the custodian of the hut was rather mean and didn't allow it to be lit. These were our sleeping quarters for two weeks and, with twenty six of us in the same room, you can image the condensation was considerable and duly turned into ice. Downstairs one end of the building was a sitting/dining room which was nice and warm from the heat of the kitchen, where the owner of the hut prepared the food. I remember they made quite a presentable Austrian cuisine, although I don't recall being particularly hungry at any time.

There was no alcohol or TV, so apart from skiing, eating and sleeping that was it. Only on one occasion do I remember going down to the valley and staying one night (this would have been mid-course). The ablutions were even more memorable. They were located at the other end of the hut from the dining area/kitchen. The hut was perched on the edge of a cliff. A small stream came down the mountain, was diverted through the hut by an open channel and went out over the side of the cliff. The cold water gathered in a trough as it came into the building and there were a number of plastic wash bowls, so that each person could scoop water up for a very invigorating wash-down and shave. The toilets themselves were rudimentary, with a wooden seat set on the edge of the building, next to the cliff. When the seat was lifted a blast of cold air came up from below, so you didn't spend long in the sitting position and hoped that you could get your business done as quickly as possible. There was never a queue. We never saw where the waste went, but I am sure the ground below must have been stupendously fertile once the snow had melted.

The skiing was excellent. The candidates were enthusiastic and good fun. They knew that if they did well and passed they would be sent back to this site with their own candidates for the rest of the winter, or at least they would get two or three skiing trips away from guarding Herr Hess in Berlin. It was a lovely skiing area, rather similar to the White Lady and with just that one T bar. We were hemmed in by five peaks at the top of the slope, where there were many wild goats and chamois, and across from the slope there were mature pine trees which we ventured into with our prospective instructors. The course culminated in the usual passing and failing, followed by departure the following day, when we flew back to the UK.

Doug and I returned to Sonthofen many times after that and it was on one of those memorable trips that, due to lack of snow, we had to move from our usual accommodation to the youth hostel in Garmisch Partenkirchen. The skiing was to be on top of the Zugspitze, which has access via a well-used narrow gauge railway, taking you through the heart of the mountain. Hitler's hide-away had been here - several films and documentaries have been shown with regard to the rather exquisite property at the top of the mountain. On this occasion our group was on rest and recuperation from the Troubles in Northern Ireland.

On the first evening, sharing a room with five others in three double bunks, Doug and I were very amused by the Germanic tannoy system announcing: "The lights will go out in five minutes". We all looked at each other and then four minutes later: "The lights will go out in one minute". Eventually the crack of the switch being thrown left the whole place in darkness, except for safety lights in the corridor. The windows in the bedrooms either opened back from the top or, if you could undo the lock, they opened like a door. However, the locks wouldn't open so theoretically you couldn't get out. The locks weren't very big and with the help of a screwdriver we sprung them open. The whole place felt prison-like as there were no lights on the inside, but floodlights on the outside. I think we had around five days of merriment and skiing around Garmisch and survived being thrown out. The food was only average to meagre although we supplied the management with very good British military rations. We didn't see much of these and I believe they were kept and sold to the other clients, who were paying for their food and accommodation. As usual most of the guys were given a pass mark for their skiing.

Chapter Ten
There'll Be A Welcome On The Hillside

The whole world was young then. Outside, anyway. I was so lucky to have entered a profession in its infancy: there were very few instructors with the experience to run the outdoor centres which had been established, unlike today when we're producing too many for the available jobs. In North Wales there was the Plas y Brenin, run by John Jackson and his pioneers. He had a great team of instructors and they became firm friends. We'd go down from the Lodge to our sister centre for courses in canoeing with national coach Oliver Cock, to polish up our skills and learn their system. They would send staff to us, particularly in the winter for skiing sessions - there was a small plastic slope down there but little chance of snow skiing, and the Welsh experts specialised more in rock climbing and canoeing. Whenever Plas y Brenin staff came to the Lodge they were made very welcome and given the treatment: skiing by day and singing, drinking and dancing by night. We each took turns in taking them out, but what we didn't tell them was that between coming off the hill and going out for dinner at seven we'd have been to bed.

Dave Humphreys, who was to become the first instructor to reach retirement age, had wonderful ability on skis, while looking just like Arthur Askey ("Hello playmates!"). He could make one turn in either direction, stem Christiana, nearly parallel but he could never manage two turns as he didn't have the take-off ability. But we had great fun teaching, and of course he could ski down the slope, although he fell over quite a bit. One evening we went out to Carrbridge Hotel for the folk night, which finished at midnight, then on to Jimmy Ross's which was absolutely dead. We then drove over to the Nethy Bridge Hotel, which was packed out and its doors locked. Fortunately Colin Sutton, the owner/manager, was in the foyer and caught my eye, beckoning us to go round the back, which got us into the dance for nothing. It finished at one thirty and, on the way home, we just happened to try Jimmy Ross's again...and found it absolutely heaving! The music was going, the drink flowing and we finally made it back to the Lodge by three o'clock. Our Welsh counterparts always enjoyed their Highland jaunts, with the world so dramatically different up here.

Then there was John Jackson who, well into his seventies, was still doing

Himalayan expeditions and Antarctic surveys. They continued until his death in 2005. I think his wife Eileen is still alive and I was very close friends with their sons. I taught Jacko to ski and got him through his BASI Grade 3: he had such a good time that he gave me a signed copy of his book (which I still have). On one particular evening there was news that the Ferranti electronics company in Edinburgh had a climbing club, some of whose members were fairly high-powered climbers. It was their AGM in the Laggan Inn, where there was a bothy, a hotel and a long dog-leg bar. We decided to join them after the evening programme at the Lodge. So, at around 10.30, Jacko, Eric Beard, Lolli and I set off for the party. I had a carfull, a Morris Traveller loaded with guitars in the back and one extra passenger, Ray Greenall. He was a comical figure and a great friend and I'm sure he'd remember the evening. Ray had a slight paralysis on the left side of his face which he played on: it caused a tear in his eye sometimes, especially if he was laughing at his stories of frightening old ladies on buses in Manchester until they offered him their seats. I haven't seen him for ages, sadly. He lived and worked at Ogwen Cottage in Snowdonia. Anyway, off we set for Laggan in a storm, a gale blowing snowdrifts over the roof of the car all the way. We got there safely in the end, and met up with the climbing fraternity: Haston, Brown, Patey etc. The evening was noisy and only punctuated with respectful silence when my Lolli sang a couple of ballads. When the others sang, the place reverted to its rowdy state, celebrating the rough, tough mountaineering culture of their world. We set off for home at about two in the morning with Ray sleeping in the boot of the car. After dropping Lolli off at Kingussie, where she was staying at Columba House, we ploughed on up the glen, finally getting back to the Lodge a mere four hours after lock-up time. Ray was sound asleep, until we rolled him out into his freezing feather bed of fresh snow.

Such was life for the full-time Scottish Sports Council instructor. Oh so many characters at Glenmore in those days. We had Beardy with his fell-running – he was a record-holder for all the long-distance races, the four Cairngorm tops[4], the Irish, the Skye Ridge, the Welsh 3000, the 24-hour Lake District marathon. All these titles he held in the early sixties, and some remain unbroken to this day.

Then there was Plumb Worrall, the son of a plumber, with his thick Mancunian accent. He was a fanatic on skiing technique. In those days Austria was ruled by Krukenhauser, in charge of the country's ski instruction for more than two decades. They allowed English and other foreign nationals to join their courses at St Christoph and Plumb

[3]Editor's note - In 1963 he went round the four main Cairngorm peaks in 4 hours 41 minutes from and back to Glenmore Lodge – see Scottish Mountaineering Club District Guide – *The Cairngorms,* 6th Edition, p.14

was one of those people. Later on I was privileged to join a similar course with Krukenhauser at the Bundersportheim on Kitzsteinhorn. Doug Godlington and I spent a very enjoyable fortnight learning how to short ski, after the "blizzard ski" craze was introduced in the late sixties. But, as I said, Plumb was a fanatic. His first wife Robbie (who sadly died of cancer and is buried at Rothiemurchus's Five Stones graveyard) came with him to Scotland. He had worked as a plumber himself, and had some properties in Manchester which he let to students, which I think financed his skiing exploits. His fanaticism was such that, on returning from Austria, he produced a large piece of card which folded out to show circles representing all the different points which triggered the turn, depending on whether you were doing one which began with a check, a down movement, an outward movement or whatever.

As my sons go through life in skiing, they'll find that the wheel goes full circle: they'll end up talking the same language we used forty years ago. Today the skis have changed but the release technique of how you execute a turn remains: French, rotational Austrian, counter-rotation and so on. Plumb was hot on this and whenever he had an audience he would get on the table to demonstrate the knee and ankle movement in making these turns. In fact, he could be fanatical to the point of being boring about it, but he was good company for all that, a child at heart and a wonderful teacher of children – and anyone else prepared to listen. Coupled with that, he was as hard as nails: didn't wear gloves or a hat and the storm could do whatever it liked, since he was oblivious to the pain. This was borne out by the fact that he was a member of one of Manchester's big climbing clubs and tackled the Cuillins with them, surviving a fall near Glen Brittle which punctured his stomach. The story has it, and I've no reason to doubt it, that in order to save himself he used a whole crepe bandage, rolled up, as a plug and wrapped another one around himself before walking three miles to the hospital. He wasn't prone to telling porkies and it is said that on another occasion, after a terrible day on the hill, he finally had to check his foot which had been nagging him: when he got his boot off, he found a spark plug in it, which he simply hadn't noticed. Hard to believe, yes, but it fits the man's character to a T. Plum taught me just about everything I know about skiing; what he didn't teach me, I learnt from Frith Finlayson and Karl Fuchs. Plumb had worked for Karl before coming to Glenmore, and before that he had taken a tent for six months through the winter at the top of Corrie Cas – near the steep part – long, long before lifts. He and his wife Robbie dug themselves in and spent the whole winter skiing. The only time they ever came down was for provisions, and they would walk down. Doug Godlington was writing a book about his exploits, but I don't know how far he got.

There isn't enough paper in the world to tell all the stories of the hill and its characters, but one I want to include was told me by a folk-singing legend, Alan Bell of the Taverners, one of the many guests from the floor at the Carrbridge folk night. He played guitar and concertina, a gifted singer/songwriter and very big around Manchester for years, with audiences of up to 2000 at the Corn Exchange. Alan was a skier, mainly here for the sport. He told me there was a ski club in the Lake District, which got snow often enough to warrant a lift, even although it was a fair old hike to get to it. On heading up there once he came across Plumb in his tent, with his little lurcher dog, a snappy thing that would have your hand off if you weren't careful. There was the usual meeting and greeting and Plumb asked if he fancied a brew. "OK" said Alan, sitting down. The tea was made and passed to him, whereupon the dog growled menacingly. "What's up yer dog, Plumb?" he asked. "Oh it's all right" came the reply, "it's just that you're drinking out of 'is mug, but it'll be all right".

Plumb had surprises for everybody. One of his favourites was the "now turn". He would set his students off at the top of a hill and they'd traverse across the field. Just before they hit a dry stone wall he would shout: "Now! Turn!". I can still chuckle at his methods. Many years later, on a winter survival course, we tried snow-holing. Although he was a great camper, mountaineer and skier, he hadn't done much in the way of snow-holing while some of us had become quite expert at it. The thing was, Plumb was utterly oblivious to pain and it was a nightmare for the rest of us, trying to keep dry while working in the hole. We built some epic igloos and snow holes and rode out some fierce storms. The students weren't very good at it, but those challenges were some of the best times we spent away from the Lodge, with no telephones, nobody calling you and no early starts. We had many remarkable sessions with school children, both boys and girls, on two-day expeditions deep into the Cairngorms, sleeping in monstrous snow holes which might have been cornices which had turned back on themselves, leaving a tunnel we could dig into. On one such occasion I had a dozen girls with me and in the morning they had to go out to relieve themselves. I gave them a row when they eventually returned covered in snow, but it was only an hour later when I went out to discover that an 80 mph gale was blowing and that there had been three feet of snow overnight. We almost lost the stretcher we'd taken with us, and it was as much as we could do to drag it back to Glenmore through the forest.

Talking of the Lodge, there were many girlfriends. Well, not that many. A few. One of the ladies who came to work with us was one Sally Fraser. She'd been working for

Captain Wells, head of the Aviemore Centre while it was being built, and had seen an advertisement for a secretary at the Lodge. I was still involved with Lolli at that time, but it wasn't to be for much longer. Sadly, Lolli had a serious illness which left her unable to bear children and she finally decided to go home to America rather than live childless with me. It took the wind out of my sails, until I decided that the "playboy" life wasn't so bad. Besides, my mind was also made up about going it alone in business. I had meetings with Captain Wells about setting up a lease for Loch Morlich, planning to establish my own Cairngorm Canoeing School Ltd. He wanted sailing as well and, since I could sail too, I didn't see a problem. The thing is, I also wasn't seeing that the real reason for my enthusiasm was that, actually, I was getting bored with teaching. I was also being approached by a lot of people wanting to join my group (which they couldn't, as we were only allowed to include people who were resident at the Lodge). To cut a long story short, the playboy came first and he missed his chance: it was Sandy Caird who took the Loch Morlich lease and Cairdsport got under way.

When I came to my senses I made friends with the new secretary, who did my typing for me. She was a good skier too. In fact, Sally was a cut above the rest in every way. We became good friends, courted for a short time and the rest, as they say, is history. What she saw in me I've no idea.

And there were more surprises.

In 1969 I got a lease from the Forestry Commission to operate on Loch Insh – the same Forestry Commission which, I know, had not been too keen to see me on Loch Morlich. The big surprise about getting Loch Insh was that it gave me access to the Spey, despite the known hostility of the big landowners. Colonel Grant of Rothiemurchus, father of the present laird, Johnny Grant, had had me up to the "big hoose" and made his feelings very clear, suggesting that I might like to start a canoeing and sailing school south of Perth. I got much more sympathy from Fergus and Anne Williamson, owners of the Alvie estate, when I thought of Loch Alvie, but there was another riparian owner involved, Lord Bilsland, of Bilsland's Bakery in Glasgow, who had Kinrara estate, so I approached him. He was a very old gentleman, well into the foothills of Mount Dementia, so I had first been vetted by his 50-year-old secretary at the new Strathspey Hotel (very plush)[5]. She had travelled from Glasgow specially to interview me and must have been impressed, since I was then invited to Glasgow to meet the old boy. After a long conversation he had wandered off into raptures about teaching children to do anything and singing sailing's praises. "What do you need of me?" he had inquired. "Well sir, I need a site, somewhere to operate, and you have the beautiful Loch Alvie". "Oh yes, that will be fine. How much

---

[5]Now the Macdonald Four Seasons Hotel   94

land?" In those days I hadn't a clue, so I'd suggested an acre, to which he agreed. It had all been looking so good and I had returned to the Highlands on cloud nine. But, as I said, this was the time of surprises: before long I heard from his factor, an Inverness lawyer who had the farm at nearby Lynwilg and had been appalled at the very idea of my running an outdoor school next door. His lordship was awfully sorry old boy, but he would not be able to let me operate on the loch.

That's when I'd gone back, none too hopefully, to the Forestry Commission, to receive the biggest surprise of them all: a one-year lease at Loch Insh. Before long Fergus Williamson was visiting, wondering if I had any interest in acquiring the village hall. "What village hall?" I replied. So he took me up to the top of the bank and showed me. The place was used for badminton and dances and had been very popular in its day. Built in 1899 – as verified by a piece of wood bearing the carpenter's name, one J. A. Robertson of Feshiebridge - it was really the first place of its kind between Newtonmore and Aviemore. Before World War II, one of its celebrated guests had been Benny Lynch, the world champion flyweight boxer, who'd fought an exhibition bout there. During the war, the Newfoundlanders, cutting timber for the war effort, would leave their Nissen hut billets in Glenfeshie for a few hours to entertain the ladies of the district at the village dances there. The older generation in the Strath still reminisced about it, but I had no use for it – and I certainly didn't have the £2000 asking price. Next I got a call from the minister at Insh Church, who thought it would be ideal for me. But it was all pointless pestering me, since neither I nor my parents had the cash. "But you should at least put some kind of bid in", everybody insisted. "I haven't got two hundred pounds, let alone two thousand", I told everybody. I was even doing a night school in Fort William for a tenner a time, hoping to buy a Firefly (which, it turned out, was useless for teaching with anyway).

To shut everybody up I eventually did bid, but only a thousand. The phone duly went and the minister suggested I should raise my bid. I wondered if he was simply trying to tell me something or if he could possibly have been "at it". I put the thought out of my mind, since gentlemen of the cloth could never be "at it", could they? With no money to back it up, I raised my bid to £1200. It was successful, but I found later that I'd ended up paying £200 over the odds, with the only other bid - from the Girl Guides in Inverness - at the bare thousand. You live and learn, while teaching.

I carried on travelling to the Fort for ten nights over the winter, teaching canoeing in the swimming pool at the High School, where another of my old flames, Caroline Hill, had become the PE teacher (hence the trek across country). Caroline and Sally pulled me in different directions, until Sally won my heart once and for all. I remember crossing the threshold with her: of the village hall, that is. After hauling her down there, to show off my new possession I realised I didn't actually have a key. The poor lass had to climb through a broken window, and her duties started before she'd even got her breath back – I told her to start sweeping the place up while I explored. I feel terrible about it now, but it must have been love, since she actually did sweep the place up, and very thoroughly too. We had a really good look around and found nothing at all – no electricity, no water, just a tin building.

I tell a lie: actually, we found a beautiful friendship in that ugly building. It led to marriage and our move, eventually, to Insh Hall. Far from finding nothing at all, we found everything.

Chapter Eleven
Dislodged

By this time the Sports Council, who had been quite supportive, had a new boss in Ken Hutchison. His predecessor, May Brown, had been very helpful, offering some timely advice on whether or not I should go it alone. After I'd taken the plunge she had some more: "Clive, if you are starting your own place, just make sure it's up and running before you leave here...". I thought that was very good of her, but the new boss, with a nudge from Eric Langmuir (who was then the Lodge Principal) didn't share her sentiments. At that time each new day brought a new surprise and my new venture was to provide a beauty. I had a contract which said the Lodge couldn't sack me, but that's just what they did. The Sports Council weren't too keen on my having a limited company of my own, even less that I should be running it while still at Glenmore, so I was summoned to Edinburgh and invited to resign. I declined the invitation and my employment was promptly terminated. I see in the Lodge's 60th anniversary literature that I "resigned" in 1969, but we shouldn't always believe what we read, should we?

My sacking left me bitterly disappointed, since my entrepreneurial activities in no way impinged on any of my colleagues there: I had two of my own people running the Loch Insh venture. One of them was Eleanor McFadden, an 18-year-old Aberdeen University student, who did a great job before heading off to America for a spell... of 30 years. I'm delighted to say she's now back in Kincraig, running a highly successful charity, correlating global cancer research for the medical world.

The shock dismissal was a miserable end to my Glenmore Lodge career, giving me no leeway while I fought to get things off the ground and into the water at Loch Insh. For the first time in my life I had to sign on the dole, at a time when there were no jobs going for schoolteachers. So for a while I got some of my money back from the government. My parents had a caravan at Glenmore, which we brought down to the Hall. It was somewhere for an unemployed teacher to sleep while he set about developing his investment. The first task was to get the old spring up the hill flowing, then to set about repairing what was left of the old pipe network. There had been a water supply and a generator, but it was

Top - Glenmore Lodge Group 1967/68 – back row L to R - unknown, Duncan Ross, Clive, Liam Carver, Archie Scott (Chairman, Cairngorm Chairlift Company); front row L to R - Brian Hall, Jack Thomson, Eric Langmuir

Above – Helicopter snowfield survey group 1978. L to R - army pilot, Iain Fraser (Outdoor Education – Highland Region) , Bob Clyde (General Manager, Cairngorm Chairlift Company, Jack Thomson (Glenmore Lodge), Hans Kuwall (Ski School Director, head down), army technician, Guy Chilver-Stainer (Scottish National Ski Council), David Paterson (Manager, Glenshee Ski Centre), army pilot, army sergeant, Clive

obvious that the place needed re-wiring. Of course, I didn't have the money to do this, but I did have friends and by this time we'd formed a company, Cairngorm Canoeing and Sailing School Limited, which had officially bought the Hall. There were three shareholders: Jack Maxwell, Willie McKenna and yours truly. Willie was courting Lorna then and they had a residential caravan which needed a home, so they drew it up alongside the Hall on the understanding that Willie would give me a hand two days a week, digging drains and the like.

It was a complete repair job. The lead pipes under the sinks were all burst. My friend Ray Pettit was a great welder and engineer, but had to throw in the towel at welding lead. We didn't have the money for new plastic pipes, or any other kind for that matter, so Plumb was brought down. For all the years that I knew him he had always had a shaky hand and you sat next to him during breakfast at your peril – most of his food ended up on your plate and he needed two hands, one for holding the spoon and the other for holding the hand holding the spoon. For all that, when at work he only had to take hold of the stick of tallow, the mohair pad, the blowtorch and he was away, making magnificent lead joints. He repaired all of those pipes and we got the place going with a small water supply.

By this time Sally was pregnant with Duncan, so we were going to have to improve our bathroom facilities. The toilet was at the back of the hall, which had a stage and exits from either side. Having no money for timber, the show had to go off: we decided to pull the stage apart, but it was so well put together, with old-fashioned square nails, that we had to cut it up instead; to this day part of the old passageway to the hall is a section of the stage which was fashioned into a ceiling, just before entering the main building. On the right hand side, just where there are now cupboards, the piece of wall between the kitchen and those cupboards is another section of the old stage. That became a bathroom with a window into the hall, and we installed a new cast iron bath. Another friend, Louis Grant, gave us a small Aga. Plumb fitted two radiators into what would have been the tea room and we closed off the section of the main hall and tea room to form what today are rooms 1, 2 and 3. Room 3 became our bedroom, 1 and 2 were our sitting room and Andy Muir, the jazz pianist from Jimmy Ross's days, built the first chimney, which is still there although not in use, with a Baxi fire. It was a cosy little place, even in winter. The only problem for Sally was that the loo was still at the back of the Hall and, from memory, it was just resting on bits of the wall. We did improve on that, but had to leave it in the same place since it had to be connected to the existing cesspit.

There was no septic tank in those days, just a stone-built pit within 10 yards of the building. It worked, but we knew a purpose-built septic tank was essential and we noticed that the neighbouring cottage, Legerwood, owned a strip of land literally five or six feet from our back boundary. I spoke to the owners, the Watsons, a delightful couple in their 70s, and showed them the deeds, which revealed that they, under the name of Naismith as previous owners, owned the strip. They agreed to sell us the area, for £200 I think. He was an artist and his somewhat eccentric behaviour was put down to an accident in earlier life, when a horse owned by his well-to-do family had reportedly kicked him in the head. All the activity suddenly going on at the Hall might have been a headache for both the Watsons, but they were always very understanding and accommodating. They loved Duncan when he finally arrived (and the other boys when they did too) and were eventually to ask us if we wanted to buy their cottage too, since they were moving back to their roots in Bath. It was an offer we couldn't refuse – even though we still didn't have any money.

We beavered away at the Hall and made it as homely as we could. There were no carpets, but at the Lodge I had met Ray Hetherington, a Geordie who worked at Fort William. I'd taught him to ski, along with his friend at the Hydro Board, and they had both heard about the Hall and its bare floors. They advised us to get hold of some of the conveyor belt used at the Wiggins Teape pulp mill near Fort William. A lot of people bought it and dyed it for flooring, since it was brilliantly hard wearing. This was arranged and I took a trailer to the Fort. I found the stuff was pretty bomb-proof and weighed half a ton, but it was very thin. Still, it was better than nothing and carpeted the bedroom and the sitting room, keeping the draughts out. But we didn't dye it - we left it in its dark white hue. Some years later the same guys, learning that we were building the Boathouse and that the electricity had to be taken from the Hall (for we had power by then) identified the weight of wire we'd need: a four-core cable, 200 yards. They had some in Newcastle and they'd get us a coil if we travelled down with our big Seafarer trailer. It was all legal and above board: a pound a yard and we bought 250 metres. That cable, until two years ago, was the sole supplier of electricity to the Boathouse and four chalets. Some might say that we were always sailing close to the wind but I would say we were simply eco-friendly; we were "recycling". From day one, everything at Loch Insh was done through a friend and in the first 20 years nothing was bought new, except Mhairi McKenzie's Wayfarer. I don't regret that – and I still find it very difficult to spend hard-earned cash without ensuring we get the best price.

Talking of which, I had made an enquiry about tarmac with one company, simply asking about prices, but awoke one morning to hear the hiss of brakes outside and a voice bellowing: "I've got twelve ton on here. Would you want it...?" I looked out of the window to see an enormous lorry – what I didn't see was a driveway ready for tarmac. There followed a frantic phone-around and we managed to track down John Clarke, who had literally just returned from Loch Morlich Youth Hostel, and between us we cleared the topsoil while the lorry driver hung around for four hours, maybe five, outside the Hall. It transpired that the driver had turned up because he and his colleagues were doing repair work along the road from us, with a small vibrator roller. When the ground was prepared, they reversed the lorry up against the embankment, put two planks of wood between the tail-gate where the big larch tree is, and brought the roller down off the back of the vehicle. How the planks held I have no idea. Then we worked all day. Even if the timing was wrong, the day was certainly right, the conditions ideal: a hot, sunny day in March, a week before our wedding day. As we were finishing, another lorry drew up: "We've got another drop in the back, would you like it?" It's had no cover for four hours so it'll be hard soon, better be quick about it...". We had finished but there were still one or two thin patches so we took this load as well, but we had to start again with fired rakes, pushing it all to get it clear so that we would not have mounds in our nice new driveway. It was an exhausting twelve hour shift.

They came back the next day to collect their roller and, again, those planks held miraculously. We were very grateful for their efforts and even more delighted when my parents decided to pay for it all as a special wedding present. Price to them: £60. To Sally and me, utterly priceless. We now had a professional drive and didn't have to go ankle-deep in mud when it rained. The day marked the civic improvements to the Hall and we never looked back – just a little black.

So, within a year of leaving the Lodge I was married and had a charming son. On one occasion when Sally was out with him in the pram, a lady leaned into it and said, not knowing who Sally was: "Oh, he does look like Clive!" Realising what she'd said, she then asked if mummy was Clive's wife. Just as well she was! Duncan had a hard time of it, growing up. As a boy he didn't have much in the way of possessions, just plenty of love and affection, although he may disagree. My favourite story of him is this one: he was five or six, in the Cairngorm Ski Club, and writing a letter to Father Christmas asking for a new pair of skis "and not one out of Daddy's hire". That touched us and he did get a new pair that year.

Top – Clive crating the canoes he built to the order of the Army

Above – loading the canoes for transport to Canada

The folk scene continued apace and during my last four years at the Lodge, in the mid-sixties, we were running a folk club somewhere for four or five nights a week. Some new faces came on the scene, such as Mugsy Morgan from Birmingham, a ukulele player in the George Formby mould and a very good guitarist. To this day he's still singing professionally in Australia. He married Jimmy Ross's barmaid and has three children. Sadly they've now separated, but he does come back to see us now and then. Oh they were hectic nights: five a week singing, two at the Lodge on the evening programme and the rest of the time was my own. Somehow, in the summer, I managed to find time for building canoes. My friends Jack Maxwell, who used to live in the School House at Insh, Iain Fraser and I managed to get our hands on a lease of the school at Insh, which was soon being put to an even better use: as a factory turning out fibreglass boats. We had one mould at first, but soon had two or three including a Canadian canoe mould, which we still have. The boats were churned out. I would work in the day and come down to Insh at seven in the evening to make half a boat, possibly a whole one if I had help, and then return later to join the parts together, creating something of a production line. The two halves were laminated together and then finished off. Once the seats were fitted they were out the door. Slow, but progress nevertheless.

We had a remarkable order once. Four Canadians were needed for shipping out to the Army in Canada. I remember the huge wooden crates which we required – they were made by a local ski instructor and joiner and cost more than the canoes. But the Army paid for them, then turned up with their four-ton truck to collect them. I'm not sure that those canoes would have stood the test in the British Army, but I heard no complaints from our Canadian cousins. We sold quite a lot of boats, all over Scotland and in the south too. On one occasion my father, who'd be in his late sixties, helped me to build five Canadians in one week. That was the fastest production rate we ever managed, selling them for £100 to £120. At the Outward Bound school in Minnesota where I worked on secondment in 1964, as previously described[6], the whole school worked on Canadian paddling. We were in the Great Lakes, to the west of Lake Superior up in Ontario. Long ten day trips covering 400 miles, big paddling, big portaging. That's why I came to have Canadian canoes at Loch Insh – we were probably the first business in this country to have a fleet of them. They weren't popular anywhere in those days, unlike now – they're now just as popular as the kayak, maybe more so.

Another great friend at the Lodge, Divison 1 slalom canoeist Ray Pettit, came to Loch Insh in those early days and with his teaching skills proved an immense help. He

[6]See Chapter 9, above   103

Clive building canoes in the early days

could hold any audience with his in-depth presentations on technique. He and I raced C2's (Canadian closed racing boats) in slalom and competed at various venues. In those days the Witter brothers were the British champions and we were the Scottish ones. It wasn't a big deal actually, as there were only about five pairs competing for the Scottish title and probably only another ten pairs in the British. Sadly Ray succumbed to cancer in 2008. The last time I saw him he gave me one of the BCU annual ranking lists, pointing out our position in the C2 rankings.

Back to the factory. The arrangement with Highland Council was that schools could use the moulds to make their own canoes. Jack Maxwell, who was the PE teacher at Kingussie school at that time, questioned whether the school got much of a return but I said there were never very many children at Loch Insh anyway. He was a tremendous help, putting in many hours at a time when there wasn't much money around. Not so long ago we discovered the returns Eleanor came up with after our first season: we'd turned over £600 in total and out of that we had to buy food and pay for any non-volunteers. They said at the time they weren't paid very much and I can understand that now, but it wasn't because the money was going anywhere else. It's still the same, with the competition, the grant aid and government bodies. We're in the sharp end of the business, we have to make everything pay and it's not easy. However, I hope those who do work here enjoy the lifestyle and appreciate the work that had to go into the place before them. I just hope they can feel some gratitude towards all those who helped so selflessly over the years. We've had so many laughs out of it, such wonderful adventures, and I think it's important that these things are said before we all pop our clogs.

One of the stalwart helpers I must mention is Walter Lester. He came on the scene some five or six years after we started and was certainly here when the original boathouse was being built. He was a wiry, wily handyman, an electrician to trade from the Perth area. He'd worked on the dams and hydro-electric schemes knocking through concrete channels with hammer and chisel, moving along the tunnels to install the cabling. Nobody could match him. Away from work he was a sailor, a kayaker and canoeist, a skier and terrific company. He'd just got married when I first met him and he and his wife had lived at the youth hostel in Glenmore, but had separated after about five years. The young lady went further north and Walter stayed in the Strath, eventually living at the Hall, up the opposite end from us. He carved some lovely furniture for himself: cupboards and grills over the radiators in the Austrian style, cut-away patterns in timber. We both spent a couple of years building the stonework at the Boathouse around the block work. We bought a

Top – Early days at the original boathouse. L to R - Iain Allen, Quentin Mitchell, unknown, Jock Lennox (in front)

Above – Friends sharing a bonfire at Insh Hall in 1971, including May Maxwell (left) and from right Maureen Hynes, John Hynes and Jack Maxwell

Top left – Clive and son Duncan at work; Top right – Walter Lester building
flood defences in the Boathouse

Above – Clive digging holes, a favourite occupation

hundred yards of dry stone dykes from the Forestry Commission for £50 (50p a yard) and it took us most of the winter. I can remember the worst part of the day was taking the trailer to the dyke, loading four huge piles of rocks, getting them down to the beach, tipping them off and scattering them around so that we could check what we had to work with, and then finally building the walls which you see today. The first one went under the ramps, so that if we bungled it we could bury it. But actually it turned out pretty well and is still standing today, unlike the old boathouse, which we pulled down in 1974, on the very day the miners pulled down Edward Heath's government once and for all.

As Harold Wilson weaved his web in Westminster, the construction of the Boathouse proceeded apace. Walter and I beavered away through the winter and into the spring, when not enjoying great skiing sessions. The stonework was finished in the first year and the concrete slab roof was put onto the middle floor. The next year I acquired about 150 used telegraph poles off the A9, at varying prices from as little as 50p to as much as £3.50. All the poles were hand-sawn with a chainsaw, drilled with an auger and wooden pegged. My father made the pegs while Walter and I matched up the logs to fit. They were a bit rough compared with the ones we were to fashion in later years, but the caulking hemp worked and it's still there today, keeping out the worst of the weather. We had copied the idea from, of all places, Grantown Sewage Works, where there was an imported building from Finlog, in Finland. I had a close look at it and noticed that chainsaws had been used to taper the logs, which had then been assembled in opposite directions. It was surprisingly effective, with the walls marrying beautifully.

Just like Sally and Clive. In April 1971 we were married in Insh Church by the Reverend Alec Hutchison, the trustee of the hall who had wanted me to spend so much more on it than I needed to, but all's fair in love and marriage. Of course, I didn't even have the £1200 that clinched the deal – I was only earning £800 a year and my parents, although hugely supportive of everything Sally and I did after we married, didn't have the money either. The school had to paddle before it could swim and we relied on the friendship and enthusiasm of others, like Jim Jardine, a Glasgow skier who happened to be an electrician with the know-how to install our initial power supply. Another valuable friend was Norman Walker, whom I met through Glenmore Lodge. I visited him in Glasgow and he offered to help. He was able to, having gone it alone himself to start Pitlochry Knitwear, which was to end up with thirty six shops up and down the country – not to mention those in Paris and London's Bond Street. It was the hey-day of Scottish woollens and I was in awe of him, starting in Pitlochry – one of the hotbeds of the industry – and beating the competition's prices by 20%. He never looked back and eventually sold out very lucratively to Edinburgh Woollen Mill, years later.

Norman lent us £500 to buy a red minibus from a school in Edinburgh, with the intention of ferrying guests from the Coylumbridge Hotel to the loch. It seemed like a good idea, but as it turned out our daily service wasn't particularly popular, with most people by then preferring to travel in their own cars; but it was a learning curve. The bus was put to better use when we started doing extensive river trips (there was more demand in those days) right down to the sea; 10-12 times a year we'd travel as far as Aberlour, Fochabers and even Spey Bay. The canoes we used were all hand-built to last: we only sold them off about fifteen years ago and they owed us nothing. They were replaced with plastic Canadian boats, but fibreglass had always proved very cost-effective material, being easier to repair than plastic. Like any new business, we had always cut every cost we could; it proved economically sensible to repair canoes which had broken in half and eventually sell them on for a small profit.

And there was so much to prove. I had been sacked by Glenmore Lodge, blown out at Loch Morlich and told that my sailing school would sink inside a year. And there were many hoping against hope that it would: no sooner had we launched our canoes in 1969 than the hills were reverberating with rumbling landowners. Even before we'd dunked our first paddle, the Scottish Council for Physical Recreation (later the Sports Council), who ran Glenmore Lodge, were looking into the question of canoeing rights on the river (and Loch Insh is of course itself a broad section of the river). Their solicitor was a bit of a stuffed shirt, or a toff you might say, as so many of them were in those days. The landed gentry, the tradition merchants, held sway it seemed with the legal profession, which seemed to have no interest in our developing sport.

A Loch Insh Water Users Association was hastily formed, led by Sir Andrew Forbes-Leith of Dunachton and incorporating Uncle Tom Cobbley and all. One of the faithful, I remember, was Faucett Farquhar of Farr – Treble F, I called him. He refused to speak to me at the Association's meeting, simply referring his questions to the chair. "Would the chairman ask Mr Freshwater if...?", "would the chairman ask Mr Freshwater why...?" I actually found it faintly amusing, in an Ealing comedy way. Their meetings may have been organised to deter me in my efforts, but the effect of them was, of course, exactly the opposite. Had I needed any galvanising, I certainly got it from the Treble F world and I was resolved to reply with a few treble effs of my own. It wasn't just for me and mine – I knew right from the start that it wouldn't just be the Cairngorm School needing access at Loch

Insh. Kingussie school and Lothian Regional Council's outdoor centre at Lagganlia were also going to be needing it. Lagganlia was just in the process of being built – I had actually applied for the job of Principal, through Edinburgh Corporation, on leaving the Lodge. I'd had an interview with six others and been asked how I saw the position of teachers in outdoor education. I'd told them that, from my experience, they were very good at getting children up in the morning and dealing with log books, but this hadn't been the answer they were looking for, and the interview had been cut very short. I had told them my eight years at Glenmore had shown me there were very few teachers with the ability to lead children on expeditions to the hill and on the river, but the leader of their outdoor education programme said there'd be no problem with teachers coming from the capital, that every one of them would be capable of doing the job. So, sadly the job had gone elsewhere. Even more sadly, the leader's assessment had been shown to be utterly wrong – there was a tragic incident involving one party of youngsters trapped in a snowstorm on the Cairngorm plateau, six of them dying in the tragedy[7]. It had not been the fault of the instructors leading the party, just a fault in the system: those people had already driven all the way up from Edinburgh having done a half day's work there, only to be criticised for being late on the hill. They'd had to cook breakfast, issue the children with their kit and get themselves to the top of Cairngorm in mid-winter. It was an appalling event, but the tragedy at least gave the outdoor education programme and its administrators the jolt they were due.

Being turned down at Lagganlia had at least left me free to mind my own business. As I have mentioned, our first set of accounts showed that we turned over £600 in the first year. The outgoings show that the instructors' wages were pretty meagre, but the incomings show why: it really was all we could afford, as we struggled to get things off the ground and into the water. The average wage may only have been between three and five pounds a week, but a week-long course only brought in 10/6d (52½p) a head. All the same, reading through those accounts again reminds me of the time and energy given to the school by all those pioneers and friends, but I'm confident that the vast majority of them got a real a buzz out of the adventure. So many have told us that while they weren't rewarded with riches, they found the whole thing richly rewarding.

---

[7]Editor's note - the Feith Buidhe disaster, November 1971

Chapter Twelve
And, Having Writ, He Moves On

When you're a serious businessman with your feet firmly on the ground it's great sticking your head in the clouds for a few days. I savoured the rarefied air of the Alps, leading a BASI course for raw instructors a million miles from the stormy waters of the Spey, with all those summer skirmishes forgotten. I was blissfully unprepared for the outcome when I finally got back to my wife and parents at the Loch. Pop was at a loss too, as he handed me the writ which had arrived in the post.

A court action had been raised against us for canoeing on the river. We had been intercepted at Knockando more than once and told in writing that we had to desist forthwith; I had written back to apologise for any upset and to assure the landowners that I would only be using the river on Thursdays. There had been no cheek intended, no impertinence, no bravado, just a willingness to pour oil on troubled – but public – waters. My own letter, though, had seemingly been written not on Basildon Bond but on blue touch-paper, since a rocket had gone up. The next week, Ray Pettit and his group, which included Sally, had been intercepted by a solicitor, a factor, a ghillie, Uncle Tom Cobbley and all.

So we had a problem. The writ was served on thin white paper and looked like an old five pound note, with the Queen's head running through it. We had to move quickly, as there was a time limit: anyone fighting the action had to reply within two to three weeks and the thing had already been sitting there a week. One of the people who used to come to the Lodge was a chap called Cromar. I'm tempted to call him Arthur, but Arthur Cromar was a warden. This one was a solicitor, who'd been involved with Jock Kerr Hunter and others, investigating the rights and wrongs of canoeing on the Spey, or any other river for that matter. He was my first port of call, but sadly he had just quit working privately and taken a job with Stirling Council, so he couldn't represent us. But he recommended the man who had succeeded him, the secretary of the Scottish Rights of Way Society, Bill Davidson. Bill, of Scott Moncrieff & Trail, a firm of lawyers in Edinburgh, turned out to be a remarkable man and to become a very good friend.

Oliver Williams, another Edinburgh solicitor, had done our conveyancing and some may wonder why we didn't turn to him for help. He was after all a keen skier and acted for the Forestry Commission. The problem was, I knew he was also a keen fisherman and, with all those angling interests weighted against us, I didn't fancy putting him in a tricky situation. Things were tricky enough. What riled me more than anything else was that in simply chucking the weight of civil law around - using the last resort first - our opponents really did think we would buckle at the start. They fully expected to win by default, as it were. They knew we had no money, so they never expected for a moment that we would defend the action. Ignorance is bliss, as they say, so I didn't make a snap decision. I decided to find out just what sort of cost would be involved before doing anything. A meeting with Bill was arranged, to seek counsel's opinion in Edinburgh, and I was gravely informed that if we defended ourselves and lost, it could all cost something in the region of £5,000. Like I said, it was tricky enough.

Many people have asked why I chose to fight and I suppose the answer lies somewhere between nature and nurture. My basic instinct always was to fight and it was nurtured by my headmaster, HJH Dyer, who refined it with his sheer, unremitting competitiveness. I want to see fair play at all times and I want to see justice done - I believe in playing by the rules, but with the sole intention of winning. Let me tell you about my car.

I bought a Morris Traveller, but was to become bitterly disappointed with it. I liked Morris travellers and I'd already enjoyed three or four, but this was my first brand new one - yet it needed three engines. The third developed a squeak in the water pump and the garage decided the easiest way to resolve it was to put a handful of liquid soap into the radiator. That certainly stopped the squeak, but by the time I had got it back from Edinburgh on its inaugural run it sounded like Jimmy Ross from the Rowanlea on his fiddle. The pump was knackered, and I cleaned that up, and so my car needed three engines and four water pumps. I wrote to Morris on Glenmore Lodge's headed notepaper, suggesting that the company who had sold me the car were an incompetent garage. This earned me the threat of a libel action from the company concerned, so I withdrew the comment, at least I refined it by saying instead that they couldn't possibly be a wholly incompetent garage, merely incompetent in dealing with the maintenance of my car. They accepted that. I on the other hand regretted it, because after I'd written the letter and collected the car, now with its new water pump, the speedometer failed even before I had got to the railway bridge at Aviemore. I went back to the garage and the man, seeing me driving in, said:

"Where have you had that?" I said I'd been taking it away and he told me: "We haven't put any water in the system yet. You should never have been allowed to take it away". Having already been threatened with a libel action over their alleged incompetence I felt very aggrieved at having to withdraw my initial statement. So there you are - when it came to the court case over the river access, I felt very aggrieved that the public were being told to withdraw from a right of way. Some said I was up a legal creek, but I had a legal paddle and I was going to use it.

I'm so glad I did. As I've said, teachers never stop learning and those four years were a complete master class. I attended every court sitting, did my homework, all that legwork – and I wouldn't have missed it for the world. Apart from anything else, if I hadn't decided to fight I would never have met Kemp Davidson, one of the most remarkable men I've known. As an introduction to Lord Davidson, as he later became, destined to be remembered as one of Scotland's most celebrated advocates and judges, let me share my introduction to him: at the end of a long day in court, mid-way through another case altogether, he found half an hour to address us on the complexities of ours. He did this lucidly, eloquently and virtually without hesitation. His clarity and mastery inspired us with immense confidence, even while he estimated our chances at no more than 50-50. Later, in 1979, he became Dean of the Faculty of Advocates and as such leader of the Scottish Bar, and he was appointed a judge in 1983.

So it was that Sally and I, with a baby and hoping for another before very long, decided to take on the establishment, go through with the court case and defend the action. I subsequently learned that when Bill Davidson went home to his wife he told her of his interesting new river rights case involving a chap called, "would you believe it, Freshwater". The irony in the name was to percolate to the highest court in the land and eventually spark the same amused incredulity in no less a figure than the Lord Chancellor, as you will discover.

Thinking of ironies in names, some might label the Spey case a battle of Wills – David Hugh Hamilton Wills - but I should point out that our pursuers were actually the Spey Fishing Trust. They simply happened to use David Wills at Knockando as their nominee, because he owned both banks of the river at that point. Two centuries ago the ownership of both banks by one owner wasn't so unusual, with so much owned by so few, but by the 1970s it certainly wasn't the norm. The Trust clearly felt that since Knockando owned both sides of the waterway the water course was demonstrably private and canoe-immune. We respectfully disagreed. Anyway, that's how David Wills became unwittingly

Top – Lord Maxwell, the judge at first instance in the Court of Session in the Spey canoeing case, whose decision in Clive's favour was confirmed on appeal in the Court of Session and confirmed and strengthened in the House of Lords

Above, left – Kemp Davidson QC, Clive's senior counsel, later appointed a judge as Lord Davidson. Right, Alastair Cameron, Clive's junior counsel, later appointed a judge as Lord Abernethy

involved in the case – and I must record here that when it was all over he was the first person to write and congratulate us. His reputation had always been that of a philanthropist and it still surprises me that he allowed the estate to become entangled in the fishermen's line.

I was also surprised that the case continued after the first court exchanges. Yes, we conceded, the pursuers had intercepted us on the river, but we had stopped canoeing on the Spey for two and a half years as a result, and they had nothing else to run with. That brings me to the subject of my leg-work: I was advised to find as many witnesses as possible by my junior counsel, Alastair Cameron, since one defence open to us involved the forty year rule (since reduced to twenty years) of prescription, i.e. if a right of way has been used by the public for that length of time without let or hindrance, then it is deemed to be lawful. The task was to establish the earliest evidence of canoe activity. Sources available to us were the old statistical accounts, Scottish historical records written by ministers in various parishes; others were the papers of established estates such as Ballindalloch and Knockando. From what I remember, none of the estates was prepared to divulge any information to us and we were left with having to find a needle in a haystack, looking for evidence of other transportations on the river. We got nowhere until Alastair discovered a case on the Ness dating back to 1774, two years after a case had been taken up on the Spey. The Ness case was identical: the people at Ness Castle owned most of the river, having crown right to fish by cruive (stone walls across the river, with holes in them to which wicker baskets were hung for catching salmon). In Norway, at the head of Sognefjord, there's a museum devoted to salmon, where samples of the half-metre square baskets can be found, complete with sharp sticks at their entrance which allow the fish to swim in but prevent them from getting back out. As recently as ten years ago my fishing return for the River Board had to include fish caught by net, by line and by cruive, although the cruive section was usually crossed out.

It turned out that the Ness case had drawn on a previous case in 1772, where Gordon Castle at the mouth of the Spey had a crown right to cruive fishing. There were various rights in Scotland: Joe Public's, the riparian right (someone owning water frontage, usually to the middle of the river) and crown right, which takes precedence over the riparian one. From 1720 to 1772 the upper Spey proprietors had been in and out of court, up to and including the House of Lords as the ultimate civil court for Scottish cases, to have these blasted cruives removed from the river since they were inhibiting the progress of fish up the river; even though history tells us that fishing on the Spey in the upper section was

Spey floaters in the 19th century. Evidence of the use of the log rafts they constructed provided crucial evidence in Clive's successful defence in the Spey canoeing case

fantastic, the estates were greedy enough to want more and more. The papers we found directed us to the fact that in 1772, during the height of Britain's naval supremacy, there had been a further case on the Spey, where the log floating out of Glenmore, which was feeding the shipbuilding industry at Kingston-on-Spey at the mouth of the river, was having difficulties navigating over the cruives. The logging interests had gone to court claiming that the cruives prohibited the navigation of the river. The end result was that they had won, and that the cruives had had to be removed to allow the floats to pass. Because there had been 60 years of arguments, it was the decision of the courts not to make the clearance of the cruives *carte blanche* but specifically for the times when the floats wanted to come down the river. The discovery of that case and its outcome was to prove crucial to the outcome of ours.

By this time some eighteen months had elapsed from the serving of the writ to the first court hearing in Edinburgh where, as I said earlier, the pursuers could offer no evidence against us. They produced witnesses to say their piece and to put on record the time they first saw canoes passing along the river; we produced witnesses to say our piece. We had found a man who had driven a horse-drawn bread wagon over the old bridge at Grantown, round about 1932, but Kemp Davidson kept sending me back to him to "beef it up", as "one or two canoes" wouldn't necessarily be seen to justify the establishment of a navigable right. We had George Cousens of the Coffee Shop in Aviemore, who had fished regularly at Knockando with his father. As I have narrated in Chapter 8, they were wealthy farmers and drove around in a Rolls Royce and George had an interesting story to tell: he had once seen a canoe capsize and later found the canoeist's wallet at Knockando.

We had Bill Lawson, a builder from Grantown, whose family built the original toilet blocks on the campsite at Glenmore in mid-winter. I knew his father and Bill was not a great deal different. They were a hard-working family with three sons. The old man came as a witness, being one of the most prestigious fishermen with records on the Spey, perhaps by dubious means, but nonetheless he holds the record for the heaviest and largest number of salmon caught. I can remember when Bill was rattling off the different names of the pools, which were impossible to spell and get your head round, the unfortunate court shorthand writer had a bad time: indeed, when any Highlander spoke too quickly he actually rose out of his chair, still writing, and then sank back down again as the conversation dropped off.   Lord Maxwell, the judge in the case, would sometimes wave his hand and ask: "Could you speak a little slower for my friend?". It lent some much-needed levity. Another moment of comic relief came for us, it can now be revealed, when the opposition produced a photograph of an anonymous canoe on the river, to show the court what the river looked like with a canoe on it – blissfully ignorant that they had snapped the evil Freshwater himself on the spot, with fellow invader Ray Pettit.

We had our exhibits too, and thirty witnesses of our own, those whose identities we were aware of. I had travelled around Speyside for the cause and met some very interesting people. While working as Captain Wells' secretary at the Aviemore Centre, Sally had found a friend in Pincher Martin, an ex-military man who'd run the fishing school in its early days. Pincher had repeatedly suggested she spoke with a Major Waddington, famed for a number of fishing flies and for two knowledgeable volumes on fishing. He lived in Blairfindie Lodge near Tomintoul and at the eleventh hour, there being a closing date for summoning witnesses, I called on him - nice place; Silver Cloud out front, wife's mini round the back. A man of medium build, in black trousers and black T-shirt, he opened the door to me and allowed me to explain myself before ushering me into the parlour, where his wife was sitting in front of a roaring fire.

"Listen to this, darling. This man is being pursued by David Wills for canoeing on the river on the pretext that it's disturbing the fishing." He turned back to me. "I can tell you that I have fished every pool of the river. I fish regularly at Knockando, where we throw stones into the pools, to stir up the fish. Or we might go for a swim, or put the dogs in – it fairly improves the fishing. And anyone who tries to tell me that canoes will do anything other than improve the fishing is off their head!" Or words to that effect. Whatever the exact words were, it was all pretty strong stuff and I loved it. It was music to my ears and I said so: "But would you be prepared to say the same in court"? "I certainly would," he nodded. Then his brows met: "When is it? When am I fishing with Charles, dear...?" I wondered if he was meeting the Prince of Wales, but in fact it was Charles Clore and they were due to fish the Wye at some time. "Yes, that's fine, as long as I'm not kept hanging about."

We have to remember that he was one of the first people to start commercial shooting and fishing; until the sixties the toffs had held sway, but they were finding it increasingly difficult to make ends meet and the old order was changing. True to his word, the Major arrived on the given day and took his oath. It was Court 13, at the back of the Court of Session, where young Andrew was being weaned in the defenders' waiting room, having been born just before the start of the case. While Sally and I had been in the witness box, we had been asked one or possibly two questions by Lord Maxwell, but when Major Waddington took the stand there were many more queries from the bench. From the outset of the case Maxwell had admitted, as all judges have to on such occasions, that he fished and had an interest in the sport. He had told us that we had the right to a new judge altogether because of that interest, but senior counsel on both sides had advised against any change: to them, Lord Maxwell was a thoroughly decent chap with a high reputation as a judge and they were happy for him to continue. I agreed with them and I am glad I did: he did indeed turn out to be a very fatherly figure and fair in all things. He certainly made no secret of his interest in fishing that day, with so learned a witness to grill (apologies for the pun). At one stage, Kemp turned to me and said, behind his hand: "Hm, I think his Lordship is perhaps thinking of writing a book himself!" Again, the judge provided us with some timely mirth as he soaked up all that free advice from our expert witness: why did salmon feed/not feed? Why did they take/not take? Which pools were popular?

The opposition, albeit unwittingly, also provided some moments of relief through the judge. During the proceedings they cited the Manchester Canoe Club continually - the club came on regular tours of the Spey, a very enthusiastic lot with a large membership, who went right down the river. The pursuers' QC, Charles Jauncey, went on about them just once too often and Lord Maxwell finally looked over his glasses and told him: "It appears to me, Mr Jauncey, that you might have the wrong people in court".

"Good on you, M'Lord!" I shouted...inwardly. Of course, all this colour doesn't appear in the law reports or in the later House of Lords papers – they're basically the opinions of judges – so I'm putting it in here since I don't want it all to be simply lost forever. It just didn't appear in depth anywhere – in fact, I heard something of a complaint about that through Alastair Cameron, or possibly Kemp Davidson, who had been at a dinner for the press at Parliament House, the court complex in Edinburgh. The press actually found reporting the case very difficult, coming and going as they did, not sitting in court for any length of time, just giving it their attention for the odd half an hour and disappearing again. Even when Lord Maxwell was to give his final decision, not many column inches were to be given over to it in the press. I gather that Lord Emslie, the Lord President and Scotland's senior judge, ultimately said to them: "Gentlemen, you miss the biggest case on water rights in Scotland for the last 250 years in not reporting the Spey case". That really was what brought home to us how important the battle was. Alastair Cameron (later himself a distinguished judge, with the judicial title of Lord Abernethy, a lover of Speyside with a home in Nethy Bridge), recently invited me down to the Judges' annual dinner, where one of his colleagues shook me firmly by the hand and averred that he had wanted to meet me for 35 years to discuss those momentous times. It's amazing how long ago it all seems now, and I know that many who were opposed to the canoeists have mellowed significantly in their antipathy, having been allowed by the courts to see Major Waddington's testimony tried, tested and proven. Even at the time, he was pretty much in line with so many of the ghillies. Some explained to the pursuers at the time that they might not make the best witnesses against the canoeing fraternity, since in truth they had no difficulty with them.

For all that, the pursuers were not giving up the chase. They found plenty of other witnesses with backgrounds in salmon fishing. They even organised an experiment at Knockando, where canoes were brought over from the RAF base at Lossiemouth and from the toffs' school, Gordonstoun. The Top People's canoeists were asked to paddle through the pool while observers noted how the salmon reacted: in those days the pools were full of fish and you could actually see them below you. They did move, usually off their lies, circling for a while and then settling down again. As I see it, one of the problems the angler has to cope with is warm weather, when the fish get dozy and sit on the bottom. They won't go near a fly or a spinner, which is precisely why Waddington would swim or send in the dogs, to stir them up and give the poor unfortunate fisherman a fighting chance. The canoeists paddled through the pool at the top of Knockando, just below Black's Boat, the first of the pools, having sent a gamekeeper across in a boat with instructions to get into a tree and watch the fish. They then brought a roe deer stool over – thirty foot pine logs lashed together into a tall platform, perhaps forty foot high, with a ladder up the side – so they could see for themselves.

"Oh, I'm looking forward to this!" exclaimed Lord Maxwell, as they prepared to give the results of the experiment.

The pursuers described how the canoes had gone through; the man had gone up the tree; the deer stool was put in the river, probably causing far more disturbance than the canoes, and when their witnesses came to be cross-examined by Kemp Davidson they proceeded to contradict each other. The disparity finally prompted our QC to tell the judge: "Well, my Lord, here we have a major, a general and a sergeant, which only goes to show that we still need a sergeant major to keep them in order".

Much laughter. Particularly when the court was informed that the fish had mostly been agitated by the *walking* canoeists, when simply dragging their craft along the shingle at the side of the river, rather than carrying them properly, the way students of the Cairngorm school were taught. It may not all have been reported in the press but it went into the transcript which, I discovered later, had had to be retyped three times, with much of the court recorder's notes misconstrued or misspelt. When the job was finally completed, Lord Maxwell's opinion ran to 58 A4 pages. Only then did the laughs evaporate. Sally and I went to the Court of Session to hear the decision. Not knowing what to expect, we sat in dead silence as Lord Maxwell read his opinion.

In the Scots Law Times' verbatim account, I think it's only when you get to page 54 that the actual decision is made. After four or five pages more of it we suspected we had won, since it certainly sounded like it, but of course we couldn't leap up and down punching the air or anything. We had to control our emotions until the proceedings had clearly been brought to an end. Only when we were outside the court did a smiling Bill Davidson offer his hand in congratulation: "Well done! You won!"

"Thanks a..."

"But it's probably not the end of it. I'm sure they will appeal."

That, of course, was for them to decide. For us, it was straight home to celebrate.

Chapter Thirteen
All It Took Was A Little Application

Whisky never tasted better. The lairds who pursued us to court in the capital were left to grouse, but Fergus and Anne Williamson came over from Alvie with forty ounces of the capitalised stuff and toasted a capital verdict. And the spirit of celebration reached Newtonmore: Mike Heywood had been among the Top People invited to finance the fight against those awful boat people, but he had sent a postcard replying, rather boldly I thought, "If I put my money anywhere, it will be with the defenders." The Spey Fishing Trust had been launched to organise "the letting of salmon fishing" (and to fight those who launched canoes) but the Trust's trust, in Mike anyway, had been misplaced, I'm delighted to say. And we had other friends in high places, such as Lord Leven up at Furness, who'd allow us to canoe on the Findhorn when the water was high. I remember arriving once with canoes for his sons just as a lady and her ghillie were settling down on the opposite bank.

"Isn't that damnable!" huffed his lordship. "There's been nobody fishing here for a fortnight and they just *have* to turn up today. Well, we'll just sit and watch her – she'll be so embarrassed she'll move off in half an hour."

She only lasted twenty minutes. Her line snagged so often that she decided to cut it, along with her losses, and leave the river to all those blasted canoeists. As if we'd had any doubts about the good lord's support, he told me one afternoon during a regular skiing session on the hill: "I've put a donation in the kitty anonymously, so that my friends don't think I'm stepping out of line". We'd put a collection box in the Bank of Scotland courtesy of a very supportive manager, something we probably wouldn't see today, more's the pity, and I think we raised £1,500 towards our costs. To the great credit of the Scottish legal system, when I asked our solicitor, Bill Davidson, when we were due to pay our costs, he said he'd have a word with counsel and get back to me. When he did it was merely to say "That's OK" and we never paid a penny in the process of the proof, other than our witnesses' travelling expenses, which certainly didn't break us.

What might have broken us, before we had even begun, was the way our planning application for the Boathouse at Loch Insh had been handled: our enemies never were confined to the water.

We were ready to knock down the original boathouse when the application was intercepted and misrepresented by the clerk to the Council. He told the councillors that his department was in receipt of a planning application "to run a canoeing and sailing school", which simply wasn't true. I phoned him up and asked if some other organisation was applying, only to be told that the application was mine. "No it isn't!" I told him. "It's not for a canoeing and sailing school - I am asking for permission to build a boathouse; that's all the application concerns and it should be considered on that basis." "Ah yes" came the reply, "but there are implications".

The only implication I saw was that the powers that be clearly had no intention of granting me permission. It was a battle from day one of the 1970s. To cut it short, the application was discussed at a big meeting in Inverness convened by the Countryside Commission where, not for the first time of course, the landowning fraternity lined up against me. I was given the chance to speak eventually, although by then I had little to say other than to make the point that I hadn't heard much evidence as to why we shouldn't be allowed to build a decent boathouse at Loch Insh. As I saw it, the local authority's notice of my application had been so worded – or perhaps I should say misworded – to enable all the local landowners to make objections, which of course they promptly did. For all that, the authorities did finally agree with me and gave me the green light, but it could all have been done so much more quickly, cleanly and cheaply if that gauntlet hadn't been thrown down.

By 1974 we were ready to do some building. Jim Scott had done some drawings and, after pulling down the old wooden shed, Walter Lester and I began digging the foundations and footings of the new one. John Clarke was a huge help too, but I shall come back to him later. As I have said, Walter was a master of all trades and specialised in electrics. I desperately wanted him to help out during the winter but he was committed to his ski instruction with the Scottish Norwegian ski school, so it was only in the spring and summer months that we could have him – and even then, after he'd run sailing schools for Moray Council on the coast. He was a brilliant teacher and even better company – I don't think there were more than two cross words between us, and then it was probably tiredness talking, over something utterly trivial. Sally and I had the occasional disagreement too, but they were never trivial. My love affair with recycling is far more important than that: I remember her disgust over the flat-bed trailer we had modified, to bring those 100 metres of drystane dyke down to the loch. In its hey-day it had been a

Top – Original boathouse, leased from the Forestry Commission in 1969

Above – Clive, with the new Boathouse under construction

caravan, gifted to us by the Williamses, and Sally insisted it had had its day and was only worth one more outing – to the dump. Two of the staff, one from Nottingham whose name escapes me and another, a tall lad called Jeremy, duly took it to the dump, kicked it to bits and then brought back the chassis as secretly instructed by me. The thing was too good to throw away, much to Sally's disappointment. They covered it in corrugated iron and for the next ten years we used it as a work-horse, carrying everything from cement to concrete blocks, oil tanks, walls, you name it.

By the time we had the foundations in, Bill Lawson had been persuaded to show us how to build with natural stone. He was a master of his craft and his sons had come over to put up the blockwork. They were quick workers and when you build for yourself one of the great benefits is that when you think you've missed out a window, or when something hasn't turned out too well, you can simply change it. Those guys were so quick that by the time I'd got back from an errand, even a short one such as the six-mile trip to Aviemore, I might discover that the place I had planned a window had already been bricked up. They would simply say "No problem" and take down a few rows of blocks. I would always be mortified about mucking them around, but on-the-hoof adjustments proved no big deal for them. The job was completed and, in three days at the most, the bottom section of the Boathouse (in 9-inch blocks) was up and level, ready for the concrete beams which would support the upper floor. These were ordered from Inverness Pre-cast and when they arrived we had a crane ready. Jeremy and I hooked them up and they were swung into position. We then had to roll several of them over to position them, since the crane couldn't reach far enough. We escaped with no trapped fingers and no injuries, in the days before statutory hard hats and gloves, when you thought twice as hard about your personal safety. Only when we had done the job did it really hit us: we were in the most stunning, breathtaking place in the world.

Standing there, seeing our awesome view for the first time, we knew it would have been a crime to obliterate that scenic vantage point: the floor had been designed as a garage for the precious red Transit, but we knew that would have been an unforgivable waste. We promptly banged in another planning application asking for change of use, to make the top floor a cafe instead. Fortunately, the authorities shared our respect for that view and without any fuss planning consent was granted and the Boathouse Restaurant began to take shape.

That first winter passed, then the spring, then the summer as Walter and I beavered away at the stonework. Bill Lawson had shown us how to make the first corner, giving us a good grounding in good groundings: "Rule one, never pick up a stone until you've identified the right one, the one that'll fit!" In other words, spread out your stones so that you can see them clearly and judge the next space you have to fill, and in time you'll get an eye for the task. The greatest exponent of the art I ever saw was drystone waller Alec Fairlie from Dundee, who built the distillery at Glen Tromie. He was wonderfully fast, producing amazing quality work in transforming an old tool shed there. Walter and I would never be as smart as Alec, but we got pretty good at it. To this day I can put my hand on the pieces that Freshwater built. The big lad, Jeremy, had a bash too and we gradually worked our way round the building. As I have said previously, the ramp was our trial run and if you took it away today you'd reveal a natural stone finish right the way down to the foundations of the building. We allowed ourselves a fourteen inch working distance, up against the nine inch concrete wall and, seeing some of the floods we get nowadays, it's probably just as well that the wall is effectively twenty three inches deep. There are no air bricks so that when it does flood no water finds its way inside – as long as everybody remembers to keep the doors closed.

It was very satisfying work and by the next winter it was time to log-on: with the straightening of the A9 in full swing those old telegraph poles were being whipped out like carrots and I remember passing Dalwhinnie one day on my way to see Jim Scott, the Glenmore Lodge architect, whom I had previously consulted with a sample joint I'd made. The area down towards Drumochter Pass was the first to be cleared and the poles had been laid alongside the road, with the lines already laid undergound. I stopped the car and found out they'd all been sold to a farm at Laggan. On my way back from Edinburgh I called in to see the farmer and bought half of them for 50p each. As I have said previously, we bought some 150 from various other parts of the A9, with a top price of £3.50 but all of them brilliant value for money since they were excellent building material. But as we started on the job we realised that, as with the natural stonework, it was going to take real skill to construct a building even remotely worth looking at. We didn't do badly, but comparing our first effort with the house we were to build up the hill some thirty years later, it seems pretty rough now. Our joints weren't as good as they might have been, but using cork and hemp hammered into any tiny gaps the place has stood the test of time and should last another thirty years, I'd say. We left some of the dates on the poles deliberately and at the far end of the building, in the last bay of the pool room, there's a pole stamped "The General Telegraph Company" which came out of a bog near Nairn, dated 1876. It's probably the oldest one we used and sits second one up above the window opening.

Considering we were total novices Walter and I became fairly skilled in scribing the poles to the joints, using the chainsaw to cut out the longitudinal groove and then recycling the cut segment for two-foot dowels, which would augur the poles. It was a very slow process, taking from October to May. The loch had frozen over and we worked through the snow. By the time spring was stretching its limbs our logs were touching the roof. We had met up with a joiner called Charlie Duncan from Glasgow, who proved something of a miracle worker. In fact, now I come to think of it I don't recall ever seeing him eat; he was as thin as a telegraph pole and just seemed to roll cigarettes somewhere inside his long hair, but what a worker, and what a craftsman. The first job he'd tackled up here was the squash court at the Aviemore Centre. I don't remember how I got to know him, but we roped him into making the tables that we still use today in the restaurant and the Hall. They were made out of larch bought from the Forestry Commission at Culloden, where I found a friend in the forester.

"Oh, could you do me a favour?" he asked. "My Aunt Jessie (Fraser) lives at Insh House and I have half a dozen chickens for her. Could you put them in the back of your van and deliver them?"

From little layers of eggs grew great big layers of timber: my favour was returned over the years in a very good working relationship with Culloden, where I could choose my timber, dress it myself on their planer and bring it home ready for installing. Meantime, Charlie would make a table a night, with no power drills in those days - just pump screwdrivers and hand planes. They were all magnificently crafted, tight as a drum and absolutely beautiful. All these years on they could do with resurfacing I grant you, but I'm very reluctant to let go of them, considering their durability and, of course, their role in our success here. Charlie's next triumph was the Boathouse roof. He and Philip McArdle, from Kingussie, who had been helping us at the time, set about building the rafters, the timber again coming down from Culloden sawmill. A mere human joiner might have had an impossible job with them, but not Charlie. The things were reasonably square in diagonals but they were a couple of inches out and, worse still, one corner was four inches higher than the other. With his skill and expertise Charlie Duncan managed to bring it all level by using a couple of wall plates and today if you look carefully you'll see how they make up the difference in height.

How we had time to do anything other than work in those days I have no idea. A short day was fifteen hours. Usually we worked nineteen and at the time I was still a trainer for BASI, although we weren't really offering any winter courses ourselves which did make life a little easier. All the same, by 1974 we were getting more people on our sailing courses than we do today, so a second stretch of water was considered a good idea and we established ourselves on Loch Laggan, with a decent year-long lease. The Laggan Inn was a useful base, since it had a dozen box-type chalets on the hillside with a restaurant and bar - I had many happy musical evenings there, with the climbing fraternity. Things seemed well set for us and the Cairngorm school prepared to branch out.

Guess what? No, not rampaging landowners this time, but a rampaging bulldozer, which came into view the day we arrived with the first of our Seafarers. These boats had been recommended to us by John Clarke, then working at the National Sailing Centre at Cowes, which was using the model for skippered coastal cruising; they were day boats, very sturdy still, and very good at sea. I drove into Laggan only to find a bulldozer driving away from one of the chalets and to hear that the handyman had persuaded the none-too-wise owners that the chalets were past their best and should be removed. He was taking them off their hands, only to replant them at Spean Bridge for his own caravan site. It was a smart move on his part, but a disaster for us as we were now based at Laggan with no accommodation, nothing to advertise and no locally-based staff. We ended up putting a caravan out there, which was promptly christened "The Outpost". Yes: if anybody behaved badly at Loch Insh they were instantly dispatched to the Siberia of Loch Laggan for a whole week. The place ticked over, more or less, but people didn't stop and it really wasn't an attraction. For a couple of years we had two Seafarers, a Wayfarer and some canoes based there but it wasn't a success and we finally closed it down.

"Come to Ullapool" suggested Tom Patey, when we bumped into each other in the Aviemore Centre. "There are plenty of people walking about the High Street with nothing to do except gawp at fishing boats. There used to be a PE teacher who had some sailing boats but he allowed them to get under the pier on a rising tide and they all broke up".

It sounded like a good alternative for us, so I took a trip up and before long I was talking with the local authority, Wester Ross Council, who were extremely helpful. I explained what I wanted to do, leaving them in no doubt that to be viable the venture would need a substantial lease. We were ultimately offered one of 50 years on the small jetty in front of the Royal Hotel. Accommodation was available for the clients, but instructor-wise we were back to a caravan and a tent, this time at the far end of Loch Broom, at the first little farm, where our friends Dougie and Mary still live. For seven or eight years we were allowed to stay on their patch with our caravan and staff. It was a very good relationship and we were grateful for their help, the four-mile trip into Ullapool not

Top – Seafarer fleet on Loch Insh

Above – Synchronised windsurfing. L to R – Andrew, Jonny, Eric Oldale

Top – The mobile office: Staffa in the background

Above – Clive on holiday in Antigua; the boat's name gave him endless amusement

an overly arduous one. The canoes were left on the trailer and the white van formed the office on the jetty, where we established probably the first skippered charter business – when I asked Doug Godlington to design our brochure he asked me what a skippered charter was and I had to explain that with a skipper on board we could put up to six beginners with him and teach them how to sail. For five or six years we were leasing three or four 30-40 foot boats. Walter was put in charge of the entire operation. He had a trailer load of canoes and the best - at least the most reliable - instructors at his disposal. We had two Seafarers and two Wayfarers as well as the four cruisers, which we leased from various people, both friends and commercial contacts. It was a very busy time and we were literally on the crest of a wave: six instructors at one time, living on their boats, including Walter who only came ashore on his turn-around day, when he enjoyed the luxury of a hotel bed. It was hard work for everyone involved, with instructors allowed no peace from the clients either day or night of course, until they came ashore on the Saturday morning. Then on the Sunday a new batch would be picked up and taken on board. Everybody wanted to go to Stornoway, despite the wonderful sailing up and down the west coast, north and south of bonnie Ullapool, but invariably on a Thursday afternoon Walter would phone to say where he was. The Seafarers were reserved for sailing out to the Summer Isles, approximately a twenty five mile run and a wonderful place to learn to sail, with no tide as such, just a rise and fall of about fourteen feet.

There were many epic journeys from Speyside up and down to Ullapool. Invariably there would be a puncture or something, either one of the trailers or the caravan getting into difficulties despite all the rigorous testing before setting off. It seemed after five years at Ullapool that we had bolt-holes all the way from Aviemore to the north-west coast, places where we knew we could get assistance in our predictable emergencies. Walter and I took a course in yacht-master/seamanship, although we didn't have to in those days and we didn't actually take the full qualification. A young man called Ian, a ticket-holder working at Abernethy outdoor centre, gave us an introduction to ship navigation. Sally, being a Morse operator, astounded us with her speed-of-light reading and transmission. We were only able to do three words a minute, while Sally was able to work at such a speed that you couldn't tell whether the light was on or off. Of course, modern day equipment renders the code obsolete. Everything's now computerised, but I'm no bright spark with the computer either.

Walter and I had many exciting and adventurous times on land and water, towing boats to Ullapool, sailing boats to and from Stornoway, across the Minch. It was generally

Top – First summer season, 1969. Left to Right -
Iain Baxter, Mike Anderson, Neil Baxter, Clive

Above – Building the new wing at Insh Hall, c. 1982. L to R
- Kelly Gillen, Gordon Graham, Clive

reckoned that even if we checked every wheel and brace, we could still guarantee to have a puncture or a bearing collapse between Loch Insh and Ullapool. There were however one or two places where we could get assistance late at night. We became great friends with Mr and Mrs Urquhart, who ran a cycle hire and bed and breakfast at Muir of Ord, on the main street opposite the primary school.

John Urquhart was known under the stage name of "The Bogan" and was one of the most entertaining and amusing comedians working in Scotland. He would do anything up to six nights a week at the Cummings Hotel in Inverness in a very professional Scottish night with dancers, singers, fiddlers and himself as the general master of ceremonies. His jokes were simple, West Coast and very humorous. He had been a railway porter at Muir of Ord. Sally always appreciated his joke about the tourist approaching a railway porter and asking "Why, my man, are the crossing gates half open and half shut?" - to which he replied (in good Highland accent) "Och, well we're half expecting a train". Just simple, clean, humorous fun. There was another, about the guard coming round at Perth at the time when the train split, part of it to go to Fort William in the middle of the night. The guard stops a gentleman to inspect his ticket. He asks if he realises he is travelling on a child's ticket. "Och well" says the Highlander, "That just shows how fast your trains are running!" One of his stories which I like to retell is of Sandy telling his friend Angus in Inverness that he is getting married and going on his honeymoon to Paris. "Well", says Angus, "You just be careful because you know they drive on the other side of the road in France". "Is that a fact?" says Sandy. On seeing Sandy some time later in Inverness Angus asks "How did you get on with your honeymoon?" "Och" said Sandy, "We didn't go". "Why not?" asks Angus. "Well", Sandy replies: "We tried driving on the right hand side to Nairn; man, it's dangerous!" I have fond memories of these friends we met over the years. John's wife Betty still visits us when in Speyside.

One bright spark who was of immense help to us was Gordon Graham. He and his wife Anne came to live in the village and took on the wardenship of the Badenoch Christian Centre when we were getting the Hall into shape. He helped us work round the Hall, taking off the tin and insulating the walls before building new blockwork. We also replaced floor joists, using some of the timber from the old Kincraig village hall, which had been pulled down to make way for the Badenoch Centre. There was a lot of good timber being taken down by an Irish chap – he had two tools, a short-handled pick and a long-handled pick, and he could rip out anything that caught his smiling Irish eyes. I remember going up to see him one hot day to ask about timber and see if he'd finished. On looking up at the gable he said: "Indeed sir, I am. But I'm leaving this gable until the boss comes next week, since it's full of wasps and bees and I shall drop it just as he arrives and watch the fun!" Sure enough, the following week the gable was down and the fire was on, burning the remains of the old place where earlier I had helped the minister's youth club to fire the enthusiasm of the lads who grew into the men who are still living in Kincraig.

So Gordon worked at the Badenoch Centre for a couple of years and then decided he was going to work with us for a further two. He was a self-employed electrician, so we had the ability to keep most of our electrical work in-house. He and I were both prepared to have a go at the plumbing as well, and Gordon was a very capable builder – he bought a piece of ground in the village and made a beautiful house for his family. He was a skier too, and had worked for the Christian Centre in Glenshee. Moreover, he possessed sharp business acumen as well - and what pulled him back from the brink of perfection, thank heaven, was the fact that he wasn't much of a sailor and I don't recall him doing much in the way of canoeing except on the loch. But the landlubber and I remained very good friends for all that. He was to sell the house he built and create an even finer one towards Insh after moving into the insurance assessment business, which (as he puts it) beats crawling around in people's rat-infested lofts doing re-wiring jobs.

One young man who came looking for work was Billy Burnham, a fibre-glasser who had built aeroplane wings for the Fokker Friendship. What better qualifications could anyone have? We put him to work building canoes at Kingussie. They were the heaviest we ever produced and each time I picked up a Canadian canoe at the beach I'd say: "Billy Burnham!" My staff would ask: "Pardon?" "It's all right" I'd reply, "I'm just swearing..." Billy was the nearest we came to an accident. You may find that an unusual thing to say, but when you consider the activities which have gone on at Loch Insh in forty years, with not one injury worth a visit to the doctor, you'll maybe understand. At the time Billy was with us, Maggie Thatcher launched her *Protect and Survive* campaign – there was a cold war on and we were being told that when the four minute warning went up we were to take the doors of our houses, prop them against the wall with some sandbags and get behind them. There were BOOKLETS of this nonsense produced, at the taxpayer's expense.

With no thaw in sight for the cold war, we felt we should have more than a few soppy sandbags. After the untimely passing of Jim Scott, Kincraig's Jock Lamb became our architect, even though he was trying to retire - some hope, with us around. Jock's son-in-law lived in good old neutral Switzerland, so neutral in the cold war that they needed a

Cantons Manager for fallout shelters. From him we acquired a very extensive tome on how to build a *real* shelter. Since we were about to start the bedroom wing at the back of the Hall, Gordon and I decided it would be a timely idea to have a go at building one of these nuclear shelters and we got hold of some easy-to-follow drawings, along with the hardware for the gas extraction, blast-proofing etc. We were deadly serious and Sally and I went so far as Preston to acquire massive, concrete-packed safe doors, and not just for ourselves – a young chap, Leo Vielhaber, who'd started a ski factory in Aviemore also took the idea seriously enough to ask us to bring back two sets for him as well. Our little transit only just made it back to Aviemore, but at least we were going to be safe and sound, snug and warm behind our cold war doors.

First, though, we had to dig this enormous hole at the back of the Hall – and second, Billy Burnham had to fall down it.

Chapter Fourteen
Lots To Do

There were already lots of little holes in the Hall. Jokingly, I admitted to Frances Adam, a teacher friend who'd returned to college as a lecturer in dance and gymnastics, that we were going to need a cat to keep the culprits down. On her next weekend visit she produced a beautiful ginger tom and I christened him Rastus, after the mouser they'd had at the fish shop back in Mablethorpe. Intelligent, friendly and very, very effective, he was to be a member of our family for 17 years. Our last cat, Hobbs, was not dissimilar but didn't have the track record of Rastus – I remember one morning, we were woken by the sound of fierce scratching under the bed and found Rastus with a young but well grown pheasant which was getting nowhere in its efforts to escape. Both were quickly dispatched through our bedroom window.

There were a lot of other holes in the Hall, not least the huge gaps in its fittings and furnishings. I'm not sure who introduced us to the auction rooms in Elgin, Nairn and Forres but we've lots to thank them for. Ten railway waiting room benches – cast iron frames, single plank backs and seats – and half a dozen gymnastic benches were just about the only things we inherited with our very vacant possession, and most of those we gave away to the local sheepdog trial club since we couldn't see any use for them. Only two of them remain with us, in the laundry room entrance. The side flat wasn't any better furnished, so we had to start from scratch. There would be regular trips in the Morris Traveller and the red minibus and they were great fun, meeting all the local worthies – especially at the Elgin saleroom, in the area where the cattle would be brought in and bid for. We became quite well known at the sales and acquired a great deal of interesting stuff at very reasonable prices – the £9 sideboard for Legerwood was a snip and will be worth a lot more than that today. I'd been eyeing it throughout the auction and when it finally came up I was told that it had already been sold three times but that the various buyers had never actually been able to get it into their houses. At last, we had a reason to celebrate the size and emptiness of our place.

At first Sally would only go if I accompanied her to do the bidding but eventually she found the nerve to do it herself – which was when my nerve went. I came to dread what she'd return with, since she never wanted to come home empty-handed. There were some good surprises though: once at Forres we went after two three-piece suites which we needed for the Hall after we'd started our residential courses; I remember collecting the second one, a dark brown leather thing which we snapped up for £3; as I lifted the sofa, 60p fell out from the cushions, which we took as a very good omen. Sally had some pick-ups of her own: I remember one night she was on her way home with a vanload of chairs and attracted the attention of the constabulary. In those days the RAF disowned their chairs after just five years, so we had a steady flow of top quality – Parker Knoll, even – with bedroom and dining chairs to match; they'd fetch anything between £2 and £7. On this particular occasion she'd gone for some vanity chairs and had 40 of them jammed into the back of the Transit. They were quite visible through the windows and at one in the morning she was pulled over in her dubious old banger by the "polis", one officer speaking with her while the other walked round the vehicle checking the tyres and so on. She was asked where she'd been and where she was going and when she replied in her lovely crisp hockey-sticks accent she astonished her interrogator, who until then had been convinced he'd got some local criminal.

"Well, er...it looks like you've had a very successful day, madam" he saluted. "We'd best let you get on your way."

Sally duly returned home a free woman, and some of those well-gotten gains were to serve us for thirty years. We retain a few of them to this day, along with various carpets we picked up at incredibly cheap prices. Not that we were free from court proceedings, of course – with the Spey canoeing appeal pending that summer in the Court of Session, there were to be plenty in Edinburgh. The Langmuirs kindly let us pitch our caravan beside their home there for a few days. When we returned to Edinburgh for the appeal we stayed with Mrs Ord, mother of our one-time cook Liz, whose brother Peter latterly served the Royal Family as the factor at Balmoral. Liz and her pal Izzie Johnson had been little gems, the first cooks persuaded to come and work for us in our first ever catered accommodation. We managed to hire the 16-bed ski lodge at Lagganlia as the owners, Edinburgh Corporation, never used it in July and August. We had no problem filling it for four to six weeks for two summers running but in the third year the owners had decided it wasn't good for us to be running commercial courses from it. Izzie had been known to me as one of the senior exploration girls at Glenmore Lodge. I'm not sure how we'd kept in touch, but she recalled a three-day expedition over Cairngorm and down to the Shelter Stone, up the other side and on to a night at the Etchachan bothy. We'd carried tents and food for three days. It was a long haul. And the following day we'd have walked down to Derry Lodge and round to Corrour bothy in the Lairig Ghru – the very bothy I'd passed through with the boys from Leeds on that epic expedition before starting at Glenmore Lodge. Talking with Izzie again, I remembered that long, gloomy pass, and 35 miles of nervous nostalgia. I suppose that early criss-crossing of the Cairngorms is the main reason I don't particularly yearn to get back into the hills and wander along the same tracks, much to Sally's disappointment.

Anyway, back to Liz's mum in Edinburgh: she was very kind to us all, and we were happy to leave the two children with her while we went off to court. As I started to write these reminiscences she was moving gracefully through her 90s and was still visiting us but sadly she has since died.

Sally didn't come to court with me every day during the appeal, but I found every session unmissable and hugely instructive. The appeal was heard in the Court of Session before three judges: Lord Emslie (the Lord President), Lord Johnston and Lord Cameron, in his eighties then and sharp as a tack. Senior counsel on both sides selected parts of the evidence from the proof (the first hearing) and presented their arguments again, thirty witnesses' evidence being consolidated. Over those two weeks many pointed questions were raised about Lord Maxwell's decision and how he had arrived at it, but much more interest was shown in the public's right to navigate, which by then was seen as absolutely paramount: the right was vested in the Crown for its subjects and could not be taken away by anyone except through statute, no trace of which had been found to the court's knowledge. In statute law, the Crown right to cruive fishing was held to be subservient to the public's right to navigate the waters, so we were quietly confident.

If you've ever been in the Court of Session you'll know there is a magnificent hall, the old Parliament Hall of Scotland which went out of use for its original purpose at the Union of the Crowns in 1707. There counsel parade up and down for exercise and discussing cases in private, out of range of prying ears and microphones. I found it rather unusual to be invited to join them occasionally, so that we could discuss various points. I was intrigued by the way it all panned out, counsel often disagreeing vehemently with what this judge or that judge had been opining about, and all of us with absolutely no idea which way the decision would go.

We were eventually summoned to Edinburgh for the outcome and when the decision was finally announced I again had to wait for clarification in my own, ground-level version of the English language - and even then it was not a time for leaping around punching the air. But we had won again and we held a celebratory dinner at the capital's George Hotel the following night, spending a very pleasant evening with Kemp Davidson and Alastair Cameron and their wives - the first time, so they said, that they had been treated to dinner in such circumstances - where I was equally relieved to hear that we were still not being asked to pay a penny towards our legal costs. But I was left in no doubt that it probably wasn't the end of the case by a long chalk, and I wondered just how things might still pan out.

"Well, Clive" said Alastair's wife, Elspeth, "I don't know what you plan to do of course, but I do know that if the opposition lodge a further appeal and take it all the way to the House of Lords, Alastair and Kemp are going on with it".

In other words, the decision whether or not to continue the fight was no longer in my hands. Which was perhaps just as well, since Elspeth's suspicions were duly borne out: the opposition did appeal, and there was no end yet in sight for the Spey canoeing case.

I should mention Mr Smith. At the time of the court hearing the old wooden boathouse at the loch had a telephone in it and one auspicious day a "Mr Smith" interrupted our work by ringing to ask who our legal advisors were. I was slightly suspicious and asked why he wanted to know. He explained that he was the manager at the Macallan distillery at Aberlour and they were having problems obtaining permission to drain effluent into the Spey. The company needed a good QC to fight their corner, so I gave him the name of one. They eventually won their case and the little "Swiss chalet" which stands on the left bank of the river by Aberlour, below the distillery, is in fact the result of that call to the Boathouse, which is probably why we received that cheque for £50 towards the fighting fund from the distillery. What I particularly liked was the compliment slip which accompanied it, requesting a receipt - nice touch.

We had made good friends with a farmer, Bob Maconie at Ballindalloch. He used to allow us to camp in his fields by the railway station during the river trips. After the court case was concluded he received a directive from his landowner, Sir Ewan Macpherson-Grant, that if he allowed those boat people to camp on the bank again he would lose the tenancy of his farm. That gave me cause to phone Mr Smith at the distillery and explain the situation. He invited us down to see him, since they had three miles of the river above Craigellachie Bridge, and suggested we might camp there, once we'd made an arrangement with their farm tenant.

Top and above – Canoeing through rapids on the Spey

Around that time we also had a chance meeting with a great chap, the clattery-teethed Mr Watson, at one of our barbecues. His two sons were fine accordionists and they played beautifully on the beach at Loch Insh. Anyway, their dad turned out to be the land agent for British Rail and told us that his assistant, Andrew Gilchrist, was a canoeist: if we could travel down to Glasgow he would make arrangements for us to have the lease of the disused railway station at Ballindalloch. We did have it – for some 30 years. What's more, Mr Watson continued to furnish us with details of all British Rail properties in the area as soon as they came on the market, including some shops which David Cameron, the Aviemore property tycoon, ended up buying for a million pounds. Sally drew the line at my getting involved with that kind of money, but Davie had a much freer hand.

I have very fond memories of those early Ballindalloch days, in particular the folk singing sessions in the bar with my students. There was one little old lady who used to collect the glasses. She was five feet nothing with a lovely cheeky smile. I used to sing her a song:

> A secretary in the office had a watch that didn't go.
> I asked her if the watch was broken?
> She looked at me and said 'Oh no,
> My boyfriend gave it me last Wednesday,
> It's just a strap and case - but it's all right
> Because, you see, my boyfriend promised
> He'd give me the works tomorrow night!'

I had sung this a few times to the amusement of the guests and a few in the pub, the Delnashaugh Inn. On one particular occasion Liam Carver and Graham Tiso had accompanied me on the river trip. We got to the pub and, realising it was going to be a heavy night, I had just half a pint of lager. I was standing at the bar and the afore-mentioned little lady came and tugged my arm. I looked down at her and she asked: "Did she ever get the works to her watch?" I never did tell her.

I also remember an incident when meeting the singer and broadcaster Jimmy McGregor in the process of his Speyside Way walk. On seeing me he began to talk about what the old Ballindalloch station was used for and he decided he would like to add part of it to his programme. I asked what he was finishing with and he agreed to have a little ceilidh sing-song in the nearby Delnashaugh Inn the following evening. Before that he encouraged me to take the canoes down to Knockando so that he could have shots for his film and a bit of background for the canoeing case. So M.A. Harper, myself and the three boys went to run the rapids at the railway station at Knockando. He only had one camera and after three walks up the bank, with canoe on shoulder, Andrew rather dejectedly said "And how many times have we got to do this?" Each time the cameraman had to move position to get a good shot and Andrew was not terribly patient about that sort of thing. We had the ceilidh, which wasn't as good as the locals were expecting because of the way the filming worked out. Jimmy asked me what we were singing and I said *Bonnie Lass o' Fyvie*. This was agreed and we played it through. The director asked for it to be played again so they could take different shots of people in the bar. I think we sang it about six times, which of course was not very entertaining for those who had come to the ceilidh. It went out on BBC 1 some weeks later.

Just recently, I caught Jimmy McGregor's story on the radio, comprising six episodes, about the West Highland Way, which he had walked and when he had talked about many people along the way. I was complaining to myself as unfortunately the BBC World Service, which I often listen in to late at night, were running all the episodes back to back, so the programme lasted something like two hours. Once into the theme of it, it was difficult to turn off. Next time I see Jimmy I will tell him I lost two hours' sleep over listening to that programme.

In those days Ballindalloch was a hotbed of entertainment, particularly after the hotel had thrown us out at midnight. We were invited back to various places; the station master's house, the ghillie's house etc, and it would go on until two and three in the morning. The rule of the game was that you would all be on parade at 8.30 the next morning to get the students ready for the river trip. I noticed just recently that the station master from Ballindalloch had died. Since I knew him he had moved further south and finished up being the station master at Euston, which must have been quite a prestigious promotion for him.

Coming back from the bar one night one of the locals had offered us a lift to the camp. As we climbed in to his A45 van he said "Well, who's driving then?" He had obviously realised he was not fit to drive, so one of the girls in our party drove us back to camp. This was long before we had as much traffic on the roads as now and at a time when there were certainly no problems with drink/driving laws.

On another occasion whilst canoeing down river with Dave Pirnie, a climbing friend from Glenmore Lodge, and one of the rare occasions when Sally was with us, sharing the tent, Dave became very ill. We were camped by the river and rail-bridge at Ballindalloch; Sally woke me and said we must get him to hospital, so at 3 am we summoned an ambulance, which whisked him off to Raigmore, but not before we had an epic struggle to get him up the very steep railway embankment on a stretcher. The ambulance men couldn't cope so it was just as well that I was fitter and stronger then, to be able to push the stretcher up the slippery bank. I am pleased to say that Dave made a full recovery. He had a great ability to draw caricatures, not always flattering, of staff and members of the public and some years later he joined us on a helicopter trip from Insh Hall under the local authority's auspices, to survey potential new skiing areas for development.

One of my final memories of camping at Ballindalloch, before we obtained the lease of the station building as a hostel, was the sound of an engine with bogies literally lifting the line as it moved south towards Advie. This was courtesy of our friend Dr Beeching. I believe the rails went to South Africa.

Ballindalloch provided many happy memories, and we hoped that Ullapool would too. For starters, we moved into Ullapool around the same time as the major-league gold-diggers. The "Klondykers", as we called them, were coming into Loch Broom for the fishing. Bulgarian and Russian factory ships caused all sorts of mayhem around the jetty and the beach in the early '70s, disgorging huge amounts of fish offal, as much as a foot high and covering the water surface. It affected everything we touched and ruined the place for a couple of seasons. Ironically, we had just got planning permission to build a boathouse at the jetty and one of our assistants, Henry Gibson, was a trainee architect. He had designed a beautiful building, but it didn't take into account one Alec Ross. "The Giant" - he was only about five-foot tall - had children working for us and owned a place which overlooked the jetty. He had given the Council the land on the grounds that it would not be used commercially. The Council understood that meant simply "no fishing" and duly gave us permission to go ahead with the boathouse - much to the chagrin of Mr Ross, who took us all to a tribunal, claiming that his conditions had been breached.

Another court case, another learning curve.

As I've said, teaching is all about learning and that one-day tribunal was certainly a big eye-opener for me. Until then I had been under the impression that we had actually been a big help to Ullapool. Walter, especially, had given his time and talents to the local sailors: on his arrival he'd found a number of large boats whose handlers were afraid to go beyond the Summer Isles as they simply didn't have the skills or the experience; Walter had educated them well, both he and I having completed the yacht-master syllabus. So it was quite a surprise to see just how many of our erstwhile students turned up at the hearing to speak against us. That's how life is so often, with those who succeed through hard work ultimately being put down by those who don't really make it. This has also been my experience at Loch Insh – and I hope my boys are ready for the harsh reality of life, that there are envious eyes waiting all around them.

But for all that, it's through the tough times you find out who your friends are and we found a real goodie in Robert Urquhart, our local hero. Born in Ullapool's renowned Ceilidh Place, he had been at school with The Giant but had grown into a hugely talented actor in the big world, where he had become a sizeable film star. His love of Ullapool had kept his feet very much on the ground, though, and with a genuine architectural talent too he had dreams of building his own theatre by the clubhouse. Robert topped the bill as our tribunal witness and, defying all those detractors, played the scene to perfection for us. When asked by the recorder if it really was the community's hope to have a marina he stole the show with his measured, marvellous , masterful response, delivered with all the precision of a big-screen maestro: "My Lord, I think it is more than a hope. It is a devout wish."

Our matinee idol would visit us as Loch Insh to see how we were doing, checking out Lagganlia as well, gathering ideas for his own bunkhouse at Ullapool, where so many of our students would be welcomed and treated to his wonderful stories. This one I loved: to escape when necessary, he owned a small motor boat even though he was pretty useless with motors and boats. He'd take it out to the Summer Isles and relax with a good book. His handyman used to bring the boat to the jetty and check the engine for oil and petrol and so on, since Robert couldn't be trusted to do it properly: all of which bears testament to the man's thespian prowess. See for yourself in the stirring 1958 movie "Dunkirk" where, in that little stricken boat, *whose* magical mechanical skill should save the skin of leading man John Mills but leading seaman Urqhuart, no less? German bullets fly around his oily ears, but only greasy-overalled Urqhuhart can save the day by working his magic on that crippled engine in the nick of time. Only those of us who knew him were aware how little the man understood engines, but again, only we can ever know just how good an actor, architect, businessman and wonderful friend he was. Sadly he's gone, but he's left me with the best of memories and, again ironically, the best readings I have of the Para Handy tales.

Because of Robert we nearly did commit ourselves big-time to Ullapool. We won at the hearing; the Giant left with a monster legal bill of £5,000 on hearing the Council were doing nothing illegal and that he had no axe to grind. And with at least one friend there, we seriously considered buying the old village hall when it came on the market. There was a couple living in it, who wanted to move back to Dumbarton, but as we started negotiating we got news from home that another couple were preparing to return to their roots: the Watsons, at Legerwood, the bungalow right next to Insh Hall, were heading for Bath and wondered if we wanted to buy their home to add to that strip of land we'd acquired from them when starting work on our "first" village hall. We had to admit that we simply didn't have the money to buy both properties, but when I talked to Bill Davidson, our solicitor, he told us we couldn't afford *not* to buy Legerwood – especially when the Watsons agreed to sell at the valuation price, a rare situation in those days. Bill, ever generous - he'd fought long and hard for us on the Spey canoeing case for no remuneration for the duration of the case - lent us the £4,000 deposit and we duly arranged a £16,000 mortgage. Overnight, we were the owners of both the old Insh Hall and its neighbouring cottage.

The amazing thing was that some time later we discovered we'd acquired much more land than we'd thought: the title deeds were to reveal that the grounds extended much further towards the loch than we'd realised. After the Watsons moved south we visited them a couple of times. She died quite soon after they moved, but he survived a while longer. For me, the best part of the deal was not so much the house, nor even the land, but the Nissen hut which went with it – for many years it was to serve us well as a workshop and premises for ski and cycle hire. We had had no room for those facilities at the beach and the hut was a huge help. It also had a spectacular view from the workshop end and early on I identified that corner as a perfect site for a chalet. Eventually it gave way to a double one – housing the Macallan chalet and the office which we're still using today.

By this time we had also moved into Kingussie. We had the coachworks (latterly McCormack's garage) which had served as the paint body shop for BP in the Strath. I paid a decent price on a seven year lease from the local landowner, Lord Burton, and it proved a good move: we repaired our vehicles there and churned out canoes with the help of Jim Hamilton, the best laminator we ever had (until after three years he met a Swiss girl at Loch Insh and emigrated). After ten years I had to admit the place was becoming just another glory-hole for me. They say I can never let anything go, but I did let this one go.

We were everywhere in those days. A letter came from the Royal Dutch Automobile Association, the ANWB, asking if we could arrange adventure holidays. I told them we could arrange some canoeing and wild camping across Scotland from Fort

Top Left - Clive at the helm, Staffa astern

Top Right - Clive Sally and Jonny at Laggan Dam before the start of the first
Great Glen tour for the Royal Dutch Automobile Club

Above – Inverness pick up at the end of the first tour

William to Inverness in double kayaks. Loch Ness on a bad day is no place for a Canadian canoe - although we were the forerunners of the model, our European explorers would be carrying all their equipment with them. In those days Loch Ness was no easy place to camp, let alone canoe, although the canal-side was OK. Our suggested itinerary then brought them to Loch Insh for a day's rest and an expedition on the Spey to Aberlour, taking in a distillery visit. They came back to us saying they were very interested, planning a four-week trip for up to thirty at a time on two separate courses. I have to say I was pretty pessimistic about it, as we'd heard it all before from others. Nevertheless we set about making our commitments, including the purchase of Vango Force Ten tents - we could afford to buy equipment by that stage - and built sixteen double kayaks, which we still have today.

The Dutch did come and the tours were a great success, the Great Glen expeditions advertised to the general public too. Jim Hamilton, Izzy Inglis and Quintin Mitchell were very skilled instructors who made a great job of it, running perhaps five major trips a year, which required a lot of food preparation as I recall: we weren't just supplying the four boats in Ullapool, we were feeding thirty Dutch on the canal and more members of the public on the extra tours. Muesli was brought in by the half-crate and we had a full-time girl, Lynne Williamson, splitting all the food into individual plastic bags. The Dutch came for about five years from 1977 and eventually expanded to six weeks: we had three groups and they increased their numbers. Not only did they want to do the Great Glen and the Spey: they wanted to go to Ullapool for two weeks as well. So we had fifty, and the ANWB decided they'd bring the first group in by sea to Newcastle and the last group would go home by sea, while the middle group would fly from The Hague to Inverness; they were chartering a Fokker Friendship which seated fifty two. We'd then take twenty on to Ullapool, who would spend a week at Robert Urquhart's bunkhouse, learning to sail (and living it up in the town) before moving on to the big boats for a week's cruising up and down the coast. They were extremely popular courses with the students who were, according to Walter, good hard-living types in their 20s and mid-30s who knew how to enjoy themselves. It was all good experience for us too, having to diversify in so many directions at once, doing the Great Glen and the river, schooling at Ullapool and the north-west coast, leading public river courses at Loch Insh and dinghy sailing on the Loch.

Windsurfing had just started at this time and among the Dutch group was a sixteen year old lad, Peter Bosch. We had boards at the loch, the first of the Novas (quite unstable bits of gear) and Peter asked if he could take one out. I told him it was very windy but he said he would "manage" – and promptly managed to show all of us just how it was done. He stepped nonchalantly onto the board in his wellingtons, without a life-jacket or wet suit, and roared up to the far end of the Loch and back, nae bother at all. He was the first natural windsurfer I ever saw and I hired him on the spot, along with his sister Katinka. He was with us for three years until moving on to the Mistral demonstration team and finishing up in the Navy. His folks had a caravan site and a watersports centre back in Holland, so the interest and the ability simply ran in the family.

The Dutch ran their courses very successfully through us until Irish eyes smiled at them: the tourist board on the Emerald Isle threw so much money at the recreation industry that the courses worked out significantly cheaper over there. We lost the business on price because of all those subsidies and it was the worst thing that could have happened - to the Dutch. Shortly after that the ANWB stopped providing for their members. They had over a million of them but got into financial difficulties and stopped running and promoting those courses. I haven't heard much about them ever since. For us, however, those five years were highly beneficial: we learned a lot and earned a lot, particularly with the Dutch never needing to take up any beds, at Loch Insh anyway.

We kept the Great Glen trips going for a few years until they dwindled. We had some healthy competition and maybe we didn't advertise as much as we might have done, but I'm convinced that the spirit of adventure wasn't there any more in Joe Public. Joe got lazy. By then there simply weren't the numbers of people prepared to face the thrilling challenges posed by the great outdoors. Character forming was now the job of television directors; the only lines being cast were those for actors as Joe preferred the challenge of seeing if he could stay awake until the end of the film. Of course some of the trips we did in the old days at Glenmore Lodge are still being undertaken but with nothing like the numbers experienced in the 1970s. Our grand expeditions, I remember, would come off Loch Ness, over the weir, down the River Ness – where we'd encounter fishermen even more hostile than those on the Spey – then through the middle of Inverness to the swimming pool down by the black bridge for the perfect finish: the city's beautiful setting and a magnificent hot bath. In those days we had a great relationship with the pool staff but now, of course, they've all gone the same way as the pool, into history.

I remember the day the city nearly went there with it. We had one horrendous trip down the canal with Ray, Caroline and a group of students from the Lodge. After battling with unrelenting, torrential rain, we pulled in for lunch at one of those boathouses which were about three-feet deep, where you could stand up with a roof over you to cook

Top – The site at Loch Insh in 1974. Insh Hall, with pitched roof, foreground, left of centre;
Legerwood, the bungalow in the centre, which was Clive and Sally's home until they built
Bluff House. The Boathouse is in the trees back centre

Above - the Centre as it is today

Early Scottish tourist board poster featuring Clive and son Duncan, displayed
without Clive's prior knowledge on the London Underground

lunch, have a cup of tea and dry out a little before clambering back into the canoes. We camped on a jetty half way down going east, and it was still raining as we put up our tents. A little old man came out of his cottage full of sympathy, carrying bundles of dry sticks and newspapers so we could at least light a fire. In the night we sat in our tents feeling very sorry for ourselves, only to discover in the morning that we had had the best of it: Inverness had been flooded to a depth of two feet and seemingly half the city had been evacuated to the Town Hall and a lot of other places where everybody had had to muck in – and what muck it had been.

It was all about mucking in and making do. That was the ethic at the time, especially at our own Boathouse. So many people came to help, and from all over the world at times: I remember Eric, from New Zealand, a very energetic mountaineer, skier and cross-country athlete. When he walked in one day he admitted that he'd been briefed to enquire if there was any work going for a joiner. I shook him by the hand and pointed to a window which I was in the middle of changing and he said he could help. He and the girl he was with fell about laughing, because they'd been well warned that they'd never get away from Loch Insh without doing some work. Many Kiwis came and they all left their mark. Eric made a lot of the built-in wardrobes in the Hall which are still there today. Another couple came after we'd had an incident with some army guys on rest and recuperation from Northern Ireland.

We were sitting having breakfast one morning when Duncan rushed in yelling: "Daddy, somebody's just jumped through the caravan window!" Moments later an officer knocked at the door to tell us of an "incident" and that they thought they could smell gas coming from the van. "We checked", he told us, "but couldn't smell anything and when we checked the rings on the cooker they wouldn't light. Foolishly, we inspected the oven with the match still alight, and the whole thing exploded". The caravan ended up a foot wider with no windows to speak of. Nothing fitted. None of the doors closed. Then, when he'd got his breath back the soldier asked if he could phone his HQ as one of his men had to get to a hospital for some stitches in his backside – he'd cut it on some broken glass while escaping through the window. I heard him accurately and honestly reassuring his boss on the phone that everything was going like a bomb. The caravan was written off after we towed what was left of it to the coachworks in Kingussie. Another young couple from New Zealand came, looking for work and a place to stay. I told them the only thing we had was an old caravan needing a certain amount of renovation. But they were Kiwis, to whom things were never All Black: within a fortnight they had actually managed to close the thing up and replaced the windows. They lived in it for half a year and more.

That's another interesting thing. They had arrived in a camper van, which most Kiwis did since there was a place in London where they picked them up for a friendly price. I noticed, while they were fixing up the caravan, that they were using a bag of tools which belonged to one of our Ullapool Seafarers. I asked where they'd got the bag and he said it had come with the van, in London. So I had to tell him the tools actually belonged to us and, sure enough, he confirmed that the van had been owned by the couple who'd been here before. Small world. Kelly and his girlfriend have kept in touch with us ever since. He was with us when we built the extension at the front of the Hall, which is now the Penthouse Apartment.

Which brings me back to the army and its rest and recreation trips: the sergeant often said that we could always ask him for three or four labourers and, you've guessed it, that's precisely what we did. We made an arrangement with the Forestry Commission that the army driver could go and collect the telegraph poles we were using to build the Boathouse. Some of them were monstrous 35-footers off the A9 at Dunachton, far bigger than anything Kelly and I could handle, so the Army was a huge help. The logs went up one a day, effectively three joins, and the job was finished in a single winter. It was Kingussie joiner Donnie MacDonald who fitted the roof for us. Fittingly: he had been the first friend I'd made on that inaugural visit to Scotland with the boys from Pudsey, when the victorious shinty team had raised the town's roof.

Chapter Fifteen
And I Will Duel In The House Of The Lords

"You know Clive, if we could get this thing rolled up and out of here it would pay for the whole court case."

My solicitor was giving me the red carpet treatment in the corridors of power and, as usual, he was spot-on. With that welcome to Westminster's wall-to-wall wealth, Bill Davidson got us straight down to brass tacks - or bronze ones even, in that valley of the shadow of death. The Spey canoeing case might have cost that roof we'd just put up - that and the red transit, half a dozen canoes and a trailer, since that's all our very limited company owned by then. On Bill's advice, the village hall had already been transferred into Sally's ownership. Although we had been successful in our adversaries' appeal to the Inner House of the Court of Session, they had appealed further, to the House of Lords, which at that time was the ultimate court of appeal in civil cases in Scotland.

As for costs, I had decided it was time we contributed something and Bill had suggested we might pay for the printing of the 15 copies of evidence needed for the final appeal. I'd taken a copy of the papers – an inch-and-a-half thick – up to the Rank Xerox printing service in Inverness, which did the job for £1,500. It was to be our only contribution. Our good fortune in finding a true champion would in 33 years' time be celebrated by The Daily Telegraph, in its obituary of Lord Davidson:

> In 1969 Davidson took silk, and in the ensuing years he would appear in
> many notable cases. Two of the highlights were *Wills' Trustees v Cairngorm
> Canoeing and Sailing School* in the 1970s, and what became known as 'the
> Glasgow rape case' (*X v Sweeney*) in 1982. The result in each had a lasting effect
> beyond the boundaries of the case itself. Two more different cases could hardly be
> imagined, and it was typical of Kemp Davidson that he agreed to act in them
> without any certainty of a fee.
>
> In the first, the riparian proprietors of a stretch of the river Spey and its
> valuable salmon fishing rights brought an action in which they sought to have it
> declared that they had exclusive right of navigation. They accordingly sought an

interdict to prevent the defenders, who had started up business only a few months earlier and were in no position to finance a protracted litigation, from canoeing through that stretch of the river. Davidson agreed to take the case on a speculative basis; in other words, no win no fee. The case turned on what had been decided in a very old case, *Grant v Duke of Gordon,* in 1782.

The trouble was that it was difficult to determine what had been decided: the contemporaneous law report was far from clear. The canoeists won by a narrow margin at the first stage, but the decision was appealed. By this time Davidson had been elected Keeper of the Advocates' Library, and his research among the voluminous private sets of papers in the Library's collection revealed a large amount of contemporary material which in the end proved decisive in securing success in the appeal court and in the House of Lords. It was a remarkable result, and one which might have eluded someone with lesser knowledge of the law and skill as an advocate. It was also one which he treasured for the rest of his days, not least because David had well and truly defeated Goliath...

The goodness and mercy of Lord Davidson followed us all the days of our life-or-death fight. After six years of it he was fitter than ever for the fray, his readiness matched only by mine as I arrived for the decider in London. Our friends would look after us by day and our family by night, thanks to Sally's side. As I said before, the Freshwaters had been an odd tribe: although my Dad, Jimmy, had five brothers and two sisters, I only ever met one of the brothers. They never kept in touch and so, as an only child, I knew none of my relatives. Sally, though, came from very sociable stock, with two sisters and parents who – although by now separated – still kept in touch. And she had connections with many other close families, including her godmother's husband, for whom she had worked at Butlers Wharf, long before Docklands became what it is today.

Uncle Tom and Auntie Kay were very gracious hosts to the Freshwater gang. We descended on them in the south-east, where Tom had spent his whole life commuting to the City. I was pretty soon experiencing the same delight of the one-hour sardine express with its "marked" seats for the bowler-hat brigade. I watched wide-eyed as one chap opened up his briefcase to produce the smallest set of folding chairs imaginable and sat down with his back to the partitioning door between the carriages. I was to enjoy plenty of sights during my fortnight as a commuter, training in and feeling my way around the big city to Parliament, then tracking the signposts all the way to the hub of things opposite Big

Ben: we had to travel up two or three floors to the small courtrooms with their vast,

lushly-appointed corridors. Sally was there on the first morning, along with some

supporters all the way from Speyside and some other friends of hers who'd made the

shorter trip from the Home Counties. And, of course, there was Bill Davidson, puffing

quietly on his pipe when he got the chance, between taking those copious notes of his

and organising the collections of books needed each day by counsel.

Our team alone would generally need to refer to some 25 tomes per session. We

had a tea trolley which we'd trundle along to the library, where Bill would scale the ladder

and go foraging. He'd hand down the 500-page volumes to me and I'd stack them on the

trolley, then off we'd trundle again back down the corridors, passing the learned

gentlemen and ladies of the law in their wigs and gowns, to deposit our stash at the

courtroom with the usher, who would take the books through and array them on the front

bench for counsel to pick at when the moment arose. Sometimes pages would be marked

with pieces of paper in readiness for the proceedings. Each of the five judges also had to

have his copy of anything relevant, so the proceedings moved at a pretty leisurely pace.

The judges would sit in a semi-circle in front of us. There was considerable concern that

English Law, so different from the Scottish, might be to our disadvantage, but with the

hindsight of three decades I have to say that I don't think the distinction had any effect

whatsoever upon the outcome.

The five judges were Lord Wilberforce, Lord Salmon of Sandwich, Lord Hailsham

(the Lord Chancellor), Lord Fraser of Tullybelton (one of the two Scottish judges in the

House of Lords at that time) and Lord Dilhorne – the latter promptly declaring that he was

a fisherman and that he had actually fished at Knockando. We were asked if we wished to

adjourn and we did. During the brief discussion Kemp aired his ire that Dillhorne had even

put himself forward to sit in judgment on the case. The judges, I was informed, were not

selected – they themselves chose whether or not they took part in a particular case.

However by the end of the discussion we were all agreed that it would probably be

advantageous having a judge with a self-declared interest, since he would have to be

particularly circumspect in reaching any decisions. Lord Wilberforce was the Chairman and

his reputation was impeccable.

The case opened with the usual readings of who was pursuing whom and when

the name "Freshwater" arose Hailsham looked up with a twinkle in his eye: "Is that the

fellow's real name? Rather appropriate!" I was close enough to agree with him – and his equally appropriately-named colleague, Lord Salmon – since I was just one seat behind counsel, but I thought the better of it, deciding that one introduction was sufficient.

There were no introductions in person from the other side. It surprised me that in all those weeks spent in court, I hardly ever saw my pursuers. When we were in Edinburgh I'd had plenty of time to drift from one court to another. There, in the early part of the day, 10 -10.30, they would have debates on forthcoming cases which judges would hear. With fourteen courtrooms to choose from I would go in and listen, but never saw anybody other than a QC and maybe a junior from each side putting forward an argument as to what the case was about. Then the judge would reach a decision whether or not there was a case to answer. Our case had originally been raised in the Sheriff Court in Inverness and promptly passed on to Edinburgh where it had been decided that there was indeed a case to answer.

In London it truly was a further education for me, noting how the various arguments were put forward, seeing counsel kept fully on their guard by the top judges of the land. There would be the occasional reference to one of the books we'd brought in and the junior would very quickly turn to the quoted page, the little man with his gold "scrambled egg" chain scurrying to find the same book for their lordships. By the time they were set up Kemp or Alastair would be waiting for them. Sometimes the quote would be in Latin, or some phrase would emerge in it, and Lord Hailsham would test their mettle by replying in a questioning form to the QCs in the classical tongue. Although I went to a grammar school where the subject was taught, I hadn't learned it – I hadn't even been allowed to learn French, having been judged inept at my own language. I had mixed with some of the classics boys, but their occasional conversational phrase was no preparation for what I was to hear in that courtroom. Those wise men inhabited another intellectual planet altogether and I could only sit in silent, open-mouthed awe at their erudition.

Their discussions went on for two weeks and two days, and it was only those last two days which I missed. I came back up to Scotland for a very entertaining day and night returning the hospitality of our London hosts, Uncle Tom and Auntie Kay, showing them just what all the fuss had been about, letting them know exactly what we were fighting for. For quite some time we were allowed to get on with minding our own business, while the highest judges in the land set about theirs. I still choose not to dwell on how things might have gone, I simply bless the day that the Lords finally made up their minds for us. Basically, Lord Maxwell had taken the view that there was a preponderance of public benefit - providing it was not used emulously - for those who had access to the river, which we certainly had. That word "emulously" even stumped our friend Dick Greaves. A voluntary instructor in the summer, Dick spent most of his time as a senior lecturer in English. Even Kemp and Alastair had to refer to the dictionary. Basically, it means you will not use your right to canoe to the intentional detriment or spoliation of other people's sport (for example, fishermen).

By the time the Court of Session appeal was finished the decision had centred more strongly on the public right to navigate, based upon the historical use of the river for floating timber and the floating of produce on that timber down to the sea, even though it was only in one direction. That little phrase "one direction" was picked on by some of the landowners after the court case and they argued that we only had the right to go down-river. I still maintain they were wrong and that going up-stream (if possible) is still an act of navigation. Ironically, I fish today more than I canoe, but I have a boat and go up-stream for four miles, so my act of navigation is certainly two-directional. It was made clear that it would not encompass "feats unknown to man" – whether they were having a go at jet-skis I'm not sure, since those things hadn't come on the scene in any great numbers then. This sort of activity would certainly be frowned upon, but I have to say that it's still an act of navigation.

By the time we got to the House of Lords we were still arguing about the public right to navigate, the fact that that right on rivers is held by the Crown for and on behalf of the people of the country. Under that scenario, riparian rights, where someone might own the bank to the middle of the river, or even own both banks and thus the whole river, would not take precedence over the right to navigate. The Crown right to the cruive fishing at the mouth of a river was first of all seen to be pre-eminent and it was only when the Duke of Gordon's case was decided in the 1780s that the floaters won the day – and established the right of navigation

The outcome was that their Lordships decided in our favour. In the words of the official law report:-

Held, affirming the decision of the First Division [of the Court of Session], dissenting Viscount Dilhorne, that *Grant v. Duke of Gordon* was decided upon the basis of a public right and that right was held available to the upper heritors as members of the public who had lawful access to the water; that the Spey is subject to a public right of navigation, not to some more limited right; that a public right of navigation in a non-tidal river depends not only upon the theoretical navigability of the river, but also on proof of its regular, habitual use as a channel of communication or transportation from time immemorial (customarily 40 years); that a right of navigation is not a servitude and cannot be lost by non-use; that use for mere recreation is as effective to prove navigability as use for transporting goods or other commercial use; that no question arises as to whether the use is of sufficient public benefit; that the establishment of a right of navigation in a river is not subject to the same requirements as the constitution of a right of way on land, and in particular that a right of navigation need not be established between two public places; that the public right of navigation in the River Spey would permit navigation by any vessel that could be reasonably described as a boat, including a canoe; and appeal dismissed.

So in the words of Kemp's obituarist, David had well and truly defeated Goliath. The case had far-reaching implications, since it affected every river that had any history of navigation – and not only in Scotland. My friend the BCU coach Oliver Cock, who was active in the '60s, used to travel the country in a camper van with a trailer full of canoes and taught different techniques to different groups. He was a very good friend of Lord Hailsham and he told me, shortly after the case, that the Lord Chancellor had said to him: "You will realise, Oliver, that it has equal consequences in England as well as Scotland". For all the various parties' interpretations, it was a famous victory and one which has been celebrated on the Boathouse wall ever since, thanks to a remarkable piece of poetry. There is a club in Edinburgh, The Monks of St Giles, whose members are exclusively the high flyers of Edinburgh's intellectual society. One of them at the time of the House of Lords decision was Archie Rennie, Secretary of the Scottish Home and Health Department. The Monks all used Latin names at their meetings and he was Father Pluvius, a reincarnation of the Romans' "rainy" god, Jupiter. He composed the following poem to celebrate the Freshwaters' success:

> The Lords of Appeal had a case to decide
> On a conflict between navigation
> And the Spey salmon fishing, well-known far and wide
> To be peerless for man's recreation.
>
> The agents included Field, Fisher and Trail -
> They were sportsmen whom no-one could gammon -
> And the judges could tell a fish head from a tail:
> The sederunt included Lord Salmon.

Successors in title o'er valleys and hills
The appellants, though not Dukes of Gordon,
Were the trustees of Hugh David Hamilton Wills
Whom wealth of tobacco had poured on:

They owned both the banks and the alveus (or bed)
Of a stretch of the Spey at Knockando
And their title included, as counsel had said,
All the rights de jure navigando.

These waters were claimed to give entry and ish
To the Cairngorms School of Canoeing
But the Trustees averred this deranged any fish
That an angler was skillfully wooing.

The canoeists' passage induced, it was plain
A condition akin to neurosis
And this angst of the salmon caused anglers more pain
Than the much-dreaded dermal necrosis.

This point had been won, without favour or fear
In the Court of the Lord Ordinary.
His finding, though cautious, was perfectly clear -
To disturb it their Lordships were chary.

But the case was not just a crude question of loss
To the lower, riparian heritors,
There were issues of law fit to tax Donald Ross
Or a legal professor emeritus.

Lord Fraser concluded the critical test
Was not constant use but capacity
To carry a vessel, which could, if hard pressed
Be extended by skill and sagacity

Though the water might vary in depth and in flow
According to season and rainfall
And those who canoed when the water was low
Might find it exceedingly painful.

Lord Wilberforce said that the res publicae, scarcely
Known among sinners and innkeepers
Include down-river floating, and Erskine and Blair
Held them in patrimonio principis

And the King holds this right for the good of the realm
Until the remotest futurity,
So he can't stop a boat, whoe'er has the helm
Except for the public security.

From this it had followed as night follows day
In a case in the reign of George Three
That the Dukes had no power to stop up the Spey
When the Grants wished to send down a tree.

They had floated their logs on the Aaron Hill plan
(For that poet was also a craftsman)
And a canoe can go where a timber raft can
When steered by a whisky-fed raftsman.

It is good to record that both sides had stressed
That the outcome would lead to no shindy,
Since both recognised that they would be served best
By a reasonable modus vivendi.

So all you good Monks who a fishing would go,
To eke out refection in Lent,
Be mindful of this, be the stream high or low
If you see a canoeist, tak' tent.

Though he frighten your fish, and you wish him away
Perhaps to Peru or Australia
He's as much right as you to Dee, Tweed or Tay
Navigation is inter regalia.

There have been rumblings since the case, with odd people trying to take action, including our neighbours at Kinrara. There was an ongoing saga for some two or three years after the court found in our favour whereby Stephen Ernest Scammel, who inherited the estate through Lord Bilsland, continued to write fairly strong letters protesting against our navigation of the river through the Kinrara section. Joining him was the owner of Inshriach Estate, Brigadier Curtis, some of whose property we purchased when Jack Drake sold the Inshriach nursery garden and BC (as he was known) bought the house. These two, for a good number of years, made trouble for anyone canoeing from Loch Insh to Aviemore. They actually raised an action against Glenmore Lodge for using the Feshie for canoeing on the section below the bridge. It came to court but unfortunately – as was the case in our battle – the Sports Council were not prepared to get involved and simply settled out of court. That however had no material effect on anyone else.

Of course, the Outdoor Access Code, which was introduced as a result of the Land Reform (Scotland) Act 2003, has made life a lot easier for access to land and water throughout Scotland, but I'm deeply disappointed at the level of disrespect there is from some canoeists, particularly those who run rafting expeditions. As I write this, I read in the local paper, the "Strathy", that "Soundings are being taken on banning wild camping at a Strathspey beauty spot because of fears over the escalation of anti-social behaviour, littering, sanitation and other problems. The Cairngorms National Park Authority is, for the first time, examining a series of get-tough measures to combat what it claims is 'irresponsible camping' at Loch Morlich and Glenmore". We always had an attitude of "Yes sir, no sir, three bags full sir" if we found people fishing in a pool when we were canoeing on the river. Occasionally we'd be asked to stop and stir up the fish, but most people would be pleased if you could pass one side or the other and avoid churning up the water. It was all a matter for conjecture as far as I was concerned: if they thought we were disturbing their fishing we just did as they asked. If it had been Lord Leven and his wife, as it had been a couple of times with Ray and me, they'd ask us to do a bit of rolling and ferry-gliding. In fact, during the case we had started canoeing again, and at Knockando Ray had been asked by the tenant at the time, a gentleman with a strong American accent, to arrange an Eskimo roll for him. Before the court case we had tried to get him to offer his opinion as a witness but, probably fearing he'd never be allowed to fish there again, he had declined – although he did agree that in asking us to roll the canoes he had not despoiled the fish. His name, we learned from one of the ghillies, was Sir Philip Grant-Suttie, of Canadian extraction, and he farmed in East Lothian.

Although we had won the war of the great Spey canoeing case, there were still plenty of battles ahead, as the rumbles from Kinrara and Inshriach promised. Since we had been barred from camping and landing, I had to set about finding patches where we could stay the night. Amazingly, despite all the research I had done, I was still to discover that British Rail owned four or five sites where the railway lines went close to the river - and they owned to the centre of the river, to ensure they would have the authority to protect the embankment if it ever got washed away. I managed to purchase a couple of sites, one at Kylintra Mill, near Grantown, which we later sold and on which now stands a two-storey house in the corner by the sewage works (nice), and one at Craigellachie. We still own a piece of ground, a quadrangle with fruit trees on it, bought from a couple who were running a small local hotel at Craigellachie, but I haven't been there for at least twenty years. The idea was to create hostels all the way down the river, but it proved ever less feasible after the creation of several new government bodies which started pumping money into footpaths such as the Speyside Way and establishing decent camp sites. In fact, our planning application to build at Craigellachie was refused.

The site at Kylintra was a saga in itself. I've already made the point that once you've set yourself up in business there will always be those who'll do everything they can to support you, and there will always be the others, who'll devote themselves to doing exactly the opposite. I've no reason to think that will ever change. At the time of the Kylintra Mill episode I had asked Bill Lawson if he knew who owned the ruin on the site and he told me it was a local hotelier. I went to see the gentleman and asked if the mill was available to rent or lease. He scratched his long hair to reveal his earring and told me that the ruin was far too important to the motorcycle club. I still reckoned I'd keep my ear to the ground, convinced the property would end up on the market before too long and I was absolutely right. When it did, I decided to go after it. Something told me it was not going to be easy, but then in my life nothing ever had been. I braced myself for the next challenge.

Chapter Sixteen
A Hostel Reception

It was a nice sunny day so, resplendent in my summer shirt, shorts and sandals, I decided to stroll into town and – surprise, surprise – found the hotel by the Co-op had been boarded up. In the bank next door, they told me that – surprise, surprise – the place was up for sale. It was being sold by a firm of chartered accountants in Elgin, so I decided to pop up there and see them, to establish precisely what was on the market. They told me the package included the hotel, the grounds and the house behind the hotel.

"What about the piece of land down by the river?"

"Oh yes" he said. "I'd forgotten about that..." He pulled out a triangular sheet of paper with a sketch on it. The land was about 100 x 120 x 90 yards and right next to the ground leading to the sewage plant. I left the offices after establishing that the hotel, land and house could be sold separately, and that bids would be handled by a firm of solicitors in Elgin, who had had some involvement in the canoeing case. Because of this I didn't hold out much hope for a successful bid – especially after finding out through the accountants that the place had already been on the market for six months and the closing date for bids was "Tuesday...". I was being told this on a Thursday, and the Monday was going to be a public holiday.

It all meant a very quick phone call to Bill Davidson in Edinburgh for the usual wise counsel. When he asked me for more information I had to admit there wasn't any: "Just draw a triangle and put the measurements on it," I suggested, "and bang in a bid for five thousand. Then add some braces to the belt and put in another offer in the name of Sally's father, Donald, say for an extra five hundred. That should throw them off the scent".

Full of enthusiasm, I next went to Kingussie to get a proper site plan (in those days you could get copies from the Council offices). The gentleman was very helpful, remarking that it was a very nice site as he went off down the road to another office to print it off. Then it was simply a question of waiting for the outcome. Sure enough, on the Wednesday we were phoned to say our bid had been successful. Er...our "other" bid, that is. Donald Fraser had become the proud owner of the strip of land which was going to be a super hostel for Cairngorm Canoeing and Sailing School, bought through the good offices of the Knockando solicitors. There was only one slight problem: Mr Fraser was, in fact, dead. He had passed on the year before.

Anyway, on the Friday I received a phone call to say that, unlike the new owner, the land deal was still apparently very much alive. Bill's partner, Mr Richardson, whom I didn't know at all, had been in touch with the agents to ask them for written confirmation of the acceptance of Mr Fraser's bid – only to be told that the land had gone back on the market, since the owners were now considering a higher offer. That untimely declaration had set Mr Richardson off in apoplectic rage, with suggestions of approaches to the Law Society, who could do nasty things to solicitors, etc. In my usual calmness I decided that if the place was still for sale I would simply bang in another offer – but this time with my own witness at the opening of the envelopes. This offer – our third – was made in my name, since our "cover" had been blown.

"Can you believe it?" I asked my good friend at the Council, the one who'd supplied me with the site map. "I've been gazumped".

"Oh, that's an old trick" he smiled, "just to get you to put in more money."

"Well they can stuff it" I fibbed. "If they think I'm getting involved again they're wrong."

"So you're not putting in another bid, then?"

"Well" I huffed, "would you?"

"Oh no" he agreed. "I wouldn't get into anything like that".

I promptly phoned Bill to raise the bid by another five hundred, and our man was present at the opening. Playing the daft laddie, I phoned the solicitors to ask how the bids had gone. They advised me they were still looking at the offers – three of them, no less. I told them I found that very odd, since the site had been on the market for six months or more.

"Yes, you'll know one of them", he said, mentioning a name.

I certainly did. A local businessman, he had been one of the witnesses against us in the great court battle. For all that, we were good friends and I didn't begrudge him his opinion in the matter - I had even once pulled his son out of a car which had gone off the road. Just as well too, since that lad had duly gone on to success in business, going on to become a local Round Table chairman. I well remember seeing that picture of him in the local newspaper, handing on the chain of office to...my friend in the Kingussie council offices.

Even with all these friends in high places, things can move exceedingly slowly though. As I write this, I have this week's Strathy beside me, going "Down Memory Lane" to 1st March 1985: "A local canoeing and sailing school operator may have to wait three years to provide an overnight hostel for clients in Grantown. The Cairngorm Canoeing and Sailing School Ltd this week sought the consent of local planners to build a hostel and warden's house at Kylintra, off the riverside road at Grantown. But the road junction of the existing private road and the public road requires improvement to satisfy the divisional roads engineer of traffic safety in that area. School operator Mr Clive Freshwater is unable to provide these improvements."

The road wasn't due for upgrading for another three years, and Seafield Estates, the local landowners, were also objecting, on the grounds of "road hazard" and "disturbance of amenity in the area" which was "much used by the public for walking". We never did build the thing, and the chain of hostels we had envisaged up and down the Spey never did materialise, but it left us free to get on with developing the family business at Loch Insh. And, of course, the family: marriage to Sally had brought a new one into the world - I remember my father-in-law's surprise at Duncan's arrival so soon after the wedding. Sally had always been a source of surprises for him: as a young thing she had wanted to fly off around the world as a WREN, only to be thwarted by tuberculosis. After recovering she had trained as a secretary, working for her Uncle Tom before making the break and moving to Washington DC with the Foreign Office for a spell; she then moved to Harvard, where she looked after things for two professors, who were experts in earth dams. Hers is a story worth a book or two and when I've got my own out of the way I'll start bullying her to get on with it. Her own boys have grown up, of course, and although there are now a number of grandchildren to vie for her time and attentions, I think she's long overdue for some quality time with herself.

There are all kinds of families. I was married to the skiing industry during its long infancy, dragging myself up from a non-skier aged twenty two to BASI grade 1[8] at twenty five and a trainer[9] shortly after that. For twelve years I served as the chairman of BASI (the British Association of Ski Instructors, now widened into the British Association of Snowsports Instructors, to reflect the growing popularity of snow-boarding) on taking over from founder Jack Thomson after his own twelve-year stint. In those fledgling years there was a lot of in-fighting, as there so often is in such organisations, when so many are more interested in their own ends than the common good, but it was so busy that Eric Henry, my vice-chairman, agreed with me that we needed a Chief Executive and we eventually

---

[8]The top grade of ski instructor
[9]Qualified to train ski instructors

persuaded the committee of this - I certainly couldn't afford the time to look after the office and its two staff. Hazel Bain, the Secretary, who had an amazing memory for names, and Joyce ran things efficiently, leaving me merely to sign the cheques[10]. Sadly, both ladies have since been towed to the great piste in the sky.

BASI branched out into Europe, running courses abroad through Interski, the international body of ski instructors. I didn't go to any Interski meetings for years, leaving the job of demonstrations to Hans Kuwall, Frith Finlayson and others. I didn't really get involved until I went to my first Interski in Italy, where Sally joined me, and I also went off to Banff in Canada. They were great times and I have to say I enjoyed those twenty odd years skiing, training and examining. It paid well and when working at Glenmore Lodge we took leave from there on those occasions, so I had a double pay-day – which all got ploughed back into the business we have today.

The first Chief Executive of BASI, Tony Cowan-Martin, didn't last too long after I finished as chairman and there was a bit of an upheaval. He moved on and latterly worked with the NHS in Inverness. Sometime after that Bob Kinnaird came on the scene and did a very good job of putting BASI on a sound footing. It has expanded enormously over the years and employs a large number of office staff, organising courses all over the world, some of which my sons Duncan and Andrew have been involved in as trainers. After Bob left, BASI stumbled a little, with one or two chiefs coming and going, nevertheless the qualifications it offers are still much sought after. I think one of the Association's greatest assets is that it has maintained its standards – so many want to use it as a benchmark of their own skiing ability as much as a route into ski teaching. For a long time I was actually a critic of BASI for just that reason: it always appeared that one had to be a much better skier than a teacher and I didn't, and still don't, entirely agree with that. But people were prepared to pay their money and I'm absolutely amazed at how much it is costing to run these courses aimed at the top grades. Much of it has to do, I think, with people wanting to have the BASI logo on their jacket or the rear windscreen. It's simply an emblem of their ability as a skier, and yet the qualification is probably more sought-after than those of any other sport, reflecting well on the Association and what it has achieved. I have to say that I tell young people joining outdoor education that qualification at a lower level will be enough to earn them a job, since there are, for instance, very few people who need to ski at Grade 1 level, since ninety per cent of people taking ski lessons are beginners. The same applies to most outdoor sports: it's important to be a safe and competent climber, but in most other sports the emphasis is on the beginner.

---

[10]Editor's note – This is over-modest: he was a strong Chairman – see Tim Walker's Foreword to this volume.

Top – Clive with his old friend and mentor, Bill McGuiness

Above – Celebrating BASI's 50th birthday in 2012. L to R - Sally, Liam Carver, Kate Ross, Kitty Hall, Clive, Brian Hall

My personal feeling about Glenmore Lodge is that it has become extremely expensive. It's well promoted and well-regarded - as it should be, with the staff all excellent at their job – but, as they all know, the place used to work as it was intended to work: self-sufficiently. Most such centres are inefficient today, since they are government-funded. As I write this in the grip of the credit crunch, it is very likely that some anonymous department somewhere is drawing up a list of them for "rationalising". While the government is keen for youngsters to go on outdoor courses and we need leaders, there comes a time when they will say we can't afford to go on running these centres at a loss. Students have to pay course fees and colleges are not entirely supported by the taxpayer. By and large, universities have to stand on their own feet, unlike some of these outdoor centres. When training people to be teachers of outdoor education you have to ask why there should be a difference. Maybe they are seen as "blue-eyed boys" but I don't think that will last forever.

Freshwater's little outfits at Loch Insh and Ullapool were always expected to sink or swim alone. Fortunately, they never sank: from the start there were people around who shared our love of the great outdoors and that faith in our future, and from those friends came more friends. "Networking" they call it now, but without our extended family we would never have survived. It's not a matter of bribery or corruption, nothing like that, it's simply about making the right connections and if my boys learn nothing from our family's early experiences their efforts won't bear any fruit. Pop wouldn't bear the loss of any apples, that's for sure: he worked like a Trojan well into his seventies, building canoes and looking after Sally's vegetable garden, and I remember how he was shocked to the core one day when he caught a lad scrumping our "cookers" near his chalet. He gave chase and, to his astonishment, he discovered the scoundrel was a scout master staying in the Hall with a group. For all the fine badges, the lad could never have been sufficiently "prepared" for the dressing down he got, as he planted every apple in Freshwater Senior's flat hat.

The Lennox family were always great friends. Jack and Ann's three children – Jinty, Jock and Seonaid – all worked for us when they were at school and university, and Jack himself was our accountant after our stumbling starts with various firms in Inverness. I didn't know at the time, when I asked Jock what his father did, that Jack was actually the senior partner in one of the constituent firms which merged to form Ernst and Young, but he certainly proved hugely instrumental in getting us on the right track. Jack and Ann used to rent the house behind the Kincraig village store, where Joy Anderson now lives. He liked what we were doing and his son Jock, who would have been around 18, was sailing as a

Top – Clive's Dad and Mum, James and Ivy

Above left – Clive in typical working mode

Above right – Clive with his Dad and prize turnip

crew boy for clients who had the Milton Hotel in Fort William. He sailed on a boat called "Pepsi" in the very bad storm in the Fastnet Race, where several capsized and drowned. I remember asking him how he'd got on in the event and being told: "Well, it was a bit bumpy...". An understatement, if ever there was one. His sisters worked for us regularly and still come in, now with their own children. Granddad Jack was a wonderful, fatherly figure who, while not suffering fools at all gladly, was very friendly to us and it turned out that he had actually been the senior examiner for all accountants coming out of Glasgow University – virtually every banker in the country knew Jack Lennox. If you took Jack to the bank with you, you always got a decent hearing. It was he who introduced me to Hamish Robertson.

In fact, Hamish, a skier from Dollar, was a senior civil servant at the Scottish office, in Edinburgh. His children also worked for us at Loch Insh. One day, Hamish happened to hear me complaining about the difficulties we were having getting permission to put extra boats onto the loch and before long a "Mr Donoghue" called in, to check on the number we were actually entitled to have. He asked me if various good and true bodies - the Sports Council, Countryside Commission, Nature Conservancy Council, and so on - had helped us to get extra boats on the water and I told him they hadn't done anything. Then he asked what would happen if he came along with a boat himself and I told him he would have to take the thing away with him – he simply wouldn't be allowed to put it on the water. The vice-chairman of the Highlands and Islands Development Board (now Highlands and Islands Enterprise, or HIE), Bobby Faskin, was with him and interjected, asking if *they* had done anything and I gave it to him straight: "You're the first person from the Board ever to come here." After they left. I asked Sally to check out who the men actually were and it transpired that our guest had been Lord Donoghue, a policy advisor to Prime Minister James Callaghan, which was a very pleasant surprise...for us, anyway. It clearly wasn't pleasant for somebody: one dogsbody got a real shock, because not long after "Mr Donoghue" had left I got a phone call from the Forestry saying they hoped to be able to increase the number of boats allowed on the loch. I can still picture that red Dymo sticker on the Forestry telephone trembling.   The sticker, which I'd seen on my previous visit, ordered staff DO NOT USE THIS PHONE BEFORE ONE PM, and it was only eleven in the morning.

"And how did you get on with "Mr Donoghue" the other day?" asked Hamish on his next skiing trip.

"Oh, very well. How did you know he was here?"

"I sent him!" replied Hamish. "I have to write the itinerary for these chaps" he smiled. "I just thought you might like to meet him."

These "chaps" could be very helpful at times. It wasn't too long before there was a completely different set of chaps, when Maggie Thatcher came to power in 1979. We had made a visit to Inverness to try and purchase the site which, apart from the Hall which we owned, we were leasing on a fifty year lease from the Forestry Commission. We had arranged to meet their land agents, to discuss the matter with the estates department head, Jim Jardine. I had told Jim Scott, the Scottish Office architect and designer of the Boathouse, about the meeting and he'd suggested he came too: "There will be two of them and while you're thinking of the answer to one question the other one will be thinking up the next one".

So we arrived at 21 George Street in Edinburgh and were ushered into a room where three men were working away at their desks, only to be told that Mr Jardine had forgotten about the appointment and was in Skye, so the chance of seeing him was slim. During the course of the conversation one of the men asked Jim what he did and Jim told him. "*Scottish Office?*" Well, you'd have thought somebody had stuck a hat-pin in his bum, because after shooting a glance at the other workers he left the room at high speed, excusing himself. Less than a minute later he returned to say the Conservator (the head of forestry for the Highlands) would see us in place of Mr Jardine. We had a nice, pleasant, amicable meeting and it again showed me that it helps to have friends in the right corridors - Jim didn't explain to them that he actually worked as the senior architect for Scottish prisons, but then they didn't ask. All the same, in this world of swing-doors and roundabouts you can also have friends in the wrong corridors: I had unfortunately already written to our local MP, Russell Johnston, and he had approached the Forestry Commission about the sale of the land, which gave them the excuse to answer me in the negative: the land was not available for sale since they had received formal correspondence from a Member of Parliament and would have to deal with that first. What we didn't know at that time was that the assistant land agent for the Forestry Commission was heavily involved with the RSPB.

Anyway, time moved on and we heard on the news that the new Prime Minister had appointed Sir Robin Ibbs, a leading industrialist who had been seconded to the government as Head of the Central Policy Review Staff in the Cabinet Office, with the remit to speed up privatisation. I had already heard that Mrs Thatcher's first target was to be the Forestry Commission, and I already had my own copy of the Green Paper, the precursor of a parliamentary bill. I'd also read the bill and again approached the Forestry as it was clear that our site fitted the privatisation mould perfectly, being among "the pockets of land discontiguous from the main bulk of Forestry ownership with long lease tenancy". The Forestry office in Inverness again ignored this fact and turned me down. So, on hearing about Sir Robin, I dispatched a letter to Number 10. It prompted an immediate phone call from a secretary: "Sir Robin has received your letter. He is sympathetic to your cause. He doesn't normally deal with individuals, but you will hear from the Scottish Office on Friday".

Jim Scott confirmed that the Westminster letter had landed on the Scottish Office floor like a match in a tinder-dry forest. It was green touch-paper: blue wouldn't have bothered them so much, but green was top priority and had to be answered within three days. I could visualise the minions hurtling around the place formulating their response to Sir Robin. Sure enough, on the Friday we received a letter from George Younger, then Secretary of State for Scotland, saying that the land would be sold to us. The Forestry Commission office in Inverness had been instructed to expedite matters and had appointed the District Valuer to negotiate terms. I wanted to push out our extension beyond the lease and acquire 14 acres of prime land on the corner of the loch: it was priced at a very modest £25,000 and it is where the majority of the Loch Insh Watersports buildings sit today. It could so easily have been a different story, if central government had not stepped in to keep local officials in order. There's no doubt that places like Inverness can seem a world apart from Edinburgh and, dare I say that word, London. The Forestry Commission's land agent, could have been a serious problem, having apparently been lining up our site for the RSPB. Had he won the day, we would effectively have become tenants of that Society and would certainly never have been able to build the centre you see today.

"With that major obstacle out of the way, Clive and Sally Freshwater were able to improve their centre" recalled journalist Ed Rattray in the February 1987 *Scottish Field*. He continued:

> An impressive stone and timber boat-house grew in place of a derelict shed, and above it, The Boathouse Restaurant. With superb loch views, the restaurant has earned recognition by Egon Ronay and by British Relais Routiers as a place that offers a warm and spontaneous welcome. But, such is the complexity of land tenure, the conflict of interest and lack of national planning, that further collisions seem inevitable. From the beginning, the Freshwaters have been subjected to strong background pressures which would have sunk less resilient folk.

The Nature Conservancy Council recently slapped a 'Site of Special Scientific Interest Order' on parts of the Freshwater lochside land, stating that it contained a unique stand of mature poplar trees. Shortly before that restricting order was placed, Clive had thinned out some of the trees, acting on the advice of a professional forester who described the trees as 'weeds'. Further conflict looms ahead, because Loch Insh is designated as one of nine important wetland regions in Europe...Within a short time they (the NCC and RSPB) may have the right to withdraw boating rights by declaring the 700 acres of the loch a SSSI. What happens then to the 15 dinghies the Insh Centre is allowed to operate and the canoes which are used to train young people in basic water skills?

What actually happened was that within five years of Ed's report the Nature Conservancy Council became extinct[11]. But, of course, that didn't take our school off the endangered species list. We still had plenty of adversaries, but then we still had plenty of life left in us and we were learning how to deal with our problems all the time. For example: some time previously, a group had appeared from Holland to fish for eels. It had caused quite a flurry among landowners when marker buoys had started popping up all over the loch, marking the "fyke" nets - traps suspended over a series of hoops, laid horizontally in the water. We believe they took about five tons of eels, which they stored on the Dunachton side of the loch in a perforated cage. The other landowners were worried that their patches were being exploited. The ownership of the loch had been divided into "cake slices" and there was some confusion as to how big each slice was. There was quite an investigation and Jamie Williamson at Alvie established, through his solicitors, that no-one could fish for eels in that way unless all the riparian owners agreed, and no such agreement had been reached. Jamie had sent me a copy of a 450 page legal statement on land ownership which had mentioned the interesting Latin word *solum*, describing the bed of the loch, and I had filed it away somewhere in the back of my mind. When I eventually became a landowner myself I duly received the deeds to my patch and looked for that interesting word, in vain. By then dear old Bill had relocated to the great chambers in the sky and I had a new solicitor, Tom Drysdale, who had acted for us in the purchase from the Forestry Commission and who now received a phoned question from me: "What happened to my *solum*? As I understand it, the deeds should show that I own the bed of the loch to the middle, but there's no mention of that".

"Clive, I think you're probably right, but I'll look into it", Tom assured me. By the

[11]In fact, in 1991 the Scottish part of it merged with the Countryside Commission for Scotland to form Scottish Natural Heritage.

following day he had confirmed that I was correct.

"Well please, don't say anything about this to the Forestry" I asked him. "Simply accept the titles they have offered."

Some years later the Forestry looked to sell the rest of their shoreline to the RSPB and I was shown a map depicting precisely what the Society expected to acquire. Of course, the map included the whole bed of the loch, from the top end right down to, and including, Tomdhu – the island by Insh Church. So we decided to make enquiries with our legal friends. We asked Alastair Cameron, now a leading QC, for his opinion – we could afford his fee by then – which essentially bore us out: the RSPB were not going to own the bed of the loch in our section. However Alastair felt that we should reserve our position - which we did, in no uncertain terms - and let our sleeping bird-dogs lie. Many years later a German couple, the Von Wahlerts, were staying in the chalet by the beach. He was a high-flying solicitor, travelling the world attending conferences, and was connected to a legal firm in Edinburgh which just happened to be the one used by the RSPB. He jokingly told me that we were not exactly flavour of the month with that firm, in the first place for acquiring the ownership of our land and in the second place for having had the audacity to argue that the Society didn't own the whole bed of the loch.

Not being flavour of the month with the RSPB put a big smile on my face for quite some time, but it doesn't do to get too smug: the affair was eventually to lead to a shocking revelation which would shrivel my smile.

Chapter Seventeen
The Case Of The Missing Case

How do you lose the most important water rights case in 250 years? If you're the printer, you simply run out of space.

It still amazes me. We only found out thanks to Jobst Van Wahlert, the German solicitor who had stayed in one of our chalets. After we got to know each other, he asked if he might have a copy of the Lords' historic adjudication on the epic river navigation battle and I made enquiries through our solicitor, to be told that the company which had printed the records (the written pleadings in the case) had been sold to another company in Dundee and all the publications had gone there. Unbelievably, when I contacted the company in the City of Discovery it was only to discover that the new owners of the copies had not had enough storage space for them – and had chosen to dispose of them.

Fortunately, the various legal institutions kept their own records, particularly in Parliament House and the Signet Library, owned by the Society of Writers to the Signet, so we were ultimately able to photocopy the 200 pages and the whole unfortunate episode took my further education one step further. I found that the Signet Library is one of the leading repositories of historic court papers in Scotland and we were very pleased to hear that our new solicitor had been appointed as the Deputy Keeper of the Signet and thus the WS Society's senior office bearer. The library is a magnificent building, part of the Parliament House and Court of Session complex, and through Tom we've enjoyed several visits for family weddings and birthday parties there. They were all very swish affairs where we met so many interesting people who, in their turn, had wanted to meet us and discuss our epic case and the development of Loch Insh.

My last visit to Parliament House was at Alastair Cameron's invitation. By that time he had been appointed a judge, with the judicial title of Lord Abernethy – there was already a Lord Cameron and through his involvement with our case Alistair had bought a house at Nethy Bridge. For all the position and the title, he was from the outset a very approachable man with no side at all. I think the general public have the impression that judges think of themselves as a cut above everybody else, but Alastair is certainly not of that ilk. Sally and I have long been firm friends of the Camerons and it was a really enjoyable evening at the Judges' Annual Dinner, in the Advocates' library. The great and the good were there, including Clive and Sally Freshwater – at least, until the wives were whisked away to be entertained by the judges' wives in their private residences. One of the judges, though, was a rather attractive blonde who introduced herself as Lady Smith. She asked if I remembered her and I had to admit that I didn't. "I used to go to school with Duncan" she smiled. Her parents had owned and run the High Range Hotel in Aviemore. She'd grown up there and progressed through university. I occasionally see her featuring at prestigious events and she is known to give out some fairly stiff sentences in court. Another gentleman who approached me (I forget his title) confessed he'd wanted to meet me for 35 years – to confess that he had declined an invitation to handle the canoeing case for us because of his own fishing interests.

Over dinner, a very formal affair, I discovered from Alastair that the young official who had drawn up the seating plan had put me down as "Fairweather" and, when I checked, I noted that my name had been scribbled over it in ink. It must have been something of a Freudian slip on the young man's part, since the Lord President (the head of the judiciary) had recently had a run-in with the Government's front man on Scottish prisons, Mr...you've guessed it.....Fairweather. There had been some real clashes of personality and Fairweather was not flavour of the month, or the season, or even the year, and I think the young chap who'd drawn up the list got a bit of a rocket for his slip. Ironically, we were sitting opposite the Lord President and his guest, Oliver Russell, the owner of Ballindalloch Estates. I don't think my presence put the Laird off his meal when he noticed me, and he was magnanimous enough to acknowledge my presence and we had a short conversation. There was a senior official of the European Union there too, a small Irishman with a sharp wit and a twinkle in his eye. And there was an economist, I think. Their discussion on the rights and wrongs of European economic integration went way over my head, but the good old Scottish food and the vintage French wine were superb. There was the nostalgia too, my presence enough to stimulate several of the older diners. I found it remarkable that the great Spey case was still considered to be so significant. Even today I meet solicitors and other legal eagles who are amazed at the case and that "appropriate" name Freshwater. Alistair and Kemp assured me that our fight in the Upper House was the longest running Scottish case until 2002. Solicitors dream of handling cases which establish legal precedents and go on to influence rulings in all sorts of disputes anywhere in the world where British law holds sway. Bill Davidson had helped us start something which, we like to think, will go on to help Joe Public make his way around the waters of the world.

Bill had always been a fighter. When he died some years ago, his obituary appeared in The Scotsman and Tom sent me a copy since he knew we didn't take the paper. It's not often you appear by name in somebody else's obituary. It was only then we realised what a life he'd had, particularly in the war, fighting the Japanese. He was one of those people who, when war broke out, put on his Army uniform, fought, survived, came home, put his pin-stripe suit back on and simply went back to work. Never once in the four or five years we were allied in our own war did he mention the global one, but he had obviously been in the thick of it, evidently at the capturing of a notorious hill. An order had been given that there were to be no bagpipes as the regiment began their assault, but Bill, stripped to the waist, fighting hand to hand, yelled his own and the pipes struck up, to the terror of the enemy. True or not, they won that particular battle and it was, like the one he won for us, documented as an epic success. He was a good man and we all have much to thank him for.

His successor has proved a stalwart ally too. Even though he is now retired, Tom is still quite happy to lend an informal ear to our problems. He has been involved in just about every area of the business, which is good for the boys: Tom and I have been through it all and while we're around they will have a wealth of experience to draw on as they take up the baton. I met Tom through the Cairngorm Ski Club: Duncan and Andrew were keen members and I became the race organiser. At the committee meetings Tom would take the minutes, a job he did extremely efficiently. With Bill Davidson in a care home by that stage, I asked Tom (who happened to be a senior partner with Shepherd & Wedderburn) if he would be interested in becoming our legal advisor.

Another such decision was to involve David Kidd in our financial affairs. In the early days we had plenty of difficulties with the bank, as all small businesses tend to have. We were with the Bank of Scotland for the first 20 years or so, but David, who camped at Loch Insh with a group of boys, was a banker of no small experience. A swimmer of international repute, he trained youngsters at Edinburgh Baths (now a fitness centre) and of the youngsters he had with him at our place, many seemed to belong to legal families, their parents lawyers and judges, all of whom regarded David as a good role model inspiring their interest in swimming and windsurfing. He was also an adept sailor and before long he was to steer our rocking ship to less stormy waters, over on the other bank. It was a good move: apart from the one glitch, the Royal Bank of Scotland has worked well with us. Although the staff have changed over the years at Inverness, they have nevertheless been receptive to our needs. Ian McPhail was the first of them; then there was Donald McDonald, Christine Campbell and now Brian Robson. All I can say is that, while you hear so many stories about bankers being less than helpful, that has never really been the case with us, thanks to the many contacts we've made over the years. Sadly, David Kidd died of cancer some years ago but his brother contacted us to say that in his will he had bequeathed us a very smart red sailing boat: we accepted the gesture with gratitude, on the basis that his friends would be free to come up and use it at any time. As it turned out, very few of them did and, since the boat was actually quite difficult to sail, we eventually sold it on, but I'm sure it was for a price our late financial advisor would have approved of.

We wanted to push the boat out with the building, too. It had long been our dream to have a balcony (you could say we wanted to push the Boathouse out) but we had drawn up our design during the big court case, which meant that everything was up in the air (except the balcony). No funder would commit to us while the court appeals were going on, but the moment the case was finally won we applied for grant aid. That meant we had to produce a cash-flow projection, something we had never done, and it was good old Jack Lennox, our accountant, who took on the job, journeying up from Edinburgh with his laptop. This was way back in the '80s and I'd never seen one before. We spent a whole day with one of the Ernst & Young staff in Inverness, projecting the turnover for the next five years and I am still staggered at how accurate it turned out to be. We still have it on file and it still blows me away to see how the professionals could get it so right, from the cups of tea we were likely to sell, at precisely how many tables on the projected balcony. At the same time we produced a business plan and all the ten points, including the big boat (the last item on our agenda), have now been achieved. It was a brain-numbing session with Jack and his young lady assistant, who was feeding all the data into the laptop, but it certainly did the trick and we were granted some £10,000 towards the cost of the Boathouse extension.

While we were building it later, we heard of a fire at the restaurant at the Cairngorm chairlift's middle station, known as The Shieling. Plumbing work was being carried out amid gale-force winds and it's thought that a spark had carried. The place was burned down, but its balcony had been left intact, including the brackets. These had been made by the contractor who had produced the chairlift seats, Glen Perry. Anyway, after the fire I called Harry McKay at the chairlift company to see what they were going to do

Top – Summer beach staff 1986

Above – Summer staff c. 1992

Top left – Norfolk sailing dinghy, one of the two old Loch
Morlich dinghies acquired from Glenmore Lodge

Top right – junior sail training on Loch Insh

Above – Pico dinghies on Loch Insh

Top– Sail training line-up at the Boathouse
Above – Clive at the helm of a Wayfarer

Top left – Clive fishing on Loch Insh.

Top right – his fishing partner, Dick Carr

Above left – Toasting the first day of the fishing season in 1990. L to R - Steve Newland, Dick Carr, Andrew Freshwater, Marion Ramage, Clive

Above right – One that didn't get away

with the restaurant and he told me he was waiting for the insurers to have a look at it. Some six months later I received a call to say I could help myself to anything useful, so I took the brackets and to this day we still have some of them. There used to be a problem at the middle station with the snow drifting in and blocking off the exit to the old White Lady chairlift. The decision was taken to build an extraordinarily large barrage balloon which was chained down, and when inflated would block the gap where the snow normally fell. One night a storm got up before it was fully inflated and the whole thing was ripped to pieces. It was made from white, 12oz vinyl canvas, very expensive stuff - which Walter and I recovered from the car park at the invitation of the chairlift staff. We got at least two trailer loads out of it, which went to form the dodgers at the boats up in Ullapool. They are still used as covers for the Seafarers in the winter on Loch Insh. We made boat canopies too, so the sailors could sleep on board and have the cockpit covered. I should sub-title this book "The Recycler".

I have to say that in those early days we had a much greater friendship with the other businesses in the Strath than we have today. It's nothing to do with us, it's just a sad reflection on the way society has been changing over the years, with so much more competition and dog-eat-dog now. Many businesses will support you to your face, but once the old back is turned it can be a question of "anything goes". I think one of the telling factors is that in those pioneering days of yore the chairlift company made substantial amounts of money and there was no real hint of the desperate times which lay ahead with the climate change, both economic and meteorological. It's tempting to be nostalgic about those early, innocent days, but you only find yourself making unhappy comparisons. There's one particularly uncomfortable recollection I have about pioneering innocence and it's often ugly repercussions.

Eddie the Eagle was a hero of the 1988 Calgary Olympics and meeting him face to face was a joy - it was the meeting behind his back which was torture. Eddie Edwards was a short-sighted plasterer from Gloucester who had dared to dream. With no backing at all he had competed for Britain in the ski-jump event, duly becoming last on the hill but first in the hearts of all who watched. He was given a riotous welcome at the monthly Eaton Square meeting of Britain's skiing nobs - which included C. Freshwater, since the British Association of Ski Instructors was allowed *one whole vote* on its committee (as opposed to the 20-odd afforded to the English and Scottish Ski Councils). All of us warmly shook the hand of little Eddie (he was a giant when coming down from the hill but just 5ft 8in on coming up the stairwell) and after being given a sandwich our honoured guest was escorted deferentially to the boardroom by our chairman, for a private consultation. When the meeting finally reconvened Eddie had left and it was made abundantly clear to those present that the standard for ski-jumping entries by the British athletes would be raised to a level that would eliminate any further embarrassment to the top brass – the blazered, regimental-tied brigade which was running British skiing. As a PE teacher and a leader in sport, I thought the whole episode disgraceful. I'm even more appalled today, to think that I'm in a business which turned away the one person who had sent it soaring into the headlines and capturing the public imagination for all the right reasons. In their monocular eyes it was for the wrong reasons, but I belong to another brigade altogether: the Olympic dream is not simply about "going for gold". The ethic is all about taking part, and that's always been mine too. I don't fit in with the establishment of any particular sport, since they all seem nowadays to be devoted purely and simply to the sheer misery of winning at all costs.

As I said, nostalgia can come at a price. But if you don't keep comparing the past and the present it can be great fun. As I remember the early days of skiing in the Cairngorms I'm reminded of the marvellous monologue which recounts them better than I ever could. It was put together by two senior members of staff at the Scottish Council of Physical Recreation (before it became the Scottish Sports Council, and more recently Sportscotland). This was in the early '60s when the Aviemore Centre was being built and the competition between the Rank Organisation, at Coylumbridge, and Lord Fraser, of House of Fraser, at Aviemore, was of Olympic standard. The whole thing was wonderfully observed by Charlie Wild, a great authority on the works of the British-Canadian poet Robert Service, and Jock Kerr-Hunter (Hunter Jake, as he called himself). Once Glenmore Lodge had been established, Jock was to become the driving force for the outdoor activity programme which blossomed at various venues around the country. To appreciate Jock and Charlie's masterly parody of Service's "The Shooting of Dan McGrew" you need a little background. Very recently I met Charlie's son and, although he was aware of this story, he confessed he had no copy of it, so I hope my quoting it here will rectify that. In fact, I intend sending a copy to Prince Charles, as he and I were sharing the same ski instructor – one Plumb Worrell – at the time the piece was written. I recall that May Brown, the first chairperson and one of the driving forces at the start of Glenmore Lodge, was mortified that I had acquired the words, since she'd hoped the thing would never be divulged to the rest of the Spey valley. In those days, perhaps some of the content might have been considered a little sensitive, but I believe that it's such a beautifully-written piece of work that it won't jar with anyone, even those referred to in it. One more name

to explain – Mr Nicholson was the chairman of the Scottish Tourist Board. Well, here it is:

I'll tell the tale of the high North Trail
And the men who toiled for gold -
Where the blizzard blows over the frozen snows
It would make your blood run cold.

Say, give me the makings and sit over there,
And a couple of shots of the blend
Will help us to get the picture of where
This A9 grade has its end.

You have heard of the Yukon gold rush,
Where the weakest get slammed to the wall,
Where the sun takes fear for half a year...
Well believe me, you ain't heard it all!

For the richest paid strike of the lot,
So good it looked like a freak
Was first put on stake by Hunter Jake
In these hills above Crampon Creek.

The rush ins started slow like,
Then rose to a human flood;
With hope in their eyes they swarmed like flies,
With gold-rush in their blood.

Their eyes on these hard-luck diggings,
They struggled to sweat and pant
Up a loan trail through the foot-hills fled
Of a joker named Grubstake Grant.

So he grubstaked a road to his diggings,
But this weren't enough, to be frank,
So he sold out the lots to his ranching plot
To a slicker called Raw Deal Rank.

But while Rank was building a swell hotel
He was waging a war of attrition
With another dude, a storekeeper made good
Who set up in opposition.

There Fox-Fur Fraser was a name to fear
And he aimed to bust the balloon -
And, so far on paper, he planned this sky-scraper
And an even bigger saloon.

Well, Rank's name was good at the bank
So he slapped the place up quick,
With one of the "blue bloods" of Europe
To perform the opening trick.

You can bet this got old Fox-Fur below the belt,
Seeing as how Prince Phil
Had recently been a local boy
From the school just over the hill.

It made you just start wondering
Just what was in Fraser's mind
And what fire-raiser old Fox-fur Fraser
Would get to pull up his blind

For if they had kept things in the family
They'd have made one and all quite glad,
For Phil had a son called Charlie -
Same school, too, as his dad.

It would have been a real gag and the only snag
Which might have risen to menaces
Was the fact that the Queen might not like him seen
Inside around licensed premises.

As a public figure he was blossoming forth
And I'm sure he was proving right handy,
But the problem with mum was showing his taste
For an occasional Cherry Brandy.

But my guess, old Fox-Fur
Would get up inspiration
And send his Tourist Board to find
The biggest draw in the nation.

By gum, if they failed he would have them in jail
And Nicholson in the pillory,
So I suggest that he settle the quest
And bought up a malt distillery.

An all-time spree, with drinks for free,
He had the gold rush at his door...
It hit Bonanza Square for sure,
But God help Aviemore!

In the lonely land where dog eats dog
And avarice never is rid
Fox-Fur, Grubstake or Raw Deal Rank
Will be first with the take-over bid.

Down it pardners, it's closing time.
I'll tell you more of this story
Since we're getting slung out of here
(line missing)

Thanks for your hospitality
And all those shots of blend
And sitting and patiently listening
To a story that has no end.

For there are strange things done in the midnight sun
By the men who toil for gold.
The arctic trails are their secret tales
That would make your blood run cold.

The Northern Lights have seen queer sights
So give your guns a hitch,
Get your backs to the sky and keep an eye
On the men who strike it rich.

Chapter Eighteen
Expansion, Europe, Awards And The Royals

EXPANSION AND EUROPEAN FUNDING

As our business developed and as profitability improved, we started to look towards expansion. We were soon shopping around. The Canadian system of log construction, pioneered in the UK in 1963 by Finlog, was the preferred technique, as used in the prototype Boathouse. We came across Stuarts of Old Rayne in Aberdeenshire, a father and son business, which specialised in it. They designed our first six chalets featuring inter-locking Douglas fir logs, which would prove remarkably robust. To this day they have kept their looks and have proved really popular. But as usual the bank weren't interested in providing the necessary funding. To get the first building off the ground, or rather up from it, Sally's mother, Jo Jo, came to the rescue. Jo Jo's chalet we called it, flagging it up for her retirement. The deal was that she would put up the money and we would pay her interest, but by sheer coincidence, she wasn't to be the only one showing an interest. On the very day we finished the chalet we were all sitting outside it, enjoying a barbeque, when the bank manager, Tom Forbes, drew up in his car. Never having visited Loch Insh, he found the whole concept very interesting indeed and he was soon offering to help us in building the other chalets. I had already approached the bank once and I wasn't about to start doing deals that afternoon, so he went on his way without having received an invitation to the barbeque.

Although our accountant, Jack Lennox, was continually advising me to slow down, my instinct was telling me to press on with expansion. The chalets were built and to this day I am not quite sure how we actually raised the money, but somehow we did. One of the chalets was set aside for my father (mother having passed away in 1972). In 1990 he decided he would come and stay permanently at Loch Insh. However, he couldn't cope with the fact that he would be living rent free and he insisted on paying his way. He couldn't see how he could help, so I suggested that I would get a mortgage for him and act as his guarantor. So, at the age of 80, thanks to the system in those days, he took on a

Top – Building Bluff House, Clive and Sally's home above the Loch, constructed of telegraph poles from the old Edinburgh-London phone lines

Above – the old Ptarmigan Restaurant from Cairngorm, reconstructed at Loch Insh; the seats are from the old White Lady chairlift, rendered redundant when the funicular railway was built

mortgage, with his little boy as guarantor. It was a good arrangement, since despite his age he was a first time buyer and his interest charges were a lot less than I would have had to pay a commercial lender for similar facilities. We couldn't believe it when Pop died early in 1992. The New Year was only three days old and we received a letter from Highland Council telling us he was four days overdue with his rates. I wrote back to say that unfortunately Mr Freshwater Senior was deceased and I assumed there would be no charge for "the lie in". We received a phone call (rather than a letter) saying to forget the £2.47. My father would have been amused by that.

Glenmore Lodge had gifted us their old canoe-building shed and once we had erected it our first plan was to use it as a drying room - having had a fire in the drying room at the Lodge, I was very wary of installing one inside at Insh Hall – but ultimately we decided to use it as staff accommodation. So it went full circle; having been used for that purpose at the old Glenmore Lodge (now the youth hostel), at the time of Tommy Paul, George McLeod and Jack Thomson, it was now accommodation for staff here. We made a tidy job of it and as one of our instructors, Gordon Graham, said to the occupants "If you don't look after this, the Big Yin will have you out and he will be letting it". He had hardly uttered these words when I saw the state of this rather nice two bedroom chalet/shed, which quite a number of guests enjoyed the use of. It was always very popular because it was cheaper than the log chalets. However, the staff didn't look after it and so we decided we would make better use of it. I was pestered by Sally and some of the female office staff, who said it wasn't up to the standard of the log chalets (which was true). So we took it down and built another log chalet in its place. Only after we had lifted the original structure over the fence onto a lorry, taken it to the beach car park and re-erected it (it is now the beach hut where Jonny and Jacs stay) did Alice, our accounts assistant, tell me that it was the most popular chalet, having a better cash turn-over than any of the others. I was not particularly happy that this decision was forced upon me, or that information was not put to me. We did get the occasional customer comment that they would like to be in the other chalets, but I remember an elderly minister's wife telling me that, whilst she was knitting in the sun, it happened to be just perfect for the couple, who enjoyed staying in it very much. Hindsight is a wonderful thing.

Two friends who visited us regularly at the Loch were Richard Cameron and Iain Fraser and these two gave me invaluable help in planning the next stage of the development of the business. When I first met Richard he was Deputy Director of Planning for Highland Region, later taking over the post of Director. He had a clear idea of what we might achieve in the way of the greater expansion of the business which I was always thinking about, and he was able to guide me informally as to what the local planning committee might, or might not, allow. I wanted to increase the bedroom accommodation in the Hall, expand the size of the restaurant and upgrade the lower level of the Boathouse to provide good quality changing and toilet accommodation for the school groups and other users of our watersports facilities, as well as providing secure storage for equipment. Together we worked out what might be achieved, but the problem was how it could all be financed. This is where Iain came to my rescue. He and I had been friends for 35 years. He had moved from being the physical education organiser for the Highlands to taking charge of the Youth Training Scheme (YTS), then onto the Joint Educational Training Team. He had been with Highland Council all this time. On one day in particular, having finished my shopping in Inverness, I called to see him and during the course of the conversation he asked what I was doing. "I'm thinking of building an interpretive trail, depicting the history of the area and detailing the court case", I told him. So, it would be about fauna and flora as well as the law, along with a little footpath which we had already begun to create.

"Have you looked at European funding?" he asked.

"That's all roads and bridges isn't it?" I said.

"No," he informed me, before asking his secretary to fetch two files holding application forms. "Take those home, have a read and you will see that tourism and the likes of the interpretive trail are included. I suggest you contact Dennis Malone, the senior person in Highland Council for this type of funding." Iain was known in Highland Council as 'Mr Europe' because he had to go through all the grant applications. He showed me a box containing six or seven of the plans which were to go before the main committee. He didn't have any actual involvement, but he knew a lot about the system and told me to go home, put all the things I wanted to do at Loch Insh together into an application and phone the European Regional Development Fund office. I did just that, to be told that the official couldn't come down next week, but he could come tomorrow, which for an impatient get-on-with-it guy like me was just perfect.

He arrived in his smart black car – complete with a surf board on the roof, *en route* for Tyree, which I thought was a good sign. We walked to the site and, as instructed by Iain, I had put all our thoughts into one big project, to include the matters Richard and I had discussed. On returning to the car park the official commented that I had a very active imagination. "But I am interested," he said. "Put in an application to the local development

Top – Insh Hall in winter

Above Left – Entrance to the boathouse in winter (before the latest extension)

Above Right – The Boathouse as it is today – in winter

agency and see what they can do with it".

It was an education for me looking at those papers. You would have needed a PhD to make sense of all that European jargon. What I was looking for was Objective 1 funding, as the North of Scotland was an area eligible for this benefit. As it turned out Moray, Badenoch and Strathspey Enterprise (MBSE) could not do a lot as they had never made an Objective 1 application, despite this being one of the areas of Europe which qualified for such funding.

I called Dick Ruane, the chief executive of MBSE in Aviemore, but formed the impression that he was cautious about taking the application any further forward. By this time Iain was there to hold my hand, so to speak, and certain pertinent questions were put to Mr Ruane. This made no difference as I think his powder was being kept dry for future applications like the Cairngorm funicular railway, which was then being considered, and I got the impression that he wouldn't want to see the Objective 1 funds frittered away on a small projects like mine.

Mr Freshwater, though, never was one to give way to such concerns and an application was put forward. When I asked MBSE for the application forms to be provided on disc, I was told they had never made an EU funding application and had never had a disc. This sent me back to the European Office in Inverness. We had filled in the application with Jill Gatenby, our office accountant, having spent many nights working on the figures until we eventually had an application proposal ready for £600,000.

Meanwhile, Iain had asked me if I had applied to the Sports Council for additional funding. "No" I confessed, "since we are a commercial outfit". "Yes, I know," he countered, "but funding is available for facilities such as toilets, showers etc, which are going to be used by the public."   So we promptly submitted another application. Running two applications at one time was pretty difficult, as they each had to slot in to the timing of various committee meetings, but at the suggestion of MBSE we took them to their office in Grantown for typing on the official application form.

Fortunately Sally proof read the form that evening: she found over 120 spelling and punctuation errors. The form was taken back to Grantown next day to meet a very tight deadline. The staff there were most apologetic and couldn't understand how that many mistakes had happened, especially with spell-check on. However, it was finished and delivered on time.

I then received a phone call from our man at the Europe Office in Inverness to say he had received the application, but it would need trimming back a little and would have to be put forward by MBSE, since it was their application. If they'd forward it, the application would be dealt with. In passing he said there was one small omission; we hadn't put the full costing on the front page. This rang alarm bells for us – warning us that we had, after all that palaver, ended up submitting the original copy of the form, with all the spelling mistakes. I duly apologised, but he assured me: "Don't worry about that, it is not unusual and we don't judge things on spelling". We sent the correct forms in the next day.

As a result, and after a great deal of hard work by our office staff (Jill in particular) we were successful. We won our funding 50% from Europe via MBSE and 25% from the Sports Council. Of course the bank were delighted to go along with the suggestion that they would lend the remaining money if we got 75% assistance. So with the funding secured we were able to proceed with the improvements and expansion I had wanted and these were undertaken between 1999 and 2001.

Richard and Iain, and their respective wives, remain good friends and regular visitors to Loch Insh and Sally and I can't thank those two enough for all the support they gave us over our development plans and the funding of them.

When the various projects had been completed we decided it would be a good idea to have an official opening and after we had made enquiries through official channels we were thrilled to be told that Princess Anne, with her known interest in Scotland and in watersports, would like to undertake this for us. 4 June 2001 was the chosen date. The Princess had expressed a wish to sail on the loch after the formalities had been concluded. She duly arrived by helicopter, clad not in formal Court dress but in casual sailing gear, which lent a pleasantly informal ambience to the occasion. Sadly, although the sun shone, it was a very blustery day. By the time the official programme had been completed a brisk south westerly had established itself and it was considered prudent to abandon the expedition onto the water.

AWARDS OF RECOGNITION AND THE ROYALS

Over the years we have been successful in a few of the awards that we have entered or been entered for. The first one, in 1995, was for "Best on the Water Facility in Scotland". We were rather flattered to win this, as Caithness Glass were the main sponsors.

The day of the inspection duly arrived and we decided to give the Boathouse

Top - Meeting The Queen when short listed for the Small Business Awards –
Scotland in 2000. Clive narrates how he bought a new shirt for the occasion

Above - Princess Anne, opening the major Boathouse extension on 4 June
2001. She was to have sailed on the loch and came in sailing gear, but it was
too windy on the day and she was running late

restaurant a wash and to clean the floor. The two young instructors who undertook this task had turned it into something more like a swimming pool than a mopped floor, much to the amusement of the inspection team, particularly the head man from Caithness Glass in his pin-striped suit. He reminded the lad doing the mopping that they were here to inspect the watersports facilities, which didn't include the swimming pool in the restaurant.

We must have impressed the inspectors in our own modest way since, despite being in competition with the Waverley paddle steamer, we were judged to be the best in the country. It was quite a feather in our cap and we received our award at a ceremony at the Turnberry Hotel later that year.

From time to time we would apply or be nominated for the Small Business Award – Scotland (for those employing fewer than 50 staff). In 2000 we were short-listed and duly attended the award ceremony at the Eden Court theatre in Inverness. On the way there that day I heard on the radio that The Queen and The Duke of Edinburgh were in Inverness to open a new precinct. I put two and two together and deduced that The Queen might be handing out the awards. Realising she might be there I smartened myself up with a new shirt because, as is normal with Freshwater, my shirts get shrunk at the collar and the 18.5 size doesn't fit. I made a quick stop at Iain Fraser's house, dashed into Marks & Spencer just round the corner from him, bought a shirt, duly donned it, covered its packing creases with my buttoned blazer and dashed off to Eden Court. A preliminary explanation was given to all the short-listed businesses in the theatre and there were pictures on the screen with information about them. On visiting the foyer to inspect the seating plan I noticed that Mrs Freshwater was seated next to His Royal Highness, so I suspected we must have won something, having been included at that particular table out of the 400 guests. Half an hour later we were duly meeting the entourage in the marquee and I cradled my award in one hand while shaking royal hands with the other. Sally was talking to The Queen whilst The Duke looked at me and, noticing my name badge, quipped, with a big twinkling smile, quick as a flash, "Oh, a very good name for a watersports proprietor!"

The Queen asked "Where are you?"

"We are just over the hill from you at Balmoral", I explained. "At the confluence of the Spey and the Feshie, Ma'am".

Oh yes", said she, "I know exactly where you are." We haven't seen her driving past, but she obviously knows her Highland geography.

It was a very good lunch. Sitting next to me was Judith Gray, the very pleasant wife of the Lord Lieutenant, Lord Gray of Contin, who had been the Conservative MP for Ross and Cromarty from 1970 to 1983 and a Scottish Office minister in the government; a delightful couple and they obviously knew who we were. Hearing the conversation, I decided it might be an idea to find out if we could get someone to open the new Boathouse, just to ice our cake. As I have narrated earlier, this led to Princess Anne performing the opening for us the following year. So we had the award for the Best Small Business in the Highlands; we came home feeling very pleased with ourselves; and we went out for a meal with our friends from the Ossian Hotel in Kincraig to celebrate. Happy days!

Chapter Nineteen
Family Matters

As the sacking from the Lodge pushed me to living in a caravan, Insh Hall was forced upon me. However, my better half was not forced upon me; it was our choice.

Many friends who had helped build canoes, re-wire the hall, work at the beach and so on, rallied round as we prepared to have a wedding breakfast in the newly acquired Hall. The two boats which we purchased from Glenmore Lodge (the original 1947 sailing boats, Norfolk and Clyde) were brought into the Hall, upended and filled with flowers and illumination. The Hall itself was decked out and during the day Lorna McKenna and May Maxwell, together with Eleanor McFadden, set about preparing food for the members of our team.

Through my folk singing I had made many friends and through Sally's connections there were equally as many, one of which was the gamekeeper at Invereshie, Neil Aitchison, who came round with a fresh salmon from the Loch as a wedding gift. There was to be a stag party which was held at the then popular Lynwilg Hotel (now the Rowan Tree) at Alvie. In those days it was run by a group of girls who were to marry and stay in the valley. The hotel was one of the most popular watering holes south of Aviemore. The bad news for Sally was that the salmon went with us to the stag party and was cooked as steaks on an open fire in the bar and devoured by the small number of male attendees. She really never forgave me for not keeping a piece for her.

The date was set for the 3rd April (1971), partly to dodge the tax man, as was possible in those days[12]. All was set to hold the wedding at Insh Church with the minister Alec Hutchison. Surprisingly some years later, when involved with the court case, we discovered that our lawyer Bill Davidson and his wife Jocelyn had also been married at Insh Church by the then Minister, Mr Ross; the sequel to that was that Eleanor McFadden now lives in his old house on the river bank below the bridge. We made no lavish arrangements to travel far for the honeymoon.

The day finally arrived and was cold and draughty. One of my father's old friends, Donald Brough, a railway porter and guard, provided the bagpipes as this was a

---

[12]If a man married before 6 April he could claim what was then the married person's allowance for the whole of the tax year.

Top left - Clive and Sally off to London

Top right – Clive – ski cool 1960s

Above - Wedding group, 3 April 1971. L to R – Sally's sister Joanna, her father Donald Fraser, Sally, Clive, Sally's mother Jo Jo Fraser and Clive's parents James and Ivy

supplement to his income. We had a small reception with ourselves, our parents and around fifteen others at the Lynwilg Hotel and then invited all our friends to Insh Hall for a ceilidh dance with the band provided by Frank Gail, a boat builder from Inverness. Frank made the infamous paddles for Ray Pettit and me and today they are hung in the Boathouse. He was also a double bass teacher and travelled to schools to teach. He had two other men, on accordion and drums, and the three of them provided suitable music for the evening. The dancing went well, Chic Baxter made a film of the event. Although to this day neither Sally nor I have sat down and watched it, it is in the Freshwater archives. Many friends from far and near attended, Sally's parents (although no longer together), my parents and quite a number of local old worthies, together with my folk singing and skiing friends. To my recollection nobody disgraced themselves, one or two had a few drams, but in those days we were capable of managing half a bottle without anything getting out of hand. Sally and I stayed the night at the Hall and then set off on the honeymoon trip.

Nothing had been planned and we just decided that morning to go up the west coast. The highlights of that trip are now legend. We arrived at the Dundonnell Hotel on the shore of Little Loch Broom. As we were checking in we were met with cries of "Hi Clive, have you got your guitar with you?" It was the Dundonnell Mountain Rescue Team, mainly made up of RAF personnel who knew me quite well. As it happened I did have my guitar and Sally allowed me to stay for a while whilst she had a well earned rest from the previous day.

The following day, having been fed and watered, we headed off up the coast to Kylesku where in those days, before the bridge was built, there used to be a ferry. The hotel there was very much a summer only business; we arrived late in the evening, but they were hospitable enough to give us a room. It was freezing and we needed to get some form of heat (even if we were on honeymoon) so I went to see the owner and asked if there was a possibility of a fire. He said "A fire? A fire?", but he graciously produced one which at least took the ice off the windows. We have often laughed about that particular incident. Thereafter we followed the coast round to Durness and some of the old launching points for canoes and then back down the centre of the Highlands to Garve and then home. It was a four day honeymoon, but quite long enough considering all the work we had to do when we got home. It was economical, but very enjoyable and memorable, probably more so than if we had spent a fortune on going abroad as most youngsters do today.

When we arrived home we had John Clarke with us helping to lay the tarmac, so instead of having one man to look after, Sally had two, which was quite challenging and there can't be many ladies who can say that.

Not long after there was the arrival of one young man, Duncan. He was named after my old poaching and shooting friend, Duncan Ross, who has since passed on. We were best man at each other's wedding. Young Duncan Freshwater looked very similar to me and as I have said (in Chapter 11) on one occasion a local lady met Sally whilst walking with the pram, looked into the pram and said "Oh, he is so much like Clive." Realising what she had said, she looked at Sally saying "You *are* Clive's wife aren't you?"

An anecdote regarding Andrew's arrival; Sally became very weepy whenever she was about to give birth and one morning she said "I think this is the day", to which I replied "you'd better make your mind up as I've got some canoeists to collect from Aberlour. We got into Grantown, where Andrew was to be born at the cottage hospital, and I dropped Sally off there. I collected the canoeists, brought them back to the Hall and rang the hospital.

Andrew had made his appearance about thirty minutes after I had dropped Sally off at the hospital. He had spiky black hair and had been in such a hurry to arrive that Sally had not even finished signing in at the desk. We have had many a smile with Dr Janet Henderson who, along with her husband, Lindsay (my doctor when I was at Glenmore) were the resident doctors in Grantown. They were a great couple among the old brigade of family doctors. Whenever I went to Lindsay's surgery he would have me wait until he had cleared his last patient and would then discuss any problems I might have along with a dram. In those days there was no drink driving ban and so it was a very 'Highland hospitality' type service. Lindsay and Janet became extremely good friends over the many years that we knew them. On visiting Janet recently, she told the story of our builder friend, Bill Lawson Snr, who lived in Grantown and was known as 'the moth', an apt name as when he had been out drinking, on the way home if he saw a light on in a house he would call in to see if there was a dram available.

Jonathan's arrival was nothing too spectacular. Sally was in hospital for a few days before he arrived and the birth was normal and uneventful. As time has worn on he has had plenty of eventful incidents, which I won't go into. Suffice it to say that he is as much thought of as the other two.

All the boys have moved on; all good skiers, sailors and sportsmen thanks to Bill McGuiness and many of my other friends. Believing in the adage 'never teach your wife to drive' I chose not to teach the boys to ski. Well taught by others, they picked up many

Top – Like father like sons – L to R - Andrew, Duncan and Jonny as youngsters,
on site with Clive

Above – Family business - L to R - Clive, Duncan, Sally, Jonny, Andrew

awards and qualifications which have been of great benefit to the business.

In 1990, at the age of seventeen, Duncan, having had a good run through the system in Scotland with the Scottish Ski Team and being Scottish Schools Champion, agreed with us that it would be good for him to visit our friends John Clarke and Mugsy Morgan in Australia. He was provided with a one way ticket to Perth to meet up with them there. No sooner had he arrived than we received a phone call from Izzy Skeats (who lived in Sydney) to say that she had just seen Duncan on the television. Whether it was by fate or just that John Clarke has a boat salvage business, a fifty foot yacht had run aground on a reef in Freemantle, south of Perth. John had gone down to salvage the boat with his new crew member, Duncan Freshwater, and the recovery of the yacht was national news in Australia. Duncan then went on to travel by train for two and a half days across Australia to the Blue Mountains to seek a job as a ski instructor. He was one of over a hundred applicants, but passed with flying colours since he had already passed the first stage of the BASI qualification. Nevertheless it was a selection process and he must have impressed them with his ability, even at that tender age.

Having finished his skiing, Duncan cycled some 1500 miles down through Victoria towards the south coast and then up towards Brisbane, touring and looking for work, pitching his tent along the way. To his surprise he arrived at a campsite outside Halls Gap in Victoria's Grampians National Park and saw a Loch Insh uniform fleece. This belonged to Caroline Sterritt, who had worked for us as a ski instructor the previous winter. She and her husband Wes, who had also worked for us, were from Kingussie. A friend of theirs was running Duke of Edinburgh's Award camping expeditions, so Duncan got a job with him, standing at the top of the mountain to make sure that everybody went past the obligatory post. When Wes and Caroline had first gone to Australia in the early 1980s as young adventurers. They had worked as rafting guides on the Franklin river in Tasmania They told Duncan that they thought issues involving commercial rafting on that river had parallels with our own canoeing case on the Spey.

Duncan went on to travel back through New Zealand. He stayed for a short time in the North Island with Quentin Mitchell, who had emigrated from Huntly in Aberdeenshire, and who was at that time a secondary school headmaster. On Quentin's introduction he then worked from June to September at one of the Sir Edmund Hillary outdoor pursuits centres in the North Island. After that he moved on to Canada, where he worked as a volunteer on the ski patrol at Silver Star for Norman Crerar, a longtime friend of mine and at that time President of the Canadian Ski Instructors' Alliance. At the end of the ski season he travelled to Boston for a reunion with friends he had met in New Zealand. We received a phone call from him when he was in Boston: "Hi Dad, I'm in Boston, I have to get to Los Angeles and I have nine dollars. Can you help?" This was the only time he called on us for funding. Fortunately our first beach girl, Eleanor McFadden, lived in the very same city, so we called on her to help Duncan. She generously gave him 200 dollars to get to LA. He arrived there on the day of the Rodney King verdict, when four police officers were acquitted of serious assault despite apparently convincing evidence to the contrary, leading to riots, some of which Duncan witnessed, in which 55 people were killed and over 2,000 injured. He then flew home from LA to complete his circumnavigation of the globe.

Over many years, in the '60's, '70's and '80's, as a BASI trainer, I spent most of my winter days teaching all levels of skiing on Cairngorm Mountain. As Chairman of BASI for twelve years, having to sign all the certificates etc, it is not surprising that I was quite well known in skiing circles. I was once asked to put myself forward for the 'Who's Who' book of personalities in sport. However, I declined the offer.

Understandably the boys developed as skiers and through membership of the Cairngorm Ski Club, where I was involved as an organiser more than a trainer. All three boys developed into good competitive skiers. They were Scottish Schools champions at various stages of their personal development. Duncan and Andrew progressed into the Scottish National Team and Andrew into the British Team. Unfortunately this stage of Jonathan's progress in skiing coincided with two or three seasons of very poor snow in Scotland and this drove him towards windsurfing, a discipline which he loved and at which he excelled.

Andrew had spent his time growing up here and he became a very good skier. On one particular race on Cairngorm, at which I had been gate-keeping, he and Duncan were racing and I am ashamed to say that I didn't think that Andrew would do very well. Duncan came second and on arriving home, not having stayed for the prize-giving, I asked Andrew how he got on and he said he had won. I was obviously very pleased and embarrassed at the same time. From there on Andrew grew into a very good technical skier and had his sights set on downhill racing. He was of the same age and era as Alain Baxter and while Baxter went for slalom, Andrew could only see Marc Girardelli and the big Austrian names which had graced our screens some fifteen years ago in the downhill. He was determined to succeed; we bought a small second-hand VW bus for £1,000, which had belonged to McPhail's butchers in Elgin. We insulated it so that he would have a vehicle to travel round Europe going to races. He was not part of the British Team and would not get into a race unless there was a space not taken by the British squad. He worked away at that until he finally went to America to join a club in Colorado and lived there for a season, established some good results which raised the eyebrows of the British Ski Federation, and was then invited to join the British team.

Over the next ten years Andrew achieved notoriety in racing with the Bell brothers at the British Championships and eventually beating them to become British Champion, in slalom, downhill and overall. There followed five years of lone competition in the World Cup races, as he was the only downhill racer for the British squad, with one trainer and having to do all his own maintenance, course inspection etc. It was poorly supported and he was very much thrown in at the deep end, never having raced in the lower level Europa Cup races. I believe that this did not help his progress, although it certainly put him in the headlines. He later went on to the Olympics at Nagano in Japan in 1998, having a reasonable time there, but the weather was very stormy and wet, with three delay days and a long way from the venue. His claim to fame would be when the 'Herminator' (Hermann Maier, the leading Austrian) flew out at the first or second gate through three lines of netting. Andrew came down and was equal at the split time, but went out at the second corner. His only result was in the Super G where he came in around 25th. Sometime before that, Hazel Irving had given him a good exposure on the BBC, because he and the Herminator were the only two competitors who hadn't skied the Hahnenkaam at Kitzbuhel that year and she made a distinction between those who had and those who hadn't.

It was a great education for Andrew and it was Sally's and my greatest ambition to watch him live, but this was never fulfilled, mainly because we could not afford to be away from our base at Loch Insh. Our main objective was that he should have the opportunity and we would provide the funding, which at that time was pretty limited. I believe that no-one should go into British sport, particularly skiing, unless they have adequate financial backing. Eventually, after the World Championships in Colorado in 1999 (where he did very well) he came home and he decided to retire from the racing circuit.

On an earlier occasion with the boys at the ski club, there had been a challenge put forward by Sandy Caird to see who could ski the height of Everest in a day. There was a system in place to record the runs of those taking part. In the end, Andrew and Duncan won the boys' section at the age of around fourteen, skiing twice the height of Everest, with eighty six runs on the White Lady. That evening when they got home (in those days their enthusiasm was such) they went to join the school group on an ice skating visit to the Aviemore Centre. They slept well that night.

Then we come to Jonathon, who had been overshadowed in skiing to a certain extent by his two older brothers. although still managing to achieve the title of Scottish Schoolboy Skier. He had a problem with sore knees, a growing pain problem which many school age boys get, resulting in their having to take time out from skiing. This he did and never really came back as a competitive skier, although he is now a very good snow-boarder and recreational skier. Instead he has shown the other two the way in windsurfing and was selected as a Scottish and British representative in that sport. Along with some of our instructors here, Jonathan went on to work in Moon Beach on the shores of the Red Sea, in Egypt. On one occasion Sally went out to spend a week with him on the Red Sea encampment, where there was excellent windsurfing, the biggest danger being the possibility of their being swept across to the other side. How they managed to survive with the poor security and safety I am not sure, but God was protective of them. As Alec Hutchison in christening Jonathan pointed out, it is a name that means 'sent by God'. I don't know whether that is true or not, as there are times when I think he has been sent by the other place. However, he became a star windsurfing performer and has travelled to Europe, the Middle East and Brazil and has hankered after going to the far flung places of the world, which cost an extortionate amount of money. He and his girlfriend Jacs are now fully involved in the running of the business and are planning to build a house just across from ours, above the Loch.

Jonathon has an independent mind, well illustrated by an occasion in primary school. The new headmistress had ridiculed him for writing continually in his maths book, all the sums at the top of the page and all close together, as he had been asked to do by his old headmistress, who was a frugal paper user. This did not fit well with the new headmistress, who wanted it laid out a little more tidily. On this occasion he was kept in at break and lunchtime for continuing to do exactly the same. He left school that afternoon unknown to anyone after excusing himself to go to the toilet. I was in Inverness and arrived home at three o'clock to find the headmistress in the car park shouting "well at least we know where he is now". He had walked home, gone in to Legerwood and into the bathroom, got himself up into the roof space and was hiding in the rafters; one of our instructors managed to find him. I suppose it says something about his strength of character.

It would be easy to say that the boys were not stretched academically once they went to Kingussie High School and I think that many parents would say the same of their children, but I have to say that all three got sufficient exam passes to gain university entrance, something I had not achieved. Jonathan was the first to go, in effect too young, and attended for a year and a half at Brunel University, London, at which he was going to study mechanical engineering. He very soon discovered he could swap that course for a more art/craft focussed one, which wasn't quite so demanding and to my disappointment he was allowed to do that. When Andrew retired from top level ski racing he entered Glasgow University to study computer maths. I found it impressive that he could embark on such a course after having had so much time out of education due to his skiing. He did not complete it as he found it too slow and felt he didn't need to be able to write programmes as he could just buy them.

Duncan came home one day and, as I went through the house, Sally asked if I knew if he had got in. "Got in where?" I asked. She said he had gone for an interview at Aberdeen University. He had indeed got in. There ensued four years of a Business Studies degree course, in which my only involvement was when he wanted to buy a flat. I said he could do no such thing, I would phone some of my friends in Aberdeen and get him 'digs'. He fell on his feet with a teacher friend who had a daughter studying at Loughborough and Duncan had her room whilst she was away. While in Aberdeen he met his wife Alison, and they were together through the University years. He was the second son to be married (after Andrew) and is now living in Edinburgh, where Alison is a solicitor, and they have a young son, Archie. Andrew had teamed up with Linda, a girl from Fife who had qualified as a nurse and was completing a teacher training course. She came to work at Loch Insh and at Aberlour school and they married in 2006. Their marriage has produced two lovely grand-daughters, Lucy-Jo and Tia, and a grandson, Jasper, and they live just along the road from us at the south end of the Loch.

All three boys now have a financial interest in the business and I hope this means that it will continue to thrive after I am gone.

40th Anniversary celebrations at the Boathouse - 2009

Afterword

Following Clive's passing in February 2015 Sally received many touching messages of condolence. Here are a few of them.

_____

The Spirit and the Creator of this special place - *Friend from Germany, B von W*

"The measure of who we are is what we do with what we have." Clive had a work ethic and a dogged determination which was without equal – *T W*

Clive and the Sailing School were most certainly an inspiration to me that I cherish as it shaped my life – *A H*

Clive was a most significant and much loved influence upon my young life and is someone I can never forget – *P W*

Roll on spring 2015 and a renewed vigour, proud in what Clive gave so many – *S L*

Loch Insh Watersports is such a fitting memorial for such a "big character" in Kincraig. He will be sorely missed – *H B*

Some old school mates have lost contact and hardly remembered, but everyone remembers Clive. He was a bit special even then – old school friend - *J P*

Clive's role in the development of the Centre has been both passionate and pivotal and the standards he achieved were excellent. It will be a challenge for present and future staff to maintain those standards, but by doing so, a fitting memorial to Clive will be achieved – school teacher - *L J*

Treasure your memories – they will help to ease your loss – old school friend – *B*

As a former Glenmore Lodge instructor he was a true pioneer for the outdoor sector – *Glenmore Lodge*

I was at a gig at the Nethybridge Hotel which ran over time. Clive was full of witty stories and songs and when the local bobby came in (closing time 10pm in those days) he immediately sang an appropriate song denigrating the police in a tongue-in-cheek fashion and invited the said policeman to join the party. The bobby left without a word – *R B*

There are many locally who will notice the absence of his opinions of this area in relation to business, planning decisions and local development. I suspect that wherever he is now, he will be putting forward proposals to rearrange whatever regime is in place to create improvements – *J B*

Clive leaves a legacy of achievement and a record of persistence, a template for success and often it would have been against the odds. A truly remarkable man – *H S*

Kincraig has lost one of its best. Always willing to support what he thought to be good causes and the right way of doing things – *J F-L*

Few of us will have confidence that we have left the world a better place, but I hope Clive knew what a honeypot he had created for Kincraig. From an empty Insh Hall, look what he achieved and with what courage – *A W*

Quite apart from his role in opening up the Spey and other rivers to watersports, he made a huge contribution to the development of our local tourism industry. He was definitely a national leader in 'electricity pole architecture!' – *D H*

The last time I spoke to Clive he was after some information / ammunition to have a go at some aspect of the public sector. You could sense his enthusiasm for yet another fight, something he thrived on. He was almost laughing as he was talking and I felt sorry for his opponents; they did not know what was coming! But that was Clive – God bless him – *B K*

Clive was a man of action; a man of determination and industry. If he set his mind on an objective, he went for it and would leave no stone unturned until he achieved his goal. At times the odds against him would prove to be awesome, but he persevered undaunted. He believed in himself and he had the mental capacity and the stamina to tackle and overcome adversity – *R C*

Clive was very special to me ever since freedom to use the Spey all the way up to the House of Lords. I always knew that if his help would count, he would be available. This 'wee' solicitor was proud and impressed by his tenacity – *J F*

The one attribute of Clive that I will always remember was if you did the right thing by him, he would be your strongest ally – *D F*

I will miss our chats and phone calls about a vast array of topics, but all with one thing in common, Clive thinking out of the box and always, always being alert to meeting head-on anything that might prove detrimental to the family or the business – *K H*

It was a hard few summers, but some of the greatest of my life and certainly helped me when I went for my first full time job after leaving college. He sometimes drove me mad and sometimes I wanted to shoot him, but then there was usually a big smile and always a hug. – *I I*

Clive will remain in our memories not only as the jovial, genuine and kind-hearted friend that he was, but also as a man who set many examples of what can be achieved through determination, dedication and sheer hard work – *J-H*

Index of Names

Note – In the following index, only the names of persons, not places, etc., mentioned in the text are listed. Clive, Sally, their sons Duncan, Andrew and Jonny, as well as Clive's parents, James and Ivy Freshwater, are mentioned frequently throughout the text and are therefore not listed.